# HOW TO:

# DESIGN CARS
## LIKE A PRO

A Comprehensive
Guide to Car Design from the
Top Professionals

**TONY LEWIN**
WITH RYAN BORROFF

# CONTENTS

## SECTION 01 | WHAT IS DESIGN?

# SECTION 02 | HOW TO DO IT

**02**

## SECTION 03 | TEN DECADES OF DESIGN

**03**

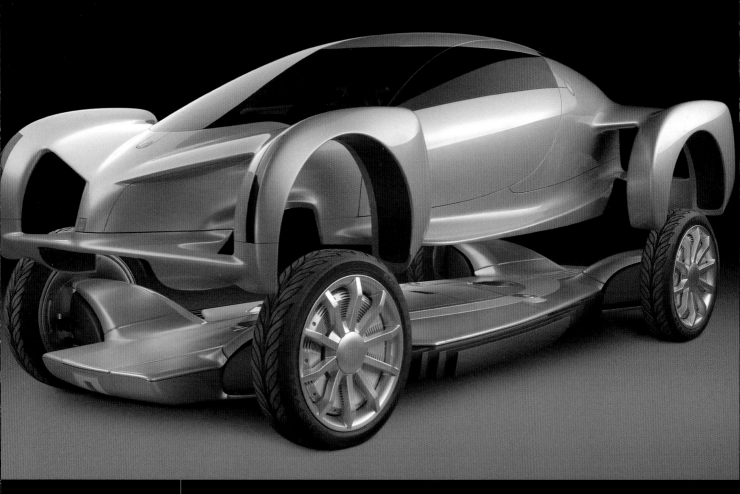

## SECTION 04 | REFERENCE

EXECUTIVE DIRECTOR OF DESIGN,

PREMIER AUTOMOTIVE GROUP, FORD MOTOR COMPANY

# FOREWORD | **PETER HORBURY**

**What is it about the automobile that gives it such a special place in our hearts compared with all those other products that form our everyday lives?**

We do not share that special relationship with the cooker, the fridge or the lawn mower that we do with our cars. Why the difference?

It is, I believe, simply because, as our personal means of transport, the car has become the substitute for the horse which, for thousands of years, was the only alternative to walking – and, as it was a living creature, the horse required certain commitments from us. We fed it, cleaned it and gave it somewhere warm to sleep at night – which is exactly what we do with our cars. We feed them at the gas station, we wash them on a Sunday and, if we can, we put them away in a warm garage at night.

What is more, just like a horse, the car needs oxygen and water as well as food for its 'heart' to function. But the greatest difference between the car and most of those other products with which we surround ourselves is that it does not remain static: it is not inanimate – it displays animal-like behaviour. The popularity of the five-spoke alloy wheel is because, at reasonable speed, we can still see the individual spokes, or 'legs', moving (any more than five is a blur) and this enhances the subconscious connection we make between the car and a product of nature.

It is no surprise, therefore, that there is more interest and debate about the appearance of the car than of any other man-made product. Of course, appearances aren't everything. There are many other properties that are essential for a car to be a success. However, no matter how powerful the engine, how brilliant the suspension or how efficient the internal layout, if it doesn't look right, then people will stay away.

'DESIGNING CARS IS ONE OF THE BEST JOBS IN THE WORLD. FROM THE AGE OF ABOUT SEVEN WHEN I DECIDED THAT I WAS GOING TO "GROW UP TO BE A CAR DESIGNER" I NEVER ONCE DEVIATED FROM THE COURSE I SET'

There is a huge responsibility resting on the shoulders of the design team. To take an idea from a simple sketch to production is a highly complex and difficult process fraught with problems and potential pitfalls where a great concept can be totally destroyed. Major obstacles could include package restrictions, which affect the basic architecture and proportions of the car; manufacturing limitations, which may not allow certain forms to be achieved by a particular supplier's production process, or one of a thousand new laws which appear each year governing everything from unbelted occupants (USA) to pedestrian protection (Europe).

Even so, designing cars is one of the best jobs in the world. From the age of about seven when I decided that I was going to 'grow up to be a car designer' I never once deviated from the course I set – and now, like many of my colleagues, I get a terrific thrill whenever I see what was once a sketch on my drawing board driving down the road.

This book will give you an insight into the world of car design; how designers think, what influences us, how we work and why we love what we do.

However, one mystery it won't solve is this one: why on earth do they *pay* us to pursue our hobby?

PETER HORBURY

## INTRODUCTION | **DESIGN MATTERS**

**It may sound obvious, but design matters. Every man-made object in the world that surrounds us has been designed in some way: someone, somewhere has decided how that object should look, how they would like people to respond when they catch sight of it.**

Yet when it comes to the design of cars, that response becomes especially complex, for cars arouse passions like no other product. The merest mention of the name Ferrari is enough to quicken your pulse: the sight of one sets that pulse really racing. Even mundane models can hot-wire straight into your intuitive reflexes: just think back to your reaction when you first saw a New Beetle, or even the born-again MINI: it's a fair bet that nine out of ten of you instantly said 'I want one!'

Cars are emotional objects, and car design is emotional design. Despite all the practical criteria that need to be fulfilled, car design still isn't ordinary, dispassionate design: when it comes to cars, everyone has an opinion, everyone feels a connection.

It is the car designer's job to spot this emotional connection, distil it, and fashion it into a product that will spark an instinctive 'must have it' response in the customer. Easier said than done, of course – but in this book we enter the secret world behind the studio doors to see how the professionals do just that – and for good measure we provide some professional tuition to help you have a go yourself.

Cars may be the products of massive, heartless industrial machines, but thanks to inspirational design they can have a life, even a spirit, of their own. They have movement, power, energy; they evoke feelings, dreams and fantasies. And at the end of the day it is these gut feelings that really sell the car.

There are of course many ways in which designers and car companies can play on people's emotions to bring the buyers in: the nostalgia evoked by the MINI and Beetle is simply one of the more obvious approaches. In this book we do much more than skim the highly polished paintwork of car design: we look at the all-time greats who shaped our design heritage, and delve deep into the design business to discover how designers tick and what really lies beneath the shapes we see on our streets; we speak to those at the top of their game to find out what influences them, what motivates them and, crucially, what the real-life pressures on them are.

Better still, we invite you to taste the design experience for yourself. With the expert guidance of top colleges and professional designers, we hand the design pencils over to you, the reader. With the help of our series of drawing and design tutorials you will be guided through the essential first steps of getting your own designs onto paper – or computer screen – presenting them in a professional manner and, if you've really got the bug, choosing a vehicle design course at one of 30-plus colleges around the world.

Two of those colleges – the Royal College of Art in London, and Coventry's School of Art and Design – have been of immense help in the compiling of this book. I have also benefited from the advice, well-filled contact book and perceptive writing of my co-author, Ryan Borroff, editor of *Interior Motives*, and the insights of industry writer Julian Rendell and historical expert and picture archivist Giles Chapman. I am indebted to Peter Robain for original photography, and the people at Car Design News website for valuable assistance too. And, finally, I would like to thank Renault for its exceptional openness in allowing me access to its senior executives, Pininfarina for its wonderful historical pictures, and Jaguar Advanced Design for letting its senior designer Mark Phillips provide us with extracts from his working diary.

But most of all, I must thank Motorbooks International for asking me to take on this ambitious project. It has led me on a fascinating voyage of discovery and deepened my understanding of what lies behind the design of the cars we all drive and dote on. I hope it does the same for you.

TONY LEWIN

# 01 | WHAT IS DESIGN?

## CONTENTS

# 01 WHAT IS DESIGN? – INTRODUCTION

There are probably as many answers to this question as there are professional designers – and non-professionals can no doubt be relied upon to supply an even richer variety of explanations.

To many, any attempt to define design is destined to be as futile as trying to define art – if not quite as explosively controversial. But while we all might pride ourselves on recognising a good piece of design when we see one, truly good design goes much deeper. A genuinely good design succeeds in achieving not just an aesthetic harmony in its visual presentation but also a harmony between the less easily visible aspects of engineering and economics, proving practical to use and profitable to manufacture.

Above all, design is a profession where, in the memorable words of Bauhaus founder Walter Gropius, the mission of the practitioner is to 'instil a soul in the product still-born from the machine'. In automotive terms this could be seen as adding personality and aesthetic quality to a product that is manufactured in large numbers in a vast factory, and which must turn a profit and satisfy thousands of tiresome regulations too.

While no designer would disagree with Gropius, each has his or her individual way of interpreting that mission – something that we in turn interpret as style. In this first section of this book we celebrate the sheer variety of those approaches, those philosophies, those styles and, above all, those beautiful shapes produced by today's designers. We examine the kind of challenges the modern car designer faces, take a look at what goes on behind the studio doors, and profile Renault to show how the visionary use of innovative design as a strategic tool can transform the image and fortunes of a major corporation. And, finally, we shadow a leading designer for a week of his busy schedule, and enter the wacky world of concept cars, where designers are let off the tight corporate leash to reveal their true creative powers.

## 01.01 | DESIGN DEFINED

'ART WITH BOUNDARIES'... 'THE HARMONIOUS AND SEAMLESS BLENDING OF FORM AND FUNCTION'... 'THE APPARENT CONTRADICTION OF DESIGNING A PRODUCT FOR MASS PRODUCTION THAT CONNECTS WITH THE CONSUMER ON AN INDIVIDUAL LEVEL'...

ASK SEVEN LEADING AUTOMOTIVE DESIGNERS TO DEFINE DESIGN AND YOU'LL GET SEVEN VERY DIFFERENT ANSWERS. BUT FOR ALL OF THESE INDIVIDUALS – AND THE COMPANIES THAT EMPLOY THEM – IT ALL COMES DOWN TO THE SAME THING: GOOD DESIGN IS GOOD BUSINESS. IT MAY BE HARD TO ACHIEVE, BUT GOOD DESIGN IS A STRATEGY FOR MOST COMPANIES AND AN EFFECTIVE STRATEGIC WEAPON IN THE BATTLE TO WIN THE MINDS AND HEARTS OF CONSUMERS.

IF THE BASIC PREMISE OF ALL BUSINESS IS TO GIVE CONSUMERS SOMETHING THEY NEED, THEN GOOD DESIGN IS THE BUSINESS OF GIVING THEM SOMETHING THEY LOVE AND ENJOY USING. IT IS THIS CONNECTION WITH CONSUMERS THAT THE AUTOMAKERS HAVE BEEN PURSUING THROUGH DESIGN, ALMOST SINCE THE VERY BEGINNING OF THE AUTOMOTIVE AGE.

FOR GENERATIONS, THE WORLD'S AUTOMAKERS HAVE KNOWN THAT THE DESIGN AND STYLING OF A VEHICLE FORM THE ULTIMATE 'HOOK' TO LURE THE CUSTOMER AND EQUALLY, IT IS CLEAR THAT THE WORLD OF AUTOMOTIVE DESIGN IS AS VARIED AS THE DESIGNS IT PRODUCES.

VICE PRESIDENT OF DESIGN

FORD MOTOR COMPANY

# J MAYS

J Mays is behind some of the most admired car designs in recent history including VW's new Beetle, the new Ford Thunderbird and the new GT. He is responsible for determining the look of future Ford, Mazda, Mercury, Lincoln, Volvo, Jaguar, Land Rover and Aston Martin vehicles. An exhibition dedicated to his work has recently been held at the Museum of Contemporary Art in Los Angeles.

### ...ON DESIGN

*Left:* **427 concept revives the US big sedan, with bold silhouette and detailing**

*Right:* **Mustang GT Coupé concept presented in 2003 is very clearly inspired by the '60s original**

*Top right, far right:* **Minimalist MA sports car and Model U show a more radical approach from J Mays**

'Design is the just a way of improving people's quality of life. What I do is not to try to create something that is just "modern" or "contemporary"– which is part of it – but at the end of the day what we are really trying to do is improve people's lives through good design.

It is important not just for the car industry but for any industry that produces products, that those products perform in such a way that there is tangible evidence to the customer that their quality of life has improved as a result of buying the product.

Up until now the car industry has been both good and bad at this. I think the car industry actually picks up the needs of the customer relatively well; this conceptual understanding of the need in their lives for the types of vehicles they need. What we don 't always get right is the execution part of this process. I don't think there is such a thing as bad car any more. This is a never-ending process: in ten years if we are still having this conversation, it will be exactly the same.

'DESIGN IS THE JUST A WAY OF IMPROVING PEOPLE'S QUALITY OF LIFE. WHAT I DO IS NOT TO TRY TO CREATE SOMETHING THAT IS JUST "MODERN" OR "CONTEMPORARY"– WHICH IS PART OF IT – BUT AT THE END OF THE DAY WHAT WE ARE REALLY TRYING TO DO IS IMPROVE PEOPLE'S LIVES THROUGH GOOD DESIGN.'

**…ON FORM AND FUNCTION**

Great car design has the right balance of both form and functional attributes, whilst good design is usually heavily weighted toward one or the other. There are cars out there that look great but which don't function particularly well, while there are other pretty good cars which function well but don't look that great. The best cars do both.

**…ON THE DESIGN PROCESS**

The overall proportion and architecture of the exterior of a vehicle is the foundation from which you build that house. You can't build a beautiful house if you have a bad layout to the house plan upon which to build.

You start with restrictions in terms of proportion, front-wheel drive and the boundaries of front overhang and crash safety and all the other considerations; by the time you get through the list you have pretty much created a pig of a foundation upon which you will begin to design. The designer ends up being nothing more than a pure stylist. The key to improving this situation, in terms of design, is to get designers involved in the engineering upfront to help determine the architecture.'

Left to right: **Evalia concept** shows Nissan design direction for versatile family car; 350Z draws inspiration from 240Z of the 1960s, while boxy Yanya is a proposal for a multi-purpose crossover vehicle

## ...ON DESIGN

'Design is the expression of passion and imagination by the creator in a visible way. A car is a very emotional product, so this is key to its success. But this is not a difficult thing to do as long as you have a clear idea in your mind of how to transfer the technical to the design after this emotional message has been determined.

Function is very important, but I don't believe that form should follow function. Emotion to me means that you should feel comfortable with both the function and the shape.

Great car design is defined by a car having its own strong and unique character. A character that no other vehicle has. Several elements have to come together to achieve great car design. This doesn't happen very often. It is determined when everything – from the head of the company to the design and the engineering divisions – are all working in harmony. No one individual can do this. The process is too complex.

## ...ON DESIGN DETAILS AND BRAND IDENTITY

Despite being a global company, we originated in Japan and so we must convey our Japanese heritage – and we want to convey Japanese character. We must do this. Design details are very important to express that. Clearly, Japanese design is about good craftmanship and paying a lot of attention to detail. Details have to be well executed and there has to be a friendliness about them.

Nissan has such a wide range of products that not only is the name Nissan the brand, but the car name too is a brand. Take a product like the Skyline: it is almost a brand in its own right. March/Micra is a brand too. Thus it is difficult to say what is a design icon for Nissan.

We want to design the best products in each of our market segments, rather than build a brand identity *per se*. Still, we want to maintain a consistency that is recognisable. We want to do both, so there should be key elements connecting one to another. The Cube, Micra, and Primera are all very different designs but still look like they came from the same company. Having the same attitude for surfacing, graphics and proportions is extremely important.

NAKAMURA

SENIOR VICE PRESIDENT, DESIGN DIVISION

NISSAN MOTOR COMPANY

# SHIRO NAKAMURA

Nissan Design has seen a revolution under the leadership of Shiro Nakamura, with Nissan developing one of the most exciting design identities in the car industry today. Under Nakamura, Nissan has presented bold new designs such as the Primera and New Micra as well as the new 350Z sports car.

'DESIGN IS THE EXPRESSION OF PASSION AND IMAGINATION BY THE CREATOR IN A VISIBLE WAY. A CAR IS A VERY EMOTIONAL PRODUCT, SO THIS IS KEY TO ITS SUCCESS.'

MANAGING DIRECTOR, STILE BERTONE

# ROBERTO PIATTI

A native Italian, born in Turin, Roberto Piatti is head of one of the world's most esteemed independent car design houses. Before working for Stile Bertone, Roberto Piatti worked at Turin's IDEA Institute as a project manager for car and industrial design projects.

## ...ON ITALIAN COACHBUILDERS

'For the Italian coachbuilders – names like Bertone Pininfarina, Ghia, Zagato, Touring – the car has always been seen as a personal object of pleasure, even to the extent that the car is considered as an integral part of an individual's lifestyle.

## ...ON THE EVOLUTION OF ITALIAN CAR DESIGN

Italian automobile design in Turin really began after the Second World War with the Cisitalia sports coupé designed by Pininfarina, which now has a place of honour at MOMA, New York. It displayed a new way of drawing and designing cars – integrated headlamps, fenders, covered wheels, and the harmonised link of hood, fender and all the body elements.

Another factor which contributed to this evolution of the development of the Italian coachbuilders was the racing cars made in collaboration with the automaker competitors taking part in the main racing competitions – names like Maserati, Alfa Romeo and Ferrari. Sometimes these specialist designs too became production models.

England remained conservative and the United States launched wild designs with aggressive front ends and fenders and enormous rear fins that symbolised the aggressiveness of the new status symbol. But Italian cars of the same era expressed speed and power in a different way, delicately linked to the formal elegance of the exterior features.

## ...ON ITALIAN DESIGN AND DESIGN 'FREEDOM'

The independent design houses and coachbuilders, like Stile Bertone, work for different automakers. This means their designers can design without the restrictions and conditioning of those who must always work on the same theme or in the same market segment. Also, Stile Bertone does not only design vehicles but many other objects and instruments as well; one day a scooter and helmets, the next day domestic appliances and even jetties used for buses in Venice or new airplane seats. Together these two factors generate a mental flexibility and a freedom of expression that influence their designers' ideas.'

Above: Birusa design study presented at 2003 Geneva motor show re-confirmed Stile Bertone as a major influence in the design world

'I BELIEVE THAT WITHIN THE APPLICATION OF NEW TECHNOLOGIES THERE IS AN OPPORTUNITY FOR DESIGN. THE OBJECTIVE OF THE BERTONE-DESIGNED FILO CONCEPT CAR WAS TO RETHINK THE ARCHITECTURE OF THE INTERIOR BY DISPOSING OF THE PEDALS AND THE STEERING COLUMN THANKS TO THE USE OF X-BY-WIRE TECHNOLOGY.'

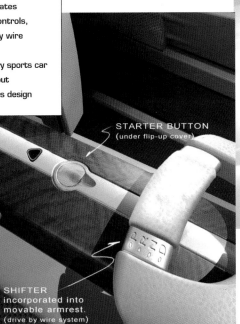

Above: Mercedes GST crossover vehicle combining qualities of SUV, minivan and station wagon was enthusiastically received and will enter production

Above right: Mercedes F200 Carving concept pushes design boundaries

Below: GST incorporates innovative interior controls, facilitated by drive by wire

Right: SL-series luxury sports car epitomises discreet but progressive Mercedes design

'FOR ME, DESIGN IS IMPORTANT BECAUSE IT GIVES A UNIQUE IDENTITY TO THE PRODUCT AND ENHANCES AND CONVEYS BRAND CHARACTER.'

STARTER BUTTON
(under flip-up cover)

SHIFTER
incorporated into
movable armrest.
(drive by wire system)

SENIOR VICE PRESIDENT

DAIMLERCHRYSLER AG

# PETER PFEIFFER

Under Peter Pfeiffer Mercedes-Benz design has been evolving for more than 30 years. A designer at Mercedes since 1968, nobody has a better understanding of car design for the German brand.

## ...ON DESIGN

'For me, design is important because it gives a unique identity to the product and enhances and conveys brand character. Design also has the role of translating technology and the fascination of it, particularly for Mercedes-Benz. But of course, design is also the platform for communication between the customer and the manufacturer.

For Mercedes-Benz, function, technology and design are one unity; they are inseparable. It differs from manufacturer to manufacturer. Some manufacturers live by design only, but this would not be right for Mercedes-Benz.

A good design is a design without fault, but great car design is something else. Great car design is fascinating and has something special, something extra, which is difficult to define. Like art, many paintings are technically good but are not masterpieces; it's the same with car design.

## ...ON STYLING

Brands differ very much with their brand strategies. Mercedes-Benz defined its design strategy back in 1975, and since then we have been expanding our design philosophy. We go by product families. Each car is styled individually with an individual character and individual features, but you should still find a family resemblance. This should be very visible to the customer. We look back at our 100-year history and keep taking familiar features and reinterpreting them and modernising them, but still making it clear to the customer that it is still typically Mercedes-Benz design. In this manner we take our customers forwards without burning the bridges behind us.'

AUTOMOTIVE, PRODUCT AND ENTERTAINMENT DESIGNER

HARALD BELKER DESIGN, SANTA MONICA, CALIFORNIA, USA

# HARALD BELKER

Harald Belker worked for Nissan, Porsche and Mercedes-Benz before a chance meeting in Los Angeles propelled him into the world of vehicle design for Hollywood movies. Since then Belker has designed vehicles for *Batman* and *Inspector Gadget* and completed vehicles for *XXX* and Steven Spielberg's *Minority Report* including 2002's Lexus-branded sports car, driven by Tom Cruise.

## ...ON DESIGN

'Design is not just styling: it includes function too. Fulfilling one but not the other is poor design. Form should always follow function, particularly in automotive design. An educated designer can tell if this has not been the case, as there is logic and a common sense to getting this right.

Automotive design is really complex. As strange as it sounds, having to have four wheels on a car really makes it difficult: it demands a complex shape, and so form must follow function.

When designing cars for movies there is much more freedom to be creative and create the boundaries.

Sure, the movie script will give me direction on what the vehicle needs to do, but ultimately the only design boundaries are set by myself.

If you work on a Batmobile, for example, you become a little boy and let your imagination go crazy with a theme. It becomes a theme vehicle, it's more outrageous and it doesn't need to be too sensible. But working on a vehicle for a movie like Minority Report, you have to do your research into the future and into future transportation systems. It still needs to be believable.

It's a double-edge sword having fewer boundaries, because ultimately people's expectations on the resulting design are much higher. They expect to see something very different in the resulting design.

Great car design has to be timeless. American car design represents a quick and emotional burst; there is no longevity to it – unless you go back to American design from the 1960s, which is far more emotional and timeless. But then something changed. Common sense in vehicle design means being innovative without destroying the overall styling. Designing a great car is not necessarily something that a designer is aware of at the time, but more something that evolves over time. Only time will tell.'

'DESIGN IS NOT JUST STYLING: IT INCLUDES FUNCTION TOO. FULFILLING ONE BUT NOT THE OTHER IS POOR DESIGN. FORM SHOULD ALWAYS FOLLOW FUNCTION, PARTICULARLY IN AUTOMOTIVE DESIGN.'

*Top, above:* **Lexus movie car, built by Belker for** *Minority Report,* **reflects research into future tranportation systems**

*Right:* **Batmobile adopts a more outrageous approach**

DESIGN DIRECTOR

ASTON MARTIN, NEWPORT PAGNELL, UK

# HENRIK FISKER

Henrik Fisker is design chief at British luxury sports car manufacturer Aston Martin and credited with some of the world's most beautiful sports cars, including BMW's Z8 and the new Aston Martin AMV8 Concept.

## ...ON DESIGN

'Design is essentially the process of making function visually attractive. Design really isn't art because art doesn't necessarily have a function and can be created just how the artist wants it. Design needs to enhance and sell the function, and the function in car design is driving.

Neither function nor design presides over the other – they are co-dependent. Today, design is more important than ever before because everybody has basically the same means and capabilities to create the function of driving.

Design is becoming the most influential part of why a consumer is buying because the function is a given. Yet there are still many car companies out there that are missing that point, not providing enough space for design to be able to make a truly beautiful car.

I don't believe that car design is product design. It's design, but they are very different. Product design is quite possible in the interior [of the vehicle] but those who try to create too literal a product design approach to the exterior of a car have failed.

For me, car design is the most incredible emotional human factor there is, and the ways that people are drawn to cars are incredibly emotional, even irrational.

To me, great car design is the connection between proportion, the surfaces and the graphics. Today, most car companies are only working with the surfaces and the graphics. The proportions are usually given by engineering, which is why people say that most cars look the same in the same class. This is due to the proportion, not the surfaces and the graphics. This is where many car companies are failing today, failing to make different and uniquely beautiful cars.

Historically, the most beautiful cars have been beautiful because of their gorgeous proportions. Take the Jaguar E-Type: its proportions are beautiful. Some of its surfaces are, too, but the graphics are not that great. Yet because the proportions are so fantastic, it overcomes those limitations.

On our latest model – the Aston Martin AMV8 – we created proportions that are great; and then we developed the surfaces and the graphics. All three – the proportion, the surfaces and the graphics – are

well executed, something I believe is extremely important.

Another car that is extremely well executed is the Bentley Continental GT. The graphics and the detailing are very well done, though I don't think the proportions are quite right. I

'DESIGN IS ESSENTIALLY THE PROCESS OF MAKING FUNCTION VISUALLY ATTRACTIVE. DESIGN REALLY ISN'T ART BECAUSE ART DOESN'T NECESSARILY HAVE A FUNCTION AND CAN BE CREATED JUST HOW THE ARTIST WANTS IT.'

think the bonnet is too short and the front wheels are in the wrong place. The cabin is way too big. In my opinion these are not the proportions of a Bentley – but maybe the Bentley people are convinced it is. It is probably more to do with the VW/Audi platform that was most likely required by engineering.

The Bertone Birusa is a wonderful show car. The best Bertone show car for many years. It has outstanding proportions, and very nice surfaces and graphics.

I believe that the face of a car is extremely important. You can argue about the side details, graphics or whatever, but it is the face that is most important. A car needs to have a face. Famous brands have tried to get rid of the face but they haven't been very successful when they have done it. This is why car manufacturers are coming back to the face of the car.

This doesn't necessarily mean that a brand needs the same face across different vehicles. Some companies have been able to take a face and modify it to the type of car – BMW and Mercedes are good examples of companies that do it well – but others do it far less well.

'Every brand should design some styling elements that become part of the brand. Those elements can then be developed and customers will identify with them. I can't think of a brand without this potential.'

...ON DESIGN DETAILS

# CHRIS BROWN

Chris Brown is an in-house hot rod designer for Barry White's Street Rod Repair Company, an award-winning street rod shop in Placentia, California, USA. One of his designs, 'Impact', recently won the America's Most Beautiful Roadster award.

## ...ON DESIGN

'We have more design freedom in that we almost always work on one-off vehicles. But the cars that we design – even though they are far more blue-sky than production vehicles – are loosely based on something else, like a '33 Ford.

Our limitations, as well as our challenges, come from the need to get into the mind of the customer to understand the car design that they desire. The challenge is to try to get some of the customer's personality into the car. They may want a car to be sporty or aggressive or elegant, depending on their personality.

Personalisation is becoming a bigger and bigger factor even in the wider car industry. But for us personalisation is everything. It is the ultimate in personalisation.

I have freedoms in the sense that I can design forms which I know cannot be stamped out of sheet metal – but which can be cut, moulded, welded and massaged into shape. This gives me more freedom. But then we don't design drivetrains, so this is a restriction for us as well. There are other parameters, too, but as far as worrying about a market, the number of cupholders required and so on, we don't need to be concerned with that.

Ergonomic issues are something I strive to work on. Obviously these cars are more sculptural forms than practical road cars, but even so the car is built around the individual and we try to set up the ergonomics as best we can. This includes the switchgear, though this varies from car to car.

## ...ON INTERIORS

Interiors are really the next big thing in hot rod design in terms of evolution. Interiors have been very smooth over the years, but now design details – within the interior – are becoming far more important. This evolution will see new directions in terms of the interior. Right now we just have regular gauges to choose from. But interiors really need to have a lot more impact. We are working towards having branded instrumentation, branded with the SRRC logo. I would love to have our own series of gauges. It is not a reality yet but I would like to create a series of specialist gauge designs, especially designed and detailed for hot rods.

Right, below right: **Agent Orange** was designed for a private client by Chris Brown and is based on a 1933 Ford 3-window pickup.

Background: **Concept 36** draws its inspiration from the 1936 Ford Roadster

'THE CHALLENGE IS TO TRY TO GET SOME OF THE CUSTOMER'S PERSONALITY INTO THE CAR. THEY MAY WANT A CAR TO BE SPORTY OR AGGRESSIVE OR ELEGANT, DEPENDING ON THEIR PERSONALITY.'

For us the distinction between good and great hot rod design really comes down to time and money. But, despite this, the best designs are not necessarily just the cars with the biggest budgets, though it certainly helps.

A hot rod needs certain details to be successful. First, the stance of the car and the rake of the windshield needs to be right. The wheels and the paint job need to be great too. Beyond this, the interior and the exterior graphics really need to be great to reward the viewer, to enhance the overall styling.'

*Left:*
Students and tutors at Coventry School of Art and Design prepare their lists of favoured models for the round-table discussion

# 01.02 | DESIGN ROUND TABLE

WHICH DESIGNS DO THE CAR DESIGNERS THEMSELVES ADMIRE? ASK ANY PRACTISING DESIGNER AND YOU COULD RISK GETTING A LIST OF OBSCURE PRE-WAR CLASSICS AND HEROIC FAILURES THAT NEVER MADE IT INTO VOLUME PRODUCTION: WHAT YOU CERTAINLY WON'T GET IS A ROLL-CALL OF CURRENT MODELS – ESPECIALLY THOSE PRODUCED BY RIVAL COMPANIES.

But what of tomorrow's designers, the crème de la crème of the design schools? These are the bright young talents who will be designing the cars we will be driving in the next five or ten years; they will be

## THE PANEL

NAME: NEIL BIRTLEY
AGE: 59
OCCUPATION:
DESIGN LECTURER
OWN CAR:
PEUGEOT 406 AND 106
ICON SUGGESTION:
**PORSCHE 911**

NAME: DAVID BROWNE
AGE: NOT STATED
OCCUPATION:
TRANSPORTATION
DESIGN LECTURER
OWN CARS:
KANGOO, 2CV, CIVIC
ICON SUGGESTION:
**RENAULT SCÉNIC**

NAME: WILL BRUCE
AGE: 23
OCCUPATION:
4TH YEAR MDES
TRANSPORTATION
DESIGN STUDENT
OWN CAR: NONE
ICON SUGGESTION:
**ALFA 156**

NAME: ROB DOLTON
AGE: 22
OCCUPATION:
4TH YEAR MDES
TRANSPORTATION
DESIGN STUDENT
OWN CAR: VW POLO
ICON SUGGESTION:
**FORD TRANSIT**

NAME: ROBERT FORREST
AGE: 21
OCCUPATION:
4TH YEAR MDES
TRANSPORTATION
DESIGN STUDENT
OWN CAR: NONE
ICON SUGGESTION:
**VW GOLF**

NAME: BENJAMIN GARVEY
AGE: 21
OCCUPATION:
4TH YEAR MDES
TRANSPORTATION
DESIGN STUDENT
OWN CAR: VW GOLF
ICON SUGGESTION:
**MERCEDES S-CLASS**

NAME: GREG HALL
AGE: 22
OCCUPATION:
4TH YEAR MDES
TRANSPORTATION
DESIGN STUDENT
OWN CAR: NONE
ICON SUGGESTION:
**SMART CAR**

the style-setters who will decide the look and the layout of tomorrow's transportation systems. As final-year masters students in a premier-league college – in this case Coventry School of Art and Design – they have been under the watchful eye of talent scouts from the major carmakers for some while; upon graduation they will be eagerly scooped up by the top car companies and swiftly put to work while their imagination is at its most fertile. Initially, their inspiration will most likely be poured into the design of original and creative concept cars, and later they will be allocated to the creation of cars that real buyers will find in their local dealer showroom.

Older designers will happily cite classics like the Citroen DS, Ford Mustang and Ferrari 250GTO as icons of the design craft that have influenced how they work and what they produce. But what are today's classics, the icons that will shape the thinking of the upcoming generation of designers? What will be their equivalent of the GTO, the Mini or the Miura, and how will the influence of these contemporary classics make itself felt in the cars these 23-year-olds go on to create?

In search of these elusive but influential automotive icons of the modern era, we convened a round-table discussion of Coventry's finest – the 2003 MDes students and their tutors. The aim of the debate was to come to some kind of consensus on what were the top design icons of our contemporary world and in the highly unlikely event of broad agreement on the make-up of the top ten we would attempt the impossible and seek to put the cars into an order of preference, too.

The rules of the discussion were simple: only current production cars would be eligible – one-offs, show-only models and concept cars were banned, as were custom designs, specials and racing cars. ❯

NAME: JENNY HANN
AGE: 40
OCCUPATION:
HEAD OF INDUSTRIAL
DESIGN
OWN CAR:
SAAB 9000
ICON SUGGESTION:
**LONDON TAXI**

NAME: NICK HULL
AGE: 40+
OCCUPATION:
MA AUTOMOTIVE DESIGN
COURSE TUTOR
OWN CAR:
HONDA CIVIC, FIAT PUNTO,
RENAULT TWINGO
ICON SUGGESTION:
**HONDA INSIGHT**

NAME: CHRIS JAMES
AGE: 49
OCCUPATION:
DESIGN LECTURER
OWN CARS:
CITROEN BERLINGO,
SMART CABRIO, CITROEN
2CV, CITROEN MEHARI,
MESSERSCHMITT
KR201, VW BEETLE
ICON SUGGESTION:
**HONDA ELEMENT**

NAME: DARREN JONES
AGE: 24
OCCUPATION:
MA AUTOMOTIVE
DESIGN STUDENT
OWN CAR:
NISSAN MICRA
ICON SUGGESTION:
**FORD KA**

NAME: EWAN KINGSBURY
AGE: 22
OCCUPATION:
4TH YEAR TRANSPORT
AND DESIGN STUDENT
OWN CAR:
VAUXHALL NOVA
ICON SUGGESTION:
**LOTUS ELISE**

NAME: JAMES SLIWA
AGE: 24
OCCUPATION:
4TH YEAR MDES
TRANSPORTATION
DESIGN STUDENT
OWN CAR:
VW GOLF GTI
ICON SUGGESTION:
**AUDI TT**

NAME: ANDREW
SOMERVILLE
AGE: 23
OCCUPATION:
4TH YEAR MDES
TRANSPORTATION
DESIGN STUDENT
OWN CAR:
CITROEN SAXO
ICON SUGGESTION:
**HUMVEE**

> Even prototypes bearing the signatures of acknowledged design masters such as Giugiaro, Pininfarina and Bertone were excluded from the analysis in our determination to narrow the focus down to the purest, most innovative and most influential of today's on-the-road designs.

In the event the discussion ranged wildly, enthusiastically – and occasionally furiously – between every known extreme, calling up myriad names in the process. In the short space of the first is minutes the roll-call of names had already taken in everything from the Twingo to Toyota's Prius, and from Bauhaus and Beetles to BMW via Citroen, Swatch and the Scénic-Espace people-carrier axis. Even gargantuan Jeeps, Hummers and Mercedes' brutish last-generation S-Class were hauled up as icons of some kind.

In the final analysis, however, once the referee had quelled the arguments enough for the full-time whistle to be heard and the frenzied debate to be wound down to a sensibly calm conclusion, there emerged a surprisingly clear consensus as to the favourite three or four designs most likely to motivate these embryonic designers in their future careers. Encouragingly, none of these designs were in the least bit exotic, expensive or obscure, though one was a US-only product unlikely to be seen in Europe or Japan.

But if the story of our panel's top choices gave us an unexpectedly easy ride with its surprising unanimity of opinions and expectations, there was no such luxury when it came to sorting out the remaining places in our icon line-up. In fact, the debate is probably still raging somewhere in a Coventry student common room.

*Above:*
**Coventry School of Art and Design trains more than 100 automotive designers each year**

*Right:*
**Final scores are added up, against the background of student designs and quarter-scale models**

'THE INTERESTING THING ABOUT THE GOLF IS THAT IT ISN'T LOOKED UPON AS ASPIRATIONAL IN GERMANY, BUT IN OTHER PARTS OF EUROPE IN CERTAIN PERIODS OF ITS LIFETIME IT HAS BEEN VERY ASPIRATIONAL. THIS ISN'T DUE TO THE BASE MODELS BUT TO VERSIONS LIKE THE GTI.'
ROB DOLTON

'GOING BACK TO ITS ROOTS, THE ORIGINAL WAS DESIGNED BY THE GUY WHO AT THE TIME WAS THE MAESTRO, AND IT KICKED OFF THE WHOLE HATCHBACK TREND. IT WAS THE CAR THAT SAVED VW.'
DAVID BROWNE

'THE QUALITY LEVELS ARE SO HIGH THAT IT HAS BECOME AN ASPIRATIONAL CAR FOR OTHER MANUFACTURERS TO BEAT TOO.'
ROBERT FORREST

'A LOT OF ITS IMAGE DEPENDS ON THE REPUTATION THAT IT HAS BUILT UP OVER THE YEARS. I JUST WONDER HOW YOU WOULD RATE THE CAR IF IT DID NOT HAVE THAT LINEAGE BEHIND IT – IF IT WAS JUST THE PRODUCT ITSELF AND YOU IGNORED ITS HISTORY.'
GREG HALL

'DESIGN IS A PROCESS, NOT JUST THE END RESULT. AND I THINK THIS HAS BEEN WELL DESIGNED.'
ROBERT FORREST

'THERE'S SOMETHING ABOUT ITS VISUAL MANNER THAT SUGGESTS SOLIDITY AND RELIABILITY. I DON'T THINK IT'S ANONYMOUS, BECAUSE IT'S VERY RECOGNISABLE.'
NEIL BIRTLEY

'I THINK IT LACKS A CERTAIN EMOTIVE EDGE THAT ICONIC DESIGN SOMETIMES HAS. AND THAT'S WHAT MAKES IT DESIRABLE TO SUCH A HUGE RANGE OF PEOPLE – IT'S A CLASSLESS DESIGN. IT MAKES A STATEMENT, BUT NOT A STRONG STATEMENT.'
GREG HALL

# VOLKSWAGEN GOLF

"I CHOSE THE GOLF BECAUSE IT IS AN ICONIC CAR, PARTICULARLY IN GERMANY. IN GERMANY IT'S JUST A FAMILY CAR – IT ISN'T TOO PRETENTIOUS, IT HAS BECOME SO UNIVERSAL THAT EVEN THE ROAD SIGNS IN GERMANY SHOW THE SILHOUETTE OF A MK 1 GOLF. THE DESIGN IS A CLASSIC EXAMPLE OF THE ULTIMATE REFINEMENT OF A THEME, AND THE WAY VW KEEPS EXPRESSING THIS THROUGH EACH MODEL GENERATION IS VERY IMPORTANT BUT ALSO VERY RESTRAINED. IT MAY NOT BE AN ICON OF DESIGN, BUT IT IS AN ICONIC CAR."
**ROBERT FORREST**

'I THINK THE ELISE IS ICONIC BECAUSE IT HAS REDEFINED THE MODERN SPORTS CAR. IT REALLY WAS A REVOLUTION FROM BOTH AN AESTHETIC POINT OF VIEW AND AN ENGINEERING POINT OF VIEW. IT WAS ONE OF THE FIRST CARS TO HAVE A BONDED AND RIVETED ALUMINIUM CHASSIS: IT HANDLES BEAUTIFULLY, IT LOOKS GREAT, IT'S VERY RECOGNISABLE AND ASPIRATIONAL – AND I THINK IT IS SOMETHING THAT PEOPLE WILL DEFINITELY REMEMBER IN 20 YEARS TIME.'

**EWAN KINGSBURY**

# LOTUS ELISE

'I HAVE ALWAYS ENJOYED THE INTERIOR MORE THAN THE EXTERIOR. WHAT I HAVE LIKED ABOUT IT IS THAT THE ENGINEERING OF THE CAR IS ON DISPLAY. IT BECOMES THE INTERIOR: THESE MASSIVE ALUMINIUM EXTRUSIONS FORM PART OF THE INTERIOR AND THERE IS ACTUALLY VERY LITTLE TRIM. YOU'RE BASICALLY SITTING IN THE CHASSIS, AND IT'S IN THE SPIRIT OF THE MINIMALISM OF THE CAR TO HAVE THE ENGINEERING ON DISPLAY.'

DAVID BROWNE

'THE MK 1 WAS QUITE A PURE DESIGN. THERE WAS QUITE A LOT OF SURFACE ENTERTAINMENT, LOTS OF COMPLEX CURVES GOING INTO EACH OTHER. BUT IT STILL RETAINED A CERTAIN VISUAL PURITY WHICH REFLECTED THE KIND OF CAR IT WAS – IT DIDN'T LOOK FAT AND IT WASN'T FAT. IT WAS LIGHT AND SMALL AND NIMBLE, AND THIS WAS REFLECTED IN THE AESTHETICS. THAT'S QUITE IMPORTANT.'

EWAN KINGSBURY

'IT'S INTERESTING THAT ALTHOUGH IT'S A VERY MINIMALIST INTERIOR, CUSTOMERS ORDER ON AVERAGE AT LEAST 12 OPTIONS.'

ROBERT FORREST

'I THINK IT'S REAL DESIGN PURITY. ITS FUNCTION AND ITS FORM ARE SO COHERENT TOGETHER, AND IT DISPLAYS WHAT LOTUS ARE ABOUT – THEIR ENGINEERING, THEIR HISTORY. I THINK IT IS ONE OF THE MOST IMPORTANT CARS OF THE LAST DECADE OR SO.'

GREG HALL

'THE NEW VERSION IS PERHAPS A LITTLE TOO FUSSY IN ITS DETAIL. IT GOES AGAINST WHAT IT WAS BEFORE.'

GREG HALL

'THE ELISE HAS SOME OF THE CHARM OF THE LOTUS/CATERHAM SEVEN – WHICH IS A REAL ICON – PLUS SOME STYLE.'

NEIL BIRTLEY

'THE DIFFERENCE BETWEEN THE CATERHAM AND THE ELISE FROM A DESIGN POINT OF VIEW IS THE DESIGN PURITY AND SIMPLICITY OF THE ELISE HAS BEEN BY PURE CONTROL OF THE DESIGNER, WHEREAS IN THE CATERHAM THERE ISN'T ANYTHING OF IT – IT'S JUST FUNCTION, BECAUSE THERE'S NO BODYSHELL OR ROOF.'

ROB DOLTON

'I NOMINATE THE HONDA INSIGHT AS THE FIRST GENUINE HYBRID CAR ON SALE. IT'S UNUSUAL IN STYLE, SLIGHTLY RETRO AND REMINISCENT OF THE CITROEN SM AND THE HONDA CRX. I'M SURE IT WILL BE VERY COLLECTABLE IN THE FUTURE.'
ROBERT FORREST

'ICONS TEND TO BREAK MOULDS, AND THOUGH WE MAY NOT REALISE IT NOW, IN THE FUTURE IT WILL BE IMMATERIAL WHAT IT LOOKS LIKE: HONDA IS THE FIRST COMPANY THAT HAS ACTUALLY BEEN BRAVE ENOUGH TO CHALLENGE THE STATUS QUO AND TRY AND CHANGE THINGS. IT'S A GENUINE ATTEMPT TO MAKE PEOPLE THINK DIFFERENTLY.'
CHRIS JAMES

'YET IT LOOKS AS IF THEY HAVEN'T PUT MUCH EFFORT INTO IT AESTHETICALLY. MAYBE THAT'S NOT WHAT IT'S ABOUT. IF YOU'RE GOING TO DO A CAR WITH A LOT OF ENVIRONMENTAL TECHNOLOGY ON IT, A CAR THAT'S ONE OF THE

ECO-FRIENDLIEST AROUND, IT SEEMS CRAZY THAT THEY DON'T PUT A SIMILAR AMOUNT OF EFFORT INTO HOW IT LOOKS. BECAUSE THAT IS THE WAY PEOPLE WILL PERCEIVE IT: PEOPLE SEE THE CURRENT GENERATION OF ENVIRONMENTALLY FRIENDLY CARS AS DULL.'
EWAN KINGSBURY

'BUT DOES AN ENVIRONMENTALLY FRIENDLY CAR HAVE TO WEAR THAT ON ITS EXTERIOR? THEY ALWAYS SAY THAT THE BEST TECHNOLOGY IS THE TECHNOLOGY YOU DON'T KNOW THAT YOU'RE USING – AND THIS CAN BE CARRIED ACROSS TO THINGS LIKE THE INSIGHT.'
GREG HALL

'IF YOU ARE GOING TO DO IT AS A DESIGNER, SURELY THE POINT IS THAT AS A DESIGNER YOU ARE BEST QUALIFIED TO CREATE THE MATING BETWEEN TECHNOLOGY AND YOUR IDEA OF WHAT A GOOD AESTHETIC IS. IF IT DOESN'T LOOK PARTICULARLY GOOD FOR WHAT IT IS, THEN MAYBE THE DESIGNER HAS FAILED.'
JAMES SLIWA

'I THINK THEY PROBABLY WANTED IT TO LOOK DIFFERENT, BUT THEY COULDN'T DECIDE HOW.'
CHRIS JAMES

'IS THE HONDA INSIGHT AN ICON BECAUSE IT WAS THE FIRST?'
JENNY HANN

# HONDA INSIGHT

'WHAT IMPRESSES ME IS THE COMMITMENT THAT HONDA THREW AT IT. THE MATERIALS AND THE AERODYNAMICS AND SO FORTH – IT WASN'T JUST A QUESTION OF SHOE-HORNING A HYBRID SET-UP INTO A CAR. THE WHOLE CAR IS A COMMITMENT TO MAKING THAT CAR AS LIGHT AND SLIPPERY AND AS SUITED TO BEING DRIVEN AROUND ON BATTERIES AS POSSIBLE. IT WAS A MASSIVE COMMITMENT.'

**DAVID BROWNE**

'I CHOSE THE KA BECAUSE IT'S THE FIRST WITH ITS LANGUAGE – NEW EDGE – AND IT HELPED MOVE THE GAME ON A LOT. THE WAY THE GRAPHICS WORK, THE SURFACES, THE FORM OF THINGS LIKE THE HEADLIGHTS – IT'S REALLY EXCITING AND THE PUBLIC HAVE RESPONDED TO IT. I LIKE THE WAY THAT ALTHOUGH IT'S A SMALL CAR, IT'S FRIENDLY-LOOKING AS WELL AS QUITE SOPHISTICATED. IT'S NOT TOO DUMBED-DOWN LIKE OTHER SMALL CARS ARE.'

**DARREN JONES**

# FORD KA

'I'M NOT MUCH OF A FAN OF IT, AND I HAVE A THEORY ABOUT IT. FORD DESIGNERS DENY THIS, BUT I HAVE THIS HALF-BAKED THEORY THAT NEW EDGE IS AN ACCIDENT OF THE DESIGN PROCESS THAT THEY WERE USING AND NOT TERRIBLY FAMILIAR WITH: WHERE COMPUTER-GENERATED SURFACES MET, YOU GOT AN EDGE.'
DAVID BROWNE

'I'M NOT SURE THE KA WAS EVEN COMPUTER DESIGNED. I THINK IT WAS A SKETCH PROCESS: IT BEGAN WITH THAT VERY METALLIC PINK CREATION THAT GHIA HAD BROUGHT TO THE MOTOR SHOW A COUPLE OF YEARS PREVIOUSLY. ALL OF ITS ELEMENTS WERE IN THAT ONE, THOUGH IT WAS ALL BODY-COLOUR – PINK – AND DIDN'T HAVE THE BLACK.'
NEIL BIRTLEY

'WHERE THE WINGS MEET THE BONNET IT IS REALLY COOL: IT'S RIDGED, AND IT DIPS DOWN FROM THE PEAK.'
ROB DOLTON

'IT HAS A LOT OF CHARM ABOUT IT. IT'S LIKE A LITTLE FROG – CUTE AND FRIENDLY. THE INTERIOR IS FUN, WITHOUT BEING SERIOUSLY FUNCTIONAL AND DESIGNERLY. IT'S A VERY NICE VEHICLE TO DRIVE, TOO.'
CHRIS JAMES

'AGAINST IT, YOU COULD SAY THAT IT IS TOO CUTE – BUT THEN FORD HAS TOTALLY ACHIEVED WHAT IT WANTED TO. IT'S AIMED AT GIRLS, AND GIRLS LOVE THEM.'
ROB DOLTON

'IT HAS GONE OVER TO BODY-COLOUR BUMPERS, WHICH LOSES THE WHOLE POINT OF IT. GRAPHICALLY, IN PROFILE, BLACK IS INVISIBLE, WHICH SHORTENS THE IMPRESSION OF THE CAR. BUT HAVING THE BUMPERS BODY-COLOURED ACTUALLY ACCENTUATES THE LENGTH OF THE CAR.'
EWAN KINGSBURY

'FOR ME IT'S TOO TOY-LIKE, AND IT'S GOT TOO MUCH BUMPER FOR ITS SIZE.'
JENNY HANN

'AS A SUB-B SEGMENT CAR THE KA IS ONE OF THE MOST INTERESTING IN ITS SECTOR. THE ONLY OTHERS ARE THE TWINGO – WHICH HAS NEVER BEEN MADE IN RIGHT-HAND DRIVE – THE VW LUPO AND THINGS LIKE THE FIAT SEICENTO. IT HAS A LOT OF CHARACTER AND A GOOD STANCE.'
GREG HALL

'I THINK IT'S VERY ADAPTABLE. YOU CAN IMPRINT ONTO IT: YOU CAN CHANGE IT THROUGH THE USE OF COLOUR.'
JENNY HANN

'IT'S A FRIENDLY, FUN CAR. IT'S VERY THREE-DIMENSIONAL.'
JENNY HANN

'THE EXTERIOR HAS THE ROLL CAGE AS A GRAPHIC AGAINST THE BODY. IT'S VERY STRONG.'
GREG HALL

'IT'S QUITE A DIFFICULT THING TO DO WITH A VEHICLE OF THIS SIZE, BUT I THINK IT LOOKS FANTASTIC. THE CUSTOMISATION IDEA MAY BE A BIT OF A GIMMICK – I DON'T KNOW HOW MANY PEOPLE WANT TO GET A CAR THEN START CHOPPING AND CHANGING IT THEMSELVES – BUT THAT FUN EDGE TO IT IS ATTRACTIVE AND THE GRAPHICS ACTUALLY MAKE IT LOOK EVEN SHORTER, WHICH IS THE OPPOSITE OF WHAT YOU NORMALLY DO.'
GREG HALL

'IN FACT IT DOES ON THE EXTERIOR WHAT THE ELISE DOES ON ITS INTERIOR. IT DISPLAYS ITS SAFETY CELL, ITS STRUCTURE.'
DAVID BROWNE

'WHAT IT SAYS IS THAT A SMALL CAR DOESN'T NECESSARILY HAVE TO BE CHEAP AND COMPROMISED – AND A LOT OF THE OTHER SMALL CARS WERE COMPROMISED IN VALUE, SPACE AND SO ON. THE SMART IS HIGH ON MY LIST AS I SEE IT AS THE MODERN 2CV BECAUSE THEY'VE ACTUALLY LOOKED AT THE NEED FOR THE VEHICLE – THE COMMUTING NEED, RATHER THAN TO TAKE THAT BASKET OF EGGS ACROSS A PLOUGHED FIELD – AND THEY'VE ACTUALLY DESIGNED A VERY STYLISH VEHICLE THAT PEOPLE WILL WANT AND DESIRE.'
CHRIS JAMES

'YOU CAN ALMOST IGNORE THE FUNCTIONALITY SIDE OF IT AND WANT IT FOR WHAT IT IS.'
GREG HALL

'IT'S OLD-FASHIONED TO DISMISS PLASTIC JUST BECAUSE IT'S PLASTIC, OR TO THINK THAT WOOD IS GOOD JUST BECAUSE IT IS TRADITIONAL: PEOPLE DON'T THINK LIKE THAT ANY MORE.'
GREG HALL

'I'VE GOT TWO OF THESE: MY PARTNER BOUGHT ONE, AND WHEN I DROVE IT I STARTED SMILING — SO I HAD TO HAVE ONE. SO THERE IS SOMETHING THAT'S FAR MORE THAN IT JUST BEING A SENSIBLE CAR.'
CHRIS JAMES

'I'M PUTTING FORWARD THE SMART CAR FOR THE SAME REASONS AS WITH SOME OF THE OTHER CARS WE'VE DISCUSSED. IT'S THE FIRST CAR TO DO SOMETHING NEW: IT'S THE SMALLEST POSSIBLE PACKAGING OF A CITY CAR, AND IT HAS BEEN DONE PROPERLY – UNLIKE SOME OTHERS. IT'S THE ORIGINAL AND BEST CITY CAR.'
**GREG HALL**

'I THINK IT'S VERY WELL EXECUTED FOR WHAT THEY'VE DONE, BUT I ALSO THINK THE CORE INFLUENCE, WHICH IS ARCHITECTURE AND THE BAUHAUS STYLE OF DESIGN PHILOSOPHY, IS MUCH MORE SUITED TO FURNITURE AND ARCHITECTURE: IT HAS A VERY VERTICAL GRAPHIC TO IT. IT'S VERY GEOMETRIC, AND HAVING THIS VERTICAL ELEMENT ISN'T SO APPROPRIATE FOR CARS. IT STILL STRIKES ME AS STRANGE THAT THEY SHOULD INCLUDE IT. IT IS AN ICON, I AGREE WITH THAT, BUT I STILL FIND IT A LITTLE PECULIAR USING THE BAUHAUS PHILOSOPHY FOR SOMETHING THAT IS MOVING.'
ROBERT FORREST

'IT'S WHAT THE GENERAL PUBLIC THINK OF AS A "DESIGNED" CAR. IT'S THE ULTIMATE KIND OF DESIGNER VEHICLE.'
EWAN KINGSBURY

'WITH ME IT'S MORE RESPECT THAN LIKING. I RESPECT THE WAY THEY HAVE GIVEN SO MANY VOLUMES A CERTAIN DEPTH, AND THEY REFLECT THIS IN THE MATERIALS. BUT I STILL FIND IT TOO VERTICAL – IT'S SO STATIC. IT'S SOMETHING YOU WANT TO SIT STILL WITH, NOT SOMETHING YOU WANT TO SEE MOVING – SOMETHING THAT YOU RESPECT AS A PRODUCT, RATHER THAN AS A VEHICLE.'
ROBERT FORREST

'WITH THE COUPÉ THE ONLY FORM THAT GIVES YOU A SERIOUS DYNAMIC IS THE ACCELERATION LINE OF THE C-PILLAR. THAT'S WHAT GIVES THE MOVEMENT.'
GREG HALL

'IT HAS VERY CLEVERLY DONE ONE THING: PEOPLE DON'T THINK OF IT AS A GOLF COUPÉ, WHICH IS WHAT IT OF COURSE IS. IT HAS CREATED ITS OWN IDENTITY: IT HAS DONE WITH THE GOLF WHAT THE FROGEYE SPRITE DID FOR THE AUSTIN A35.'
NEIL BIRTLEY

'IT'S A VERY SATISFYING SCULPTURAL OBJECT, BUT IT'S BETTER APPRECIATED FROM THE OUTSIDE THAN THE INSIDE IN MY PERSPECTIVE. IT'S SO HIGH THAT I FIND IT VERY CLAUSTROPHOBIC, BUT DIFFERENT PEOPLE WILL HAVE DIFFERENT VIEWS ON THAT, I SUSPECT – SOME PEOPLE WILL FEEL HUGGED BY IT AND ENJOY IT AS A DRIVER'S CAR.'
JENNY HANN

# AUDI TT

'YOU JUST NEED TO LOOK AT ONE – YOU DON'T REALLY NEED TO TALK ABOUT IT. IT'S JUST SO PURE, SO WELL BALANCED, WELL DETAILED. I THINK IT JUST WORKS FROM ANY ANGLE.'
JAMES SLIWA

## MERCEDES S-CLASS

'IT'S BASICALLY A STRONG STATEMENT: ITS VISUAL MESSAGE IS POWERFUL.'
BEN GARVEY

'IT'S JUST SUCH AN ACHIEVEMENT – IT'S VISUALLY STUNNING AND STILL BEATING EVERYTHING ELSE THAT HAS COME OUT SINCE. THE ONLY PROBLEM IS THAT THE REST OF THE RANGE IS STARTING TO USE IT AS AN ICON, RATHER THAN HAVING THEIR OWN AESTHETIC.'
ROBERT FORREST

'IT SHOWS THE TRANSITION FROM THE 1980S TO THE 1990S, FROM THE BRASH AND SELFISH TO THE LESS SELFISH, MORE SENSITIVE. THE OLD VERSIONS WERE NICKNAMED CATHEDRALS, THEY WERE SO LARGE. THE NEW ONE NOW IS A VERY ELEGANT CAR AND IT IS TECHNOLOGICALLY EXCELLENT, TOO.'
BEN GARVEY

## ALFA ROMEO 156

'THIS BUCKS THE TREND FOR CURRENT VEHICLES TO FOLLOW THE GERMANIC FORM. IT HAS GONE FOR A MUCH MORE ELEGANT SHAPE, MUCH MORE EMOTIONAL – AND IT HAS WORKED: THE CAR HAS DONE VERY WELL FOR ALFA.'
WILL BRUCE

'I THINK IT IS FANTASTIC FOR THE PRICE. IT HAS SOME VERY NEAT TRICKS SUCH AS THE DOOR HANDLES.'
GREG HALL

'IT COULD ONLY BE ITALIAN.'
JAMES SLIWA

'I THINK IT IS WELL STYLED, BUT I DON'T THINK IT IS AN ICON. I DON'T THINK IT HAS ENOUGH RELEVANCE TO BECOME AN ICON: IT'S JUST ANOTHER RIVAL FOR THAT MARKET THAT LOOKS DIFFERENT, HAS A BIT OF PERSONALITY. BUT I DON'T THINK IT ACTUALLY CHANGES ANYTHING.'
ROBERT FORREST

## RENAULT SCÉNIC

'I PUT THE SCÉNIC FORWARD BECAUSE IT WAS THE FIRST ONE IN THE MOVEMENT TOWARDS THAT TYPE OF VEHICLE – SO I SUPPOSE IN THAT SENSE IT ESTABLISHED A TREND AND WAS INFINITELY MORE SUCCESSFUL THAN IT WAS EXPECTED TO BE. I THINK MORE OF THIS THAN I DO OF THE ESPACE, WHICH I HAVE NEVER SEEN AS MORE THAN A VAN WITH WINDOWS.'
DAVID BROWNE

'THE NEW SCÉNIC MOVES THE GAME ON ONCE MORE. IT MAKES QUITE A DRAMATIC COMPARISON – THE NEW SCENIC COMING OUT AT JUST THE SAME TIME AS THE VW TOURAN AND THE FORD FOCUS C-MAX, WHICH ARE BOTH VERY CONSERVATIVE. RENAULT HAS CLEARLY MOVED THE GAME ON WAY PAST WHERE THESE TWO ARE.'
NICK HULL

## HONDA ELEMENT

'IT'S ONLY AVAILABLE IN THE US, BUT I THINK IT'S GREAT THE WAY THEY ARE MARKETING THIS VEHICLE MORE OR LESS AS A BLANK CANVAS FOR PEOPLE TO IMPOSE THEIR OWN LIFESTYLE ON. IT'S SOLD AS A LIFESTYLE VEHICLE, BUT NOT AS ONE FITTING INTO A CATEGORY SUCH AS A SPORTS CAR OR A VAN. IT'S TODAY'S SUCCESSOR TO THE VW MICROBUS, WHICH COULD MEAN VERY DIFFERENT THINGS TO MANY DIFFERENT PEOPLE. IT FALLS INTO MY DEFINITION OF WHAT TRANSPORTATION BY CAR IS ALL ABOUT: IT'S THE CHEAPEST WAY OF TRANSPORTING PEOPLE OR MOVING YOUR STUFF. HONDA HAS GONE TO GREAT PAINS TO AVOID IT FALLING INTO EXISTING CATEGORIES: SOME OF THE PROPOSALS WERE REJECTED FOR BEING TOO CAR-LIKE, TOO VAN-LIKE OR TOO MUCH LIKE AN OFF-ROADER.'
CHRIS JAMES

'IT'S MARKET LED, IT'S LISTENING TO WHAT PEOPLE WANT – IT'S NOT WHAT DESIGNERS WANT TO FORCE UPON US. IT'S LISTENING TO GENERATION Y, WHICH WANTS SOMETHING DIFFERENT.'
ROBERT FORREST

## FORD TRANSIT

'JUST AS THE GOLF WAS PICKED FOR WHAT IT HAS ALWAYS BEEN, I'M PICKING THE FORD TRANSIT. THE TRANSIT REVOLUTIONISED THE WAY PEOPLE CARRY THEIR THINGS AROUND, AND THE NEW ONE IS QUITE A STYLISH PIECE OF DESIGN. WITH THIS ONE THEY WENT BACK TO WHAT THEY DID WITH THE ORIGINAL ONE – IT'S QUITE A SEXY BIT OF DESIGN, FOR A VAN.'
ROB DOLTON

'THE TRANSIT IS MORE FUNCTIONAL, WHEREAS THE NEW RENAULT TRAFIC IS MORE FUNKY AND HAS MORE STYLE. BUT IN TERMS OF LOAD CUBE VALUES THEY ARE PROBABLY ABOUT EQUAL.'
NEIL BIRTLEY

'IT'S FUNCTIONAL, DOES WHAT IT HAS TO DO EXTREMELY WELL, BUT IT HAS SOMETHING ON TOP OF THAT WHICH ADDS AN EXTRA NUANCE OF DESIGN. IT WILL BE AN ICON.'
ROB DOLTON

## HUMMER

'A LOT OF ICONS WE HAVE BEEN TALKING ABOUT – LIKE THE VW BEETLE, THE JEEP AND SO ON – HAVE COME ABOUT FOR A PURPOSE. THE HUMMER HAS AN OBVIOUS PURPOSE, BUT IT HAD SUCH AN ICONIC STATUS THAT PEOPLE ACTUALLY DEMANDED TO BUY IT. FROM THAT IT HAS GIVEN US A NEW LANGUAGE, WHICH WE INDICATE AS BEING TOUGH, FOR EXAMPLE. THE 'CIVILIAN' H2, LIKE A LOT OF CURRENT CAR DESIGN, IS NO MORE THAN A PASTICHE, TAKING INSPIRATION FROM WHAT'S GONE BEFORE AND REHASHING IT. AN ICON HAS TO STAND UP AND SHOUT "I'M HERE!". IT DOESN'T HAVE TO BE ORIGINAL, BUT IT DOES HAVE TO BE THE BEST. THE H2 JUST ISN'T – IT'S SECOND BEST.'
ANDREW SOMERVILLE

'THROUGH PEOPLE'S DESIRE FOR IT, THEY HAVE CREATED A BRAND – JUST AS WITH JEEP AND LAND ROVER.'
ROB DOLTON

## PORSCHE 911

'THE PORSCHE 911 IS A MODERN CLASSIC OF ITS TIME. IN SCULPTURAL TERMS IT'S A REALLY BEAUTIFUL PIECE OF WORK. THE SURFACE DEVELOPMENT IS EXQUISITE, THE USE OF SHUT-LINES IS EXQUISITE, THE USE OF SHEET METAL IS EXQUISITE.'
NEIL BIRTLEY

'THE LATEST GENERATION HAS LOST THE POWER THE 993 HAD. THE NEW ONE IS MORE ELEGANT, BUT IT HAS LOST THAT REALLY GORGEOUS REVERSE-S HIGHLIGHT ON THE REAR ARCH NOW THAT THEY HAVE FLATTENED IT DOWN A BIT. IT'S A SHAME AS THAT WAS A REALLY STAND-OUT BEAUTIFUL BIT OF AUTOMOTIVE SCULPTURE.'
ROB DOLTON

## RENAULT TWINGO

'THE TWINGO HAS A CUTESY CHARM LIKE A FORD KA, FOR SURE, BUT ITS PACKAGING IS VASTLY BETTER. IT WAS DESIGNED INSIDE OUT, WITH A VERY INTELLIGENT INTERIOR. IF YOU STICK A SCÉNIC AND A MEGANE TOGETHER THE POSITION OF THE DRIVER IS EXACTLY THE SAME, WHEREAS THE TWINGO ACTUALLY MOVED THE DRIVER FORWARD BY MOVING THE BULKHEAD FORWARD, WRAPPING IT ROUND THE ENGINE AND REALLY MAKING THE MOST OF THE INTERIOR SPACE AND DROPPING THAT SLIDING SEAT IN. IT COMBINES THE CHEEKY, CHARMING EXTERIOR WITH AN EXTREMELY FUNCTIONAL INTERIOR.'
CHRIS JAMES

'THE PACKAGING IS UNCOMPROMISED. IT IS LEFT-HAND DRIVE ONLY, ONE ENGINE ONLY, AND WITH ONLY ONE SET OF WHEELS – SO THE PACKAGE CAN BE ABSOLUTELY TIGHT, BUT THERE IS NO ROOM FOR MANOEUVRE.'
DAVID BROWNE

## 01.03 | FROM SKETCH TO SHOWROOM

IT IS OFTEN SAID – ESPECIALLY BY ENGINEERS – THAT DESIGNING THE SHAPE OF THE CAR IS THE EASY BIT: THE REAL HARD WORK COMES IN THE HUNDREDS OF SUBSEQUENT STEPS REQUIRED TO TRANSLATE THE DESIGNER'S ARTISTIC VISION INTO A REAL CAR FOR REAL PEOPLE TO BUY. ALL TOO OFTEN, THE COMBINATION OF INTERNAL COMPANY TENSIONS, PRICE PRESSURES AND THE STRICTURES OF OFFICIAL LEGISLATION CONSPIRE TO STRIP THE ORIGINAL IDEA OF ITS SPIRIT AND ORIGINALITY; IT'S RARE INDEED FOR A DESIGN TO MAKE THE JOURNEY FROM SKETCHBOOK TO SHOWROOM WITHOUT ITS ESSENTIAL ESSENCE IN SOME WAY BEING DILUTED.

HERE, HOWEVER, WE TRACE THROUGH FIVE REAL-LIFE MODEL PROGRAMMES WHICH HAVE DONE JUST THAT: THEY HAVE SAVOURED THAT VITAL FIRST GLINT IN THE DESIGNER'S EYE, PROTECTED IT AGAINST THE CHILL WINDS OF RATIONALISATION, GLOBALISATION AND FOCUS GROUPS, AND DELIVERED IT INTACT TO THE CUSTOMER, FAITHFUL TO ITS ORIGINAL INSPIRATION AND INSIGHT. IN EACH CASE THE DESIGNERS HAVE BEEN FERVENT IN THEIR BELIEF IN THE PRODUCT; IN MANY OF THE CASES THEY HAVE HAD TO BATTLE AGAINST ENORMOUS ODDS TO SEE THOSE IDEAS BROUGHT TO FRUITION. BUT WHAT NO-ONE WOULD DISPUTE IS THAT IT WAS WORTH THE STRUGGLE.

# RANGE ROVER

LIKE MANY BRITISH CARMAKERS, LAND ROVER HAS A HISTORY OF PRODUCT AND DESIGN INNOVATION HAMPERED BY FINANCIAL CONSTRAINTS STEMMING FROM TROUBLES AT ITS PARENT COMPANY. AGAINST THIS BACKGROUND, THE DESIGN AND ENGINEERING OF THE THIRD-GENERATION RANGE ROVER INTRODUCED IN 2002 OFFERS A REFRESHING CONTRAST AS AN EXAMPLE OF A COMPANY FREED TO CREATE A PRODUCT IN LINE WITH ITS IMAGE AS THE BUILDER OF THE WORLD'S MOST LUXURIOUS AND CAPABLE 4X4.

M. SAMPSON

Before BMW bought Land Rover, the cash-strapped British company planned a major face-lift of its Range Rover, budgeted at £176 million ($280 million). Once BMW got involved, the project mushroomed to £650 million – enough for an all-new car and a refit of the factory too. In 2000, BMW sold Land Rover to Ford Motor Company.

Land Rover design director Geoff Upex and chief designer Don Wyatt tackled the project detail, while Ford Premier Automotive Group boss Wolfgang Reitzle provided the strategic direction: to create the world's best Sports Utility Vehicle (SUV).

*Above:* Design concept work on the new Range Rover began in 1996, five years before the eventual launch

Mike Sampson.

*Above:* **Near-final rendering of exterior shows more conventional proportions – a retreat from earlier themes with long hood**

Design concept work started at Land Rover's Gaydon, Warwickshire, design centre in 1996, five years ahead of launch. The starting point was to identify the essence of Range Rover design, an exercise that took the team back to the design theme of the 1970s original.

An internal design competition produced 12 one-third scale models, which were judged by the design team of about 20 people. Designers from BMW contributed two models and UK consultancy DRA a third.

From this meeting, a design by Phil Simmons, now chief designer of Mercury, emerged as favourite. Simmons's car mixed the proportions and dimensions of the original, while adding a sportier style inspired by the upmarket Riva Aquarama speedboat. A nautical theme was to feature later in the project as the Range Rover neared production.

But the Simmons car wasn't yet cleared for production. Four proposals – two each from Land Rover and BMW – went forward to a further competition in August 1997. Eventually the choice was narrowed down to one each from the British and Germans.

After further fine-tuning, Simmons's car was chosen in November 1997 as the production design, 18 months after the project started in earnest. The sportier elements of his design were toned down, exaggerated features like the long engine bay and set-back cabin taking on more conventional proportions. But the links with the original Range Rover remained strong.

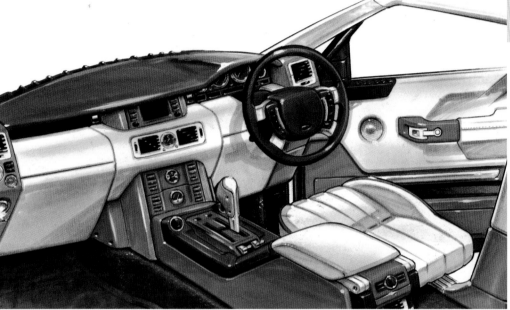

*Left:* **Many interior themes were explored before the final choice fell upon Gavin Hartley's solution, inspired by classic powerboats**

*Above:* **Early exterior design themes had set-back cabins and exaggerated hood length**

A further seven months of detailed design work – split between studios in England and Germany – contributed to the final clay model signed off in July 1998.

Around the same time the interior got the green light, although its detail took longer to freeze than the exterior. Eight models were produced for BMW and Land Rover to choose from, although two themes developed – one dubbed 'architectural' and another 'luxurious'. The former, the work of Gavin Hartley, was the design that went forward to production, its lines characterised by a strong cowl, subtle strips of wood decoration and a dominant centre console.

Interior textures borrowed from Simmons's nautical influence, with a 'foundry-finish' effect for items like the centre console, borrowed from high-quality sailboat fixtures.

Too often, the move to series production can rob a design of such unique elements but the Range Rover's carefully controlled design process, guided consistently towards a clear goal, has delivered a highly attractive luxury 4x4 that is now a strong commercial success, too.

# AUDI TT

NO DESIGN CAN CLAIM TO HAVE BEEN AS INFLUENTIAL IN THE LATE 1990S AS THE AUDI TT. SHOWN AT THE FRANKFURT MOTOR SHOW IN 1995, THE DRAMATIC TT SPLIT OPINION THE MINUTE IT WAS UNVEILED. THE PAGES OF THE WORLD'S MOTOR MAGAZINES WERE FILLED WITH LETTERS ATTACKING ITS STYLING, WITH ONE CORRESPONDENT GOING AS FAR AS DESCRIBING IT AS A 'COWPAT'.

But three years later, after its launch as a production car in September 1998, the TT had customer waiting lists all over Europe. And within a couple of years it had become market leader in many European countries, shaking up the establishment.

Like any forward-thinking idea, the TT challenged established norms to a huge degree. Its curvaceous body with flowing roofline and tight front and rear overhangs, combined with its dominant detailing, were

a major departure for a small coupé. But they were well considered, making the most of the compact, Golf-derived transversely mounted front engine and four-wheel-drive transmission set-up.

In previous decades, coupés had tended to follow classical design proportions, derived from their longitudinal front-engined, rear-drive mechanical configuration. The TT proved that a transverse front-engined coupé could be credible.

It wasn't all innovation with the TT, however, and there were precedents for the challenging shape. This was created in a top-secret works outside Audi's main design studios by exterior designer Freeman Thomas, an American now working for Chrysler, and interior designer Romulus Rost, whose credits later included the Audi A2.

Back in the 1960s VW had spun off a coupé version of the Beetle by coachbuilders Karmann and Ghia, and some of its proportions can be seen in the TT. Ironically, while the TT was in development a new Beetle was in the pipeline, its prominently arched roofline a perfect companion to the curvaceous TT.

The original TT exterior was created in top-secret works outside Audi's design studios. It proved sensational. The interior set the style for dozens of imitators, with impeccable metal detailing

Of equal significance is the TT's interior design, which has spawned dozens of imitations. The fascia mixed high-quality plastics with jewellery-like details for components previously treated as functional and not worth emphasising by clever design execution. For example, the circular air vents were detailed with high-quality chrome rings to control the airflow, and between the instrument panel and centre console were alloy buttresses of architectural merit. The beautifully lit instruments moved cabin detailing to another level for a mid-priced car.

But as with any challenging design, good timing played a big part in the TT's commercial success. The concept spawned a production car launched at a period of unprecedented economic expansion in Europe and North America and growing design literacy among affluent 30-something urban-dwellers.

A measure of the TT's incredible design integrity must be the way it easily survived a safety scare in the US and Germany. Wayward high-speed handling was fixed with suspension modifications and a boot-lip spoiler, which interfered with Thomas's swooping trunk line but failed to dent the car's sales.

A measure of any design's influence is the flood of imitations appearing in its wake. And there are plenty of those on the market.

# NISSAN 350Z

**DESIGN AND FLAIR ARE WORDS NOT USUALLY ASSOCIATED WITH JAPANESE CARMAKERS, BUT TODAY'S RENAULT-OWNED NISSAN IS NO LONGER A TYPICAL JAPANESE CARMAKER. CREATIVITY AND DESIGN INDIVIDUALITY ARE NEW PRIORITIES FOR A COMPANY AMBITIOUSLY SHAKEN UP BY PRESIDENT CARLOS GHOSN AND DESIGN DIRECTOR SHIRO NAKAMURA.**

*Right:* **Nissan 350Z coupé draws inspiration from the Datsun Z sports cars of the '60s, identified by Nissan designers as one of the highlights of the company's history. Comparison of sketch and final product shows how faithful to the original concept the series car has remained**

Key to this strategy are niche models, and none is more significant than the 350Z, a mid-size sports coupé revealed to widespread acclaim as the Z Concept at the Detroit Auto Show in January 2000. For while Nissan is seen in Europe as a brand lacking in excitement, the reverse is true in the US where the heritage of the 1970s 240Z still holds strong, giving the 350Z a strong resonance with buyers.

The previous Nissan sports coupé was the 300ZX, designed by Yoshio Maezawa, and also highly influenced by the US market. Maezawa resigned from Nissan in the late 1980s, frustrated by the lack of commitment by Nissan management to design innovation in production.

The story of the Z is a parable for a company wanting to rejuvenate its image with innovative new product, but also a case study in how a production car can remain faithful to its design concept.

Ghosn's amazing turnaround of Nissan was only just getting into its stride when the 350Z was pencilled into the product plan in 1999. Nissan had an enviable network of studios around the world – three in Japan, two in the US and one in Europe. All three continents were asked to submit designs for the production version, the 350Z, and three months after the Detroit reveal, ten one-third scale models had been whittled down to three.

Each was then developed into a full-size clay and shipped to Japan for evaluation by Nissan's top management. The winner came from the San Diego, California, studio of Nissan Design America (NDA) – although like most new models, it featured a team of international designers, its exterior being the work of British talent Ajay Panchal and its interior by Alfonso Albaisa, a Cuban. To take the concept towards production, NDA designer Diane Allen joined the team.

The design features classic rear-drive coupé proportions with tight overhangs, a broad stance and sweeping roofline. However, the detailing is more contemporary, featuring rectangular headlights, door handles mounted vertically and trapezoidal rear lights, which are neatly integrated into the curvy shutlines of the hatch.

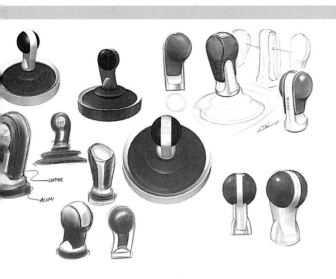

'The brief was to capture 'zee-ness' and make a design statement with a level of modernity and style that shouldn't look backwards,' said Panchal at the concept reveal.

But as is usually the case with a Japanese carmaker, the detail production design was handed over to the studio closest to the engineers and factory entrusted with production. The link is intended to ensure prime quality of fit and finish, but also top-level handling on the road. To this end, Nissan handling guru Kazutoshi Mizuno, father of the Skyline GT-R super coupé, was entrusted with the chassis design.

Nissan broke the geographic link between the creative design in San Diego and the production design in Tokyo but was highly successful in bringing the main details of the Z Concept into the production car.

## MINI

SOMETIMES A NEW CAR PROGRAMME BECOMES MORE THAN A CONVENTIONAL DESIGN AND ENGINEERING CHALLENGE. MIX IN THE BAGGAGE OF AN ICONIC ORIGINAL AND THE POLITICS OF TWO MERGED COMPANIES BATTLING TO FIND COMMON GROUND AND THE PROJECT TO CREATE THE NEW MINI FITS THAT BILL PERFECTLY.

MINI Cooper S is the most extreme version of BMW's born-again Mini. Despite numerous changes of management during the design process, the final MINI successfully captures the spirit of the original icon

Conceived in 1993 — eight years before it went on sale — the MINI became a roller-coaster ride of changed management priorities, revamped designs, technical in-fighting and board-level financial politics. That it survived to be commercially successful is as much a testament to the Alec Issigonis original as to the tenacity of BMW.

Twelve months before BMW bought Rover, the British company began exploring the feasibility of replacing the Mini, including radical city car ideas like a three-seater with central driving position.

But the arrival of BMW brought a change in direction. The German company's decision-makers were inspired by Mini's motorsport heritage and in the summer of 1994, Project R59 was born.

Design teams in the UK, Germany and the US worked on proposals – but in very different directions. British designers stuck to the utility car roots of the 1959 original, partly encouraged by the charm offensive of BMW bosses towards surviving members of the original's design team. Meanwhile BMW designers in Germany and the US followed a direction inspired by the Mini Cooper.

The tussle culminated in a design presentation in October 1995 at which six key design proposals were presented to management. From Rover there were three cars, called Evolution, Revolution and Spiritual.

Evolution, by Dave Saddington, was an update of the original, using classic cues but a more practical interior. Revolution, by consultants DRA, was a contemporary hatchback design, while Spiritual was a radical, rear-engined city car by Oliver le Grice, shown two years later at the 1997 Geneva motor show.

BMW's cars included a retro, sporty hatch, by American Frank Stephenson, and a Teutonic hatchback from the Californian Designworks think-tank.

The retro theme got the thumbs up and both Saddington's and Stephenson's cars were pushed forward to the feasiblity stage. But then the first signs of dissent emerged. British designers and

managers felt the Spiritual concept, so named because of its Issigonis links, had been unfairly sidelined and a campaign was waged to get it reconsidered. Meanwhile Saddington's and Stephenson's designs had to be rationalised into one. The new MINI, by now code-named E50, was to have Saddington's interior package with Stephenson's exterior styling adapted to fit the more practical cabin.

Engineering the car proved another test of the relationship between the British and German cultures, one that would ultimately end in the split between the two companies. Engineering was switched from Germany to Britain in 1996 and the code-name changed again, this time to R50, though overall control was exercised by a 'shadow' engineering team in Germany. By late 1999, the conflict between Germany and Britain came to a head and project manager Chris Lee was moved off the project. For a further six months a Briton continued to run the show, but in summer 1999 a German was appointed – the fourth project director – to take the all-new MINI to its on-sale date of July 7, 2001.

As an example of how not to manage the replacement of any car, let alone an icon, the MINI seems like a perfect example. Except that the car went on to sell well, its design and engineering integrity shining through the fog of its tortuous industrialisation. Its successor, wholly under BMW's control, is likely to be a much more comfortable project.

## RENAULT MÉGANE

CODENAMED X84, THE SECOND-GENERATION RENAULT MÉGANE IS A BROAD DEVELOPMENT SWEEP FOR A NEW FAMILY OF VEHICLES – FOR X84 ENCOMPASSES SEVEN DIFFERENT MODELS, CODED FROM A TO G AND RANGING FROM A FOUR-DOOR SEDAN TO A SEVEN-SEATER MINIVAN AND A TWO-DOOR COUPÉ-CABRIOLET WITH A FOLDING GLASS ROOF.

The X84 family is significant for many more reasons than the sheer variety of shapes, roles and sizes it embraces – though this had a big effect on the sheer logistics of the project. The simultaneous development of so many different models as a co-ordinated and coherent group represents the culmination of everything Patrick le Quément, senior vice president of corporate design, has worked towards since arriving at Renault in the late 1980s.

The great success of the previous family of Mégane-based models permitted a higher level of investment in the new-generation designs. Each model has much greater differentiation in external styling, for instance, and several completely different instrument panel configurations ensure there is no compromise between the conflicting requirements of, say, a family with young children in a Scénic and an affluent older couple in a Coupé-Cabriolet.

An unexpected wild card entered the equation when, in spring 1999, Renault announced its alliance with Japan's Nissan. Immediately, talk of component and platform sharing was in the air, and Renault engineers had to reassess their work in the light of this new dimension. None of this lessened the resolve of the Renault teams to bring the first new Mégane versions to market in summer 2002 – that was 29 months after styling freeze compared with the 47 months taken by the previous model.

From the start, le Quément wanted to address the Mégane's market segment – the largest in Europe – with distinctive style. 'The segment has some anonymous cars – and some strong designs,

such as the Focus and the Golf,' he says. 'Right from the beginning, we wanted a strong identity and personality – and we deliberately haven't done an average-type car clinicked down to the last detail.

'For the X84 programme we got together a group of highly motivated designers: we always open up the competition to whoever wants to participate. It's never an eight-to-five job here in any case.'

Le Quément says the five-door was strongly influenced by the Vel Satis concept car of 1999, with its long wheelbase, and short rear and long front overhangs. 'The upright, wraparound backlight is inspired by the Vel Satis, too,' he says. 'The rear end is the most characteristic, with that upright backlight and the short decklid.

'The front and rear themes revolve around the logo,' he explains, 'and on the sides the shape of the doors – especially on the three-door – becomes an element. The mass is located above the rear wheel, giving a propulsive look. It helps express safety and agility.'

The three-door has a long roofline and distinctive DLO (daylight-opening side window shape, inspired by the Koleos concept). DLO is 'even more propulsive', says the design director; in the interior, le Quément and his team chose to go with something 'extremely calm and serene, with intuitive controls and great legibility and simplicity'.

Noticeably absent from the whole process – which involved selecting from three designs for each variant and deciding to go with one – was any sense of conflict with management. But le Quément praised his 'real petrol head' programme director Carlos Savarez: 'It would have been much more difficult if we had had a business person in charge.'

# LINCOLN

·RARELY DOES A CREATIVE TEAM HAVE THE CHANCE TO CREATE A GROUND-UP REDESIGN OF A COMPLETE CAR BRAND. BUT THAT'S WHAT HAPPENED IN 2000 WHEN FORD DECIDED TO BREATHE NEW LIFE INTO LINCOLN, ITS LUXURY ARM IN THE USA.

Based in a studio in Oxfordshire, England, newly appointed Lincoln design director Gerry McGovern made up the strength of his 30 or so designers with international recruits from across the industry who started working on every aspect of Lincoln, including a ground-up redefinition of the brand. The commercial plan was to lift Lincoln from the US and make it an international luxury brand with an expanded product range, of up to 14 new models, with quality equal to Mercedes and Lexus.

McGovern's team summed up the brand as 'American Luxury' and produced two impressive show cars, the Mk9 coupé at the 2001 New York Auto Show and the Continental saloon at the 2002 Detroit Auto Show to illustrate the point.

Both concepts displayed the influence of Elwood Engel's masterpiece, the 1961 Continental, the car that McGovern's team identified as the root of Lincoln's design DNA. 'The visual language, the body side section, the simplicity of it, are wonderful. There's an elegance very appropriate to today,' said McGovern at the time. The 1961's interior, with two identical cowls making up the dashboard also fed through to the modern day.

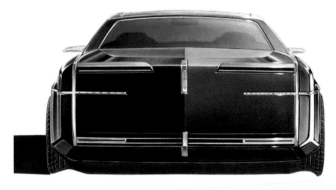

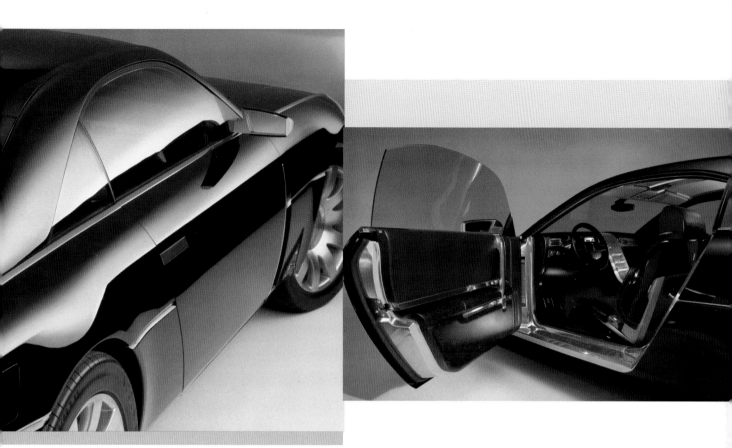

Compared to Cadillac's avant garde 'Art and Science' new design direction, the new Lincolns were conservative and traditional. They were also suitably grand, taking the proportions of luxury saloons from Bentley and Rolls-Royce as a measure of Ford's then ambition for Lincoln.

Taking the luxury theme to heart, the car's interiors became a vital element of the design and engineering, the Continental exploring rear-hinging back-doors – another influence from the '61 model.

Such design niceties need a practical engineering solution and at this stage, the ambitious Lincoln product plan sadly spluttered to a halt. Ford hit a cash crisis in 2002, shedding top managers, and the ambitions for Lincoln were put on hold.

However, the basic work on brand values still holds and the 2003 Detroit show saw the reveal of the Navicross, a crossover sedan with increased ground-clearance and four-wheel drive. Design features like the broad, brushed-chrome grille, metallic highlights over the haunches and rear-hinging backdoors still featured. Lincoln's original plan included a smaller sedan, about the size of a BMW '4-series'. The Navicross suggests some ideas on how that car might look in production.

The Lincoln concepts are also influencing the future direction of Ford North America's next generation of passenger cars. Also at 2003 Detroit was the Ford 427, a large four-door sedan with similar design language to the Lincoln concepts – characteristics such as simple body surfacing and classical dimensions.

As Ford continues with this theme, it is reasonable to predict that other US car manufacturers will absorb such influences, painting Lincoln as a significant leader in car design over the next ten years – even though its ambitions as a brand may have been put on hold for some while.

*Above:* **Lincoln Mk9 Coupé,** presented at the 2001 New York show, reflects the elegance of the original 1961 Continental, seen as the root of Lincoln's design DNA

*Far left:* **2002 Continental** concept echoes the simple visual language of Elwood Engel's '61 masterpiece

## 01.04 | THE WORLD OF INTERIORS

UNTIL SURPRISINGLY RECENTLY, THE INTERIOR DESIGN OF AUTOMOBILES WAS REGARDED BY MANY OF THE WORLD'S AUTOMOTIVE DESIGN STUDIOS AS THE POOR RELATION TO THE EXTERIOR STYLING OF THOSE SAME CARS.

IN FACT, FOR MOST CAR COMPANIES INTERIOR DESIGN WAS SO FAR DOWN THE LIST OF DESIGN PRIORITIES THAT MANY DESIGNERS BELIEVED THE LEAST TALENTED MEMBERS OF THE PROFESSION ENDED UP WORKING ON CAR INTERIORS. IT WAS HARDLY SURPRISING, THEN, THAT THE MAJORITY OF DESIGNERS REALLY DID NOT WANT TO DO INTERIORS AS THEY WEREN'T SEEN AS VERY GLAMOROUS. 'INTERIOR DESIGN, INFERIOR DESIGN' WAS THE GENERAL FEELING ABOUT CAR INTERIOR DESIGN WITHIN THE CAR DESIGN COMMUNITY.

There were exceptions to this of course: some good interiors were designed in both North America and Europe, but most were on low production runs of luxury or sporty vehicles. In the main, car interiors were never as stylish, as comfortable or as functional as they should have been: they tended to be no more than packaged spaces, dictated by exterior form restrictions and often put together as cheaply as possible.

However, by the 1990s this situation had at last began to change. The reason for this was simple. Manufacturers were beginning to find it increasingly difficult to differentiate their products from the competition through exterior styling alone. What was more, drivers were spending more and more time in their cars and often in stationary traffic. This meant that the car companies and their customers began reassessing the comfort, the functionality and the general ambience of the interiors of the cars that they built and drove.

Today, interior car design is an emerging, challenging and exciting area of product design. It is also an area of design becoming

more directly influenced by trends in fashion and home furnishings than ever before. Often, interior designers' backgrounds are in product or industrial design rather than automotive or transportation design. And the reason for this is simple enough.

For the car designer, the design of an interior presents a quite different set of challenges to those posed by the exterior styling. Outside a vehicle, the human form rarely has to interact with the car other than when entering or exiting the vehicle or opening the trunk space. Yet, inside the vehicle, the human form does virtually nothing else. Increasingly, design studios are becoming more and more involved in observing the way in which people use their cars in real-life day-to-day situations. As a result the trend is to create interiors that are far more useful than ever before. Furthermore, brand strategists are increasingly looking at ways in which the interior design of a car can add character and identity to a brand; to increase the emotional connection consumers have with their cars, in a way that has been traditionally left only to the exterior design.

The challenge for the car industry now is to create genuine design identities for the interiors of the vehicles it produces. We take a closer look at three contemporary examples of cars with exceptional or unusual interior designs that have helped to change the way in which the car industry views interior design.

# MINI

Early MINI interior proposals included many features recalling the iconic 1959 original – such as large central instruments, rev counter on steering column, and hollow door cavities. These made production, whereas ambitious seating arrangement did not

The original Mini, designed by Sir Alec Issigonis, was launched in 1959. At the time nobody had any idea that it was destined to become an automotive icon or that it would last decades in its original form – and almost without any changes to its shape or style.

To say that it was a design challenge to bring the Mini into the 21st century would be an understatement. It is a tough job to redesign an icon and it would have been very costly to get it wrong.

But BMW Group did a great job of it. Launched at the Paris Motor Show in 2000, the new MINI has been a remarkable success for the German owner of the brand. The model has been a worldwide sales success – even in the North American market, where the design is proving to be just big enough, and certainly funky enough, to hold its own.

But, according to brand owner BMW, its MINI is not a retro design car, but an 'evolution'. BMW says its designers approached the design of the car by asking themselves how the Mini would have looked if it had evolved and been continually developed over the years.

Anglophile chief designer Frank Stephenson was responsible for the MINI's design, ensuring it was just the right blend of old and new. From the outside the designers set out to really understand the emotion and character of the original car. So did they succeed?

Outside, the car has managed to capture most of the character of the original, despite being bigger and having different proportions, a wider stance, larger flanks and a bigger behind. What's more, the car is a hatchback, unlike the original. But the MINI has its hood, lights and grille and its flared wheel arches shaped to give the car a face that seems very familiar, as if it's a bigger and trendier brother of the original. Which is just what the designers set out to do, of course.

Inside the car has picked up themes of the original, with styling features (just like on the outside) which make the car recognisably Mini, though it is significantly different and sufficiently contemporary to capture the imagination of 21st century car buyers.

The interior design is a modern interpretation of the simple and straightforward look of the original Mini. The car features a dash that arcs across the car and is broken only by the hood for its characteristic centre speedometer. All of the switchgear and the buttons and dials have been designed to convey the original Mini feel but still keeping one eye on modern design requirements and trends.

Also, on some models additional instrumentation is located in front of the driver, on the steering column, very much in the manner that drivers used to personalise their original Minis with additional gauges.

The metallic-look dash dominates the interior, communicating an aggressive and sporty feel to the occupants. This is enhanced by the centre console with its vertical pillars.

The inside makes no use of metal. On the doors a large oval cut-out appears to expose structural cage-like bars that visually strengthen them. In fact, these elements do not contribute to the MINI's structural strength, but the overall feeling is that this is a fun and safe car to drive.

Low seating further enhances the Mini's sporty nature. In the rear there are 50:50 split-folding seats to make the most of the luggage space – something the original never had much of. The back seat, however, has been criticised for being too cramped – though defenders of the design are quick to retort that this is just BMW being true to the original.

## RENAULT ESPACE IV

It's hard to believe the original Renault Espace was first presented to the world as long ago as 1984. It was groundbreaking for Europe at the time as the first MPV or multi-purpose vehicle. Its success helped build a new market segment: first on the scene, it had the field to itself for several years until imitators began to offer their interpretations of what an MPV should be.

The irony is that the majority of MPVs have not been versatile enough to qualify as being truly multi-purpose. This has been especially true in terms of interior design. No wonder that for years people mistakenly thought of MPV as meaning multi-people vehicle and nicknamed them 'people carriers'.

But times are changing as manufacturers like Renault commit themselves to adding more 'multi' to the purpose of these cars. And significantly more luxury, too.

Since 1984 there have been three more generations of Espace, all of which have helped establish the roomy Renault as the premier vehicle in its segment in Europe. And for each generation Renault

has strived to set the standard in terms of comfort, adaptability and stowage space. This is particularly true for the latest, the Espace IV.

From the outset perhaps the most striking feature of the interior of the Espace IV is how the designers have set out to enhance the feeling of space and straightforward luxury.

Espace designers have created an interior that communicates light and space above all else. Space is the new luxury, insists Renault, and inside the Espace IV the interior ambience is one of tranquility. This is due to the presence of so much light entering the vehicle from its many windows and expansive glass roof panels.

A central focus for the Espace IV interior design is the 'shared' dashboard, which incorporates a surprising amount of stowage space. The dashboard sweeps across the cabin in futuristic style. Centralised instrumentation means that the information can be seen by all passengers, thanks also to a luminous blue display against a black background that allows it to be read more easily.

One of the objectives set by the designers of the Espace IV was to achieve an interior which met the needs of each individual occupant to the maximum extent possible. Thus one of the most impressive features of the design is its climate control system, available with separate controls for each passenger. Despite the ducting running over the occupants' heads, the styling of the roof has not been compromised.

Overall, with the expansive light, individualisation of design features and an interior obviously inspired by contemporary furniture design, the combined effect is that within the new Espace the occupants will be looked after on an individual level rather than just being driven around in a 'van with windows'. With the Espace IV, Renault has pushed interior MPV design towards Zen-like ambience and personalised luxury.

# ROLLS-ROYCE PHANTOM

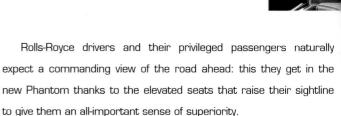

Rolls-Royce Phantom is the ultimate expression of the super-luxury lifestyle. Rear seating area offers option of twin individual seats (right) or curved three-seater theatre bench. Dashboard (below) conveys elegance and simplicity, with technical functions concealed behind panels

'Strive for perfection in everything you do. Take the best that exists and make it better. When it doesn't exist, design it...' These words of Sir Henry Royce, the founder and chief engineer of Rolls-Royce Motor Cars, have found new meaning with the launch of the latest and most ambitious example of the marque.

For, according to new owners BMW, the development teams pledged themselves to this historic principle the moment they began the design of the first Rolls-Royce produced under German ownership, the new Phantom.

The designers set out to convey traditional Rolls-Royce themes of quality, distinction and authority and combine them with modern design and technology. This is particularly true of the interior. And, unusually for any modern programme, they began with a genuinely blank sheet.

Though criticised in some quarters for its exterior styling, the inside design of BMW's new Rolls-Royce Phantom shows just how important interior design is in the super-luxury market segment. Some would argue that, historically, Rolls-Royces, even under British ownership, have never been especially attractive. But the interior of the first BMW-inspired Rolls-Royce model has taken the philosophy of design simplicity and styled it for the wealthy. It is inside that the car shines brightest, with the finest leather, Cashmere trim and fitted wooden cabinetry creating an atmosphere of simple elegance.

Access is via coach doors that open from the centre of the car with the rear doors hinged at the back. This is to give easy access for passengers to slide into the rear of the car. There is also a flat floor and generous headroom, which means that passengers can just walk in and sit down. The rear doors can be closed automatically by pressing a small button on the C-pillar once passengers are seated.

Rolls-Royce drivers and their privileged passengers naturally expect a commanding view of the road ahead: this they get in the new Phantom thanks to the elevated seats that raise their sightline to give them an all-important sense of superiority.

In the rear compartment owners can choose between individual seats, which recline luxuriously in the same manner as those in the front, or opt for sofa-style lounge seating that angles rear occupants towards one another while they sip their champagne.

And because for Rolls-Royce design has always been about the details, there are some remarkable highlights on the new Phantom. These include the major controls, which are traditionally Rolls-Royce and embrace the iconic 'organ stops' for the control of air flow to the air vents. The minor switchgear, shaped like violin keys, and art-deco inspired light fittings add to the ambience. The art-deco lighting in the front and centre roof consoles and in the C-pillars provides reading lights for passengers. There is also ambient lighting for night-time driving, supplied by LEDs in the roof, while a brighter 'boulevard' setting allows passengers in the rear to see each other without distracting the driver.

Other features include specially designed umbrellas that stow neatly in the doors for passengers (or their butlers) to ensure they are sheltered from the rain when exiting the car.

The first German-inspired Rolls-Royce was always going to be a controversial vehicle. But the design approach to the interior, attempting as it does to combine modern technology with traditional materials and traditional switchgear, is certainly brave: more certainly still, it indicates just how difficult it is to bring old conservative marques up to date without alienating traditional buyer groups.

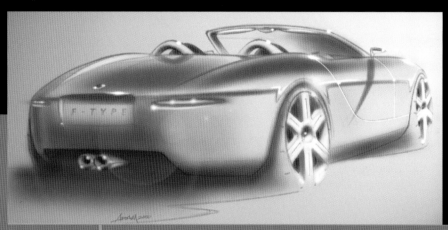

| # CONCEPT CARS: A LICENCE TO TAKE RISKS

IN THESE CASH-STRAPPED TIMES WHEN MARKET PRESSURES ARE PUSHING CAR PRICES RELENTLESSLY DOWNWARDS AND MANUFACTURERS ARE STRUGGLING TO BREAK EVEN, LET ALONE TURN A PROFIT, IT IS NATURAL TO QUESTION THE LOGIC BEHIND CONCEPT CARS.

AFTER ALL, IT COSTS MILLIONS TO DESIGN, STYLE, DEVELOP AND BUILD ANY NEW CAR AND WHEN THAT CAR IS A ONE-OFF, ALL THAT OUTLAY IS FOCUSED ON A SINGLE EXAMPLE (OR AT THE MOST TWO). FOR IT IS THE DESTINY OF EVERY CONCEPT CAR TO LIVE A FRUSTRATINGLY BRIEF, BUTTERFLY-LIKE LIFE, BURSTING INTO THE PUBLIC SPOTLIGHT FOR A FEW GLORIOUS FLASHBULB-POPPING, CHAMPAGNE-SWILLING MOMENTS AT AN INTERNATIONAL MOTOR SHOW AND THEN TO BE CRATED UP FOR RETURN TO THE COMPANY MUSEUM OR, MORE IGNOMINIOUSLY STILL, PERHAPS THE CRUSHER.

ALL THAT'S LEFT AFTER THE CROWDS HAVE GONE, THE STANDS HAVE BEEN DISMANTLED AND THE DEBRIS CLEARED AWAY ARE A FEW HAZY RECOLLECTIONS, A COLLECTION OF PRESS CUTTINGS AND, IN ALL LIKELIHOOD, A SHEAF OF BILLS TO BE SETTLED. ANDY WARHOL'S *FIFTEEN MINUTES OF FAME* COULD HAVE BEEN INVENTED SPECIALLY FOR THE LIFE OF A CONCEPT CAR.

SO WHY, ONE MIGHT ASK, DO THEY BOTHER? A MOTOR SHOW IS NOT LIKE FASHION WEEK IN PARIS OR MILAN, WHERE BUYERS WHIP OUT THEIR CHEQUEBOOKS THE SECOND THEY SEE A NEW STYLE THEY LIKE; CARS ARE VASTLY MORE COMPLEX TO PUT INTO PRODUCTION THAN THE FANCIEST HATS, COATS OR DRESSES. AND THERE ARE A MILLION TIME-CONSUMING, DOLLAR-GOBBLING STEPS BETWEEN *SALON* CATWALK AND HIGH-STREET SHOWROOM.

Jaguar's F-Type proposal *(left and below right)* successfully recreated the aura of the iconic E-type but failed to make production; XKR180 *(above)* was a one-off show car based on the series XKR

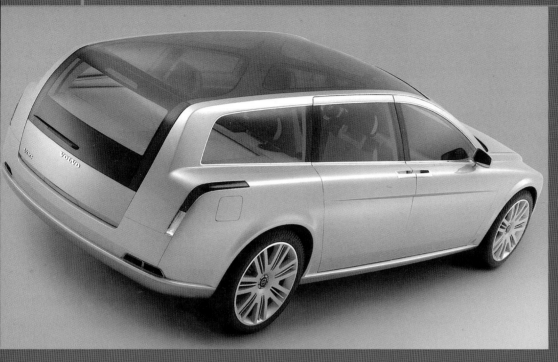

STRANGELY ENOUGH, IT IS PRECISELY BECAUSE IT DOES COST SO MUCH MONEY TO DEVELOP AND BUILD A VOLUME PRODUCTION CAR THAT THE EXTRA EXPENSE OF A CONCEPT VEHICLE IS WORTHWHILE.

Yet the fact is that concept cars are becoming if anything more, rather than less, popular among carmakers. Why?

The reason has much to do with that glory, for sure. Yet, oddly enough, in many cases it has even more to do with costs. The glory is the easiest to identify with: after all, who can fail to be awed by the futuristic aura, the voluptuous curves and the vivid colours of an exciting new concept – such as, say, Cadillac's vast 2003 Sixteen? And when, again taking Cadillac as an example, the company logo is prominently featured front and rear of the shapely machine, it's as inevitable as night follows day that one's opinion of Cadillac's more ordinary, everyday roadgoing models will notch upwards, even if only minutely and momentarily. So it's easy to see how in the complex art of car marketing, concept cars have a clearly defined role in pumping up the public perception of a brand.

Even when the brand in question is a modest, low achiever, known mainly for mundane family cars, a well-chosen showtime concept can successfully link that brand with something much more exotic and exciting – though there is rarely any technical crossover whatsoever and, again, the glory will be of the reflected variety. In marketing terms, it is akin to hiring a fashionable top 10 band to associate themselves with the brand – a glamorous and attractive face to add superficial allure to the prosaic bread-and-butter product. In auto industry argot, they're stand candy.

But the well-timed boost to the corporate image is not the most important role of the modern concept car. Strangely enough, it is precisely because it does cost so much money to develop and build a volume production car that the extra expense of a concept vehicle is worthwhile. With manufacturers often having to spend up to a billion dollars to put a new model series into the showroom, the financial stakes are so high that no-one can afford to make a mistake. The concept car is a vital part of the strategy, for it is the perfect means of flagging up new ideas and assessing public reaction. The carmaker can then get a clearer picture of whether the new idea is likely to work well in volume production, or whether it needs tweaking in order to capture the buyers' imagination.

Take Renault, for instance. Since the early 1990s it has been an enthusiastic builder of concept cars as it has explored different design avenues and sought to test out the response of the buying

**Volvo Versatility Concept**
*(left and below)* trails new ideas for a large station wagon, yet also forms an important element in Volvo's brand-building strategy

Mégane line in 1997 – though with very different styling to the showcar example. Had the concept met with a lukewarm reaction from commentators and show visitors, Renault might have thought twice about volume production.

Concept vehicles also find an important role in softening up public – and therefore buyers' – opinion in advance of an already planned model introduction or design change. Take the Mercedes-Benz E-Class, for instance. The then-new model, scheduled to launch in 1996 was to introduce a significantly different new frontal look for the brand, with four separate oval headlights rather than two large rectangular units. Mercedes, conscious that the inherently conservative clientele for this cornerstone series might feel alienated by such a step-change in the model's appearance, decided to float the four-headlight theme some considerable time in advance through the device of what was presented as the F200 concept coupé, revealed to a well-orchestrated fanfare at the Geneva show in March 1994. The new, four-eyed face was proudly revealed and duly argued over by commentators and customers, and by the time the real production model came to market the following summer all the rhetoric had run its course and the new face was already familiar – and thus appealing – to buyers. Later, the coupé shape itself emerged as the 1996 CLK – albeit minus its glass roof and hatchback tailgate.

Mercedes-Benz has been equally astute in using the concept car approach to aid in strategic as well as tactical decision-making. It may be hard to imagine now, but back in the early 1990s the idea of a 'baby' Mercedes was considered nigh-on unthinkable. While no-one doubted Mercedes' engineering abilities, few were prepared to believe that a small car could look, feel and drive like a genuine Mercedes. What could such a car possibly look like, people speculated, and how could the company prevent its peerless reputation from being dragged down to the level of volume car sellers such as Opel and Ford? Mercedes, mindful of the value of its lofty image, began to broach the idea of a small car carrying the three–pointed star. An idea was floated publicly with the deliberately radical-looking Vision A concept car, a design study whose unusual proportions concealed an innovative engineering layout that gave the tiny car the interior space of an upper-medium sector model.

*Below:* **Dodge ESX3 is just one example of the Chrysler Group's prodigious output of concept vehicles**

In a single move with the Vision A, Mercedes had signalled to the world that its interpretation of the small car would be advanced in its style, its packaging and its technology. It was to be a credible upholder of the Mercedes brand values, despite its small size and comparatively low price. In this way, the buying public had had plenty of time to get used to the idea of a baby Mercedes and was well primed for the radical and distinctive solution that emerged as the production A-Class in September 1997.

A similar softening-up approach had been used almost a generation earlier by Ford when it used the ultra-aerodynamic Probe III concept to smooth the transition from the conservative Taunus/Cortina to the then-radical Sierra. Patrick le Quément, now design director at Renault, was at Ford at the time and is a firm believer in the value of concept cars – as demonstrated by a steady stream of original, innovative and often challenging designs over the years. In addition to their PR function for the brand, they provide valuable creative freedom for the designers, he says.

'Since 1988 concept cars have always played a strong role at Renault,' he says. 'I see them as a means of accelerating evolution: we take them very seriously. That's why we try to protect them from the external environment – things like rules, standards and regulations. The concept car inspiration gives design direction, and releases designers from the responsibility of knowing that the vehicle will be produced. We try to put the target as far ahead as possible.'

Many different design directions have been explored by Renault's concepts, some more successfully than others. The distinctively curved backlight of the 1998 Vel Satis concept, designed to echo the flamboyant pre-war carrosserie era of French car design, was taken up on the Mégane II hatchback, for instance, while the Avantime of 1999 was a concept which went straight to production, though, sadly, proved too radical to sell in enough numbers to keep its contract builder, Matra, afloat.

The role of Renault concepts tends, as we have seen, to be one of signalling possible design solutions in areas of the market where Renault is not yet present. The Koleos, presented in 2000, and the Talisman the following year showed how Renault might tackle a large SUV and a four-seater GT coupé, respectively. These cars will not be manufactured in these forms, but – as with the Vel Satis concept – many of their detailed ideas are sure to find their way into the company's showroom models.

The Swedish carmaker Volvo has also made extensive use of concept vehicles in recent years – though in a dramatically different way to its old practice of solely rolling out new safety ideas on show models. Under the design direction of Peter Horbury, high-profile Volvo concepts have succeeded in shifting public opinion, repositioning the company as an organisation that values style as well as safety and environmental compatibility. The strategy has been to show Volvos becoming smoother, sleeker and less angular in their presentation, thus moving the whole brand to a younger, more

NEVERTHELESS, IN SPITE OF THE PREVAILING CLIMATE OF DISAPPROVAL, RETRO IS NOWADAYS ONE OF THE MOST-VISITED THEMES OF CONCEPT CAR DESIGN – ESPECIALLY IN THE UNITED STATES, WHERE THERE IS A SIGNIFICANTLY GREATER PUBLIC AWARENESS OF AUTO INDUSTRY HERITAGE AND PERHAPS A GREATER SENTIMENTALITY TOWARDS A SHARED AUTO CULTURE.

appealing position in the market. The strategy has worked because the promise inherent in the showtime concept cars has on the whole been fulfilled by the subsequent production model, even though the series design itself may have been more restrained. The large XC90 sports utility of 2001 was a case in point: it was previewed a year earlier by the Adventure Concept Car (AAC), described by its creators as a 'thermometer to assess the expectations and demands of the market'. Geneva 2003's Volvo Versatility

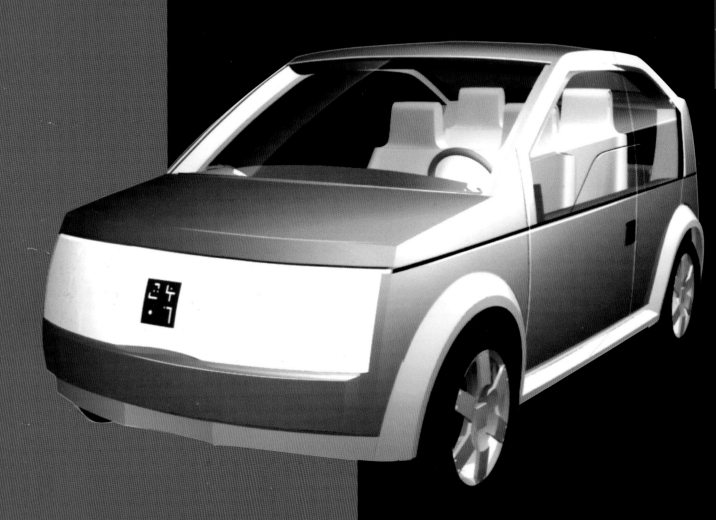

*Above and right:* **24:7 Ford's concept vehicle was derided for its boxy looks upon its 2000 debut in Detroit; its true significance lay in its all-electronic interior and focus on telematics communication**

Concept Car (VVC) clearly anticipates many of the features and much of the style likely to be found in large Volvo station wagons in the near future. However, there is a crucial and significant role difference between the two programmes: whereas the AAC was in effect a thinly disguised version of a soon-to-be released production car, the VVC – like several Volvo concepts before it – is an original concept from which a later production model might be derived or draw its inspiration. Here, the designers can be seen to have had a relatively free hand in shaping imaginative and futuristic solutions that do not necessarily have to meet every legislative requirement, let alone cost or functionality targets, in volume production.

Nevertheless, the VVC still represents a calculated step in Volvo's forward march, an integral part in the roll-out of its future model programme. In that sense, the design team were on a medium-to-long leash, free of the everyday constraints that hamper volume-sale vehicles, but nonetheless subject to the

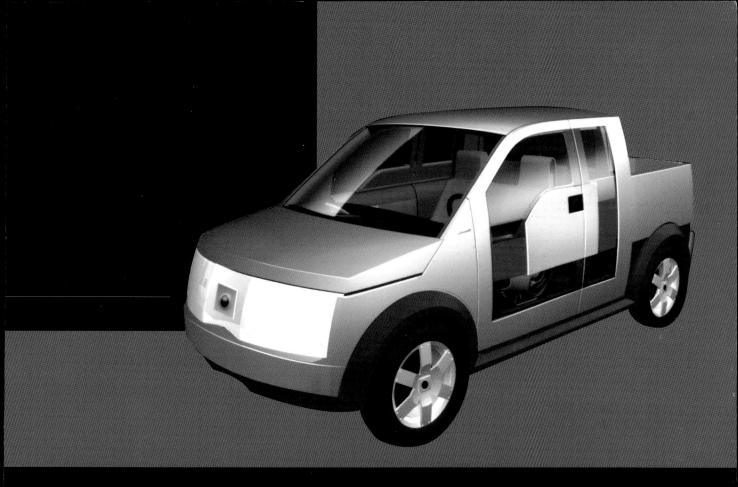

discipline of slotting in to a predetermined brand plan and model schedule.

More recently, Citroen too has been on a concept car offensive, this time with the object of restoring the once-dominant public image of the company as a technical innovator and a producer of adventurous, futuristically styled cars. A decade of dull mainstream designs, though commercially successful, had allowed Citroen to squander its market reputation as an avant garde nameplate, to the extent that it became a me-too brand selling on a commodity level rather than as an aspirational purchase. Beginning with a curvy small car design, with deliberate echoes of the old 2CV, Citroen showed a series of concept models at international motor shows – models which successfully projected the image of an avant garde Citroen for the near future. This policy had an important psychological effect both within Citroen and among the buying public: it provided the reassurance that everyone wanted that Citroen had indeed recognised the value and uniqueness of its heritage, and that it would once again begin honouring these values in its future products.

Most of all, however, Citroen has succeeded in calling up the emotive values – the spirit, the sense of advancement – from its heritage without recourse to overtly 'retro' design. The small C3 hatchback, for instance, is a thoroughly modern design: it is warm, curvy and cute in a way which reminds users of the feeling they experienced in connection with the ancient, but much-loved 2CV. Yet there is no direct design theme lifted from the 2CV, save for the arch of the roof and the front fender.

The whole subject of retro is an acutely controversial topic within design circles: it is often initially popular with the buying public – witness the US-wide hysteria for the new Beetle and Chrysler's PT Cruiser – but tends to be frowned upon by professionals intent on advancing the art of vehicle design rather than simply selling thousands of cars. And plundering the back-catalogue in search of inspiration is often viewed as the last resort of companies uncertain of which way they should move forward.

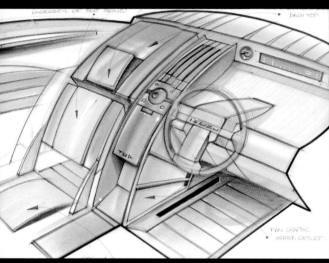

*Above:* **Isuzu Zen is one of the more outrageous design studies, but nonetheless contains many inspirational ideas**

Nevertheless, in spite of the prevailing climate of disapproval, retro is nowadays one of the most-visited themes of concept car design – especially in the United States, where there is a significantly greater public awareness of auto industry heritage and perhaps a greater sentimentality towards a shared auto culture. No-one puts out concept cars in greater numbers than Chrysler Jeep and Ford, and when it comes to honouring the past, no-one does it better than the Americans. VW's Concept One new Beetle, designed by J Mays, who now heads Ford's design worldwide, was such a show hit that VW gave in to pressure to put the concept into production. Years later, the Microbus – a West Coast sun and surfing icon from the 1960s and 1970s – received a less rapturous welcome, but is still likely to make volume production. Mays' influence at Ford has led indirectly to the reinvention of several iconic Ford models in a contemporary context, initially as concepts with all the attendant media pressure to make them production models. The Thunderbird has now been a catalogue item for several years; the Mustang will soon follow the same route, and the high-performance GT – aping the rakish lines of the mid-engined '60s Le Mans-winning GT40 – is set for low-volume build and sale to wealthy clients in celebration of Ford's centenary.

Once again, the designer's function here has been to bring the company's heritage back to life; he or she provides the cue to remind a contemporary audience of the glories of the company's past and, in so doing, to invite the user or viewer to relive those happier times, pasting in a set of warmer, more positive emotions in place of the possibly negative feelings surrounding the brand at the present time.

Of course for every Ford or Volkswagen tempted to reach for the history card in exploring its future direction, there's an Audi, a Renault or a Mercedes-Benz pushing the frontiers of forward-looking design with its concept cars. Ultimately, it's up to each company and its policy-makers to decide the type of use they wish to make of this unique opportunity for design freedom and for the public proclamation of the corporate vision. But whichever way the company chooses to go – whether it's to trail a totally new type of vehicle, to

'SINCE 1988 CONCEPT CARS HAVE ALWAYS PLAYED A STRONG ROLE AT RENAULT. I SEE THEM AS A MEANS OF ACCELERATING EVOLUTION: WE TAKE THEM VERY SERIOUSLY. THAT'S WHY WE TRY TO PROTECT THEM FROM THE EXTERNAL ENVIRONMENT – THINGS LIKE RULES, STANDARDS AND REGULATIONS.'

PATRICK LE QUÉMENT,
DESIGN DIRECTOR, RENAULT

*Below:* Renault Ellypse, shown at the Paris Salon in 2002, provides a typically imaginative approach to the design of a multi-purpose small car. Its design may well influence the five-door replacement for the Twingo

propose a dramatic brand extension into a different sector, to stir up nice warm feelings from the past, or simply to spike the guns of a competitor about to enter a sensitive segment – the concept car provides the ideal high-profile, low-risk means of staking out that territory.

More than anything else in a firm's portfolio, the concept car is a powerful statement of a company's aims, ideals and ambitions, a mirror to the visionary thinking going on in the boardroom. At its best, a concept car has the power to change the way the whole industry thinks – Giugiaro's Megagamma of 1978 and Renault's 1993 Scénic concept spring to mind. The truly good ones can indirectly boost around the fortunes of a company. Think of how the Toyota RAV4, originally just a show concept, instantly caught on as soon as it hit the showrooms – while those that are merely very good, like Ford's original Ka or Audi's TT, translate straight into successful production cars.

At the opposite end of the scale the wrong choice of concept can spell out promises that may be impossible to fulfil – Cadillac's Sixteen is a doubtful production prospect, for instance, and circumstances shattered the high hopes surrounding Jaguar's beautiful F-Type of 2000. Worse, a too-conservative concept will conspicuously fail to move the automotive game on but, worse still, one that's over-the-top,

*Below:* **9ˣ concept from Saab, the company's first for many years, began exploring new design directions**

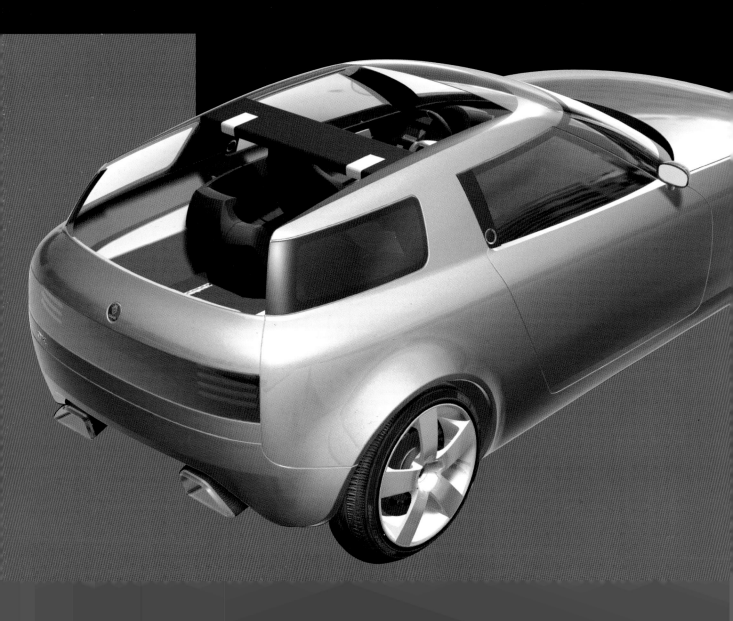

CONCEPT CARS PROVIDE A
WELCOME FREEDOM THAT DESIGNERS
POSITIVELY REVEL IN – A RULE- AND
REGULATION-FREE ENVIRONMENT THAT
ALLOWS THEIR CREATIVE POWERS
TO TRULY BLOSSOM.

*Above:* **Audi AL₂ concept pre-dated the actual A2 production car; note simpler frontal treatment without false black grille**

outrageous or simply irrelevant is likely to fall embarrassingly out of fashion the moment the show closes, if not before.

Either way, however, concept cars provide a welcome freedom that designers positively revel in, a rule- and regulation-free environment that allows their creative powers to truly blossom. But, as the wilder excesses of too many 'design-gone-mad' show cars so graphically illustrate, it needs the gentle hand of enlightened company management to ensure that those creative talents are channelled in the right direction and not wasted on superficial and inappropriate stand candy. Risky? Only if imagination is lacking or management doesn't know where it's going. For sure, a concept car is always going to be freeze-frame of future thinking at a particular instant, a shooting star whose light is destined to burn brilliantly for a few frustratingly fleeting moments before it falls, expended, to earth. And its real value, as any designer imbued with wisdom as well as experience will testify, lies in the inspiration that can later be drawn from that brief first flash of brilliance.

SENIOR VICE
PRESIDENT
OF CORPORATE DESIGN,
RENAULT

01.06 | **PATRICK LE QUÉMENT**

**THROUGH HIS CLEAR VISION AND SINGLE-MINDED DETERMINATION, PATRICK LE QUÉMENT HAS RAISED THE ART OF THE DESIGN PROFESSIONAL TO A NEW LEVEL. HIS FERVENT BELIEF THAT GOOD DESIGN CAN BE ENJOYED BY ALL HAS BROUGHT DESIGN OUT FROM BEHIND THE STUDIO DOORS AND INTO THE BOARDROOM WHERE IT HAS BECOME A POWERFUL STRATEGIC INSTRUMENT IN COMPANY POLICY.**

Today, le Quément would be quick to say that he doesn't design cars any more; he will insist he has a broad and gifted staff of designers, spread across four Renault studios in three countries and two continents who, so he claims, do the work. He will tell you that he merely supervises, encourages, facilitates, evaluates – that he's just a manager, a bridge between the top echelons of the company's management and the people who create the products.

But there can be no doubt whatsoever that Renault would be a very different company without le Quément. Some would even venture that the streets of Europe or even the world would seem different without le Quément's handiwork, and that his influences have reached beyond the confines of Renault to make their mark on the broader automotive environment.

As we head for the halfway point of the 21st century's first decade, design at Renault is on an undeniable high. The new Mégane II has established a provocative new look in the medium-car segment and took Europe's prestigious Car of the Year Award for 2003. The second-generation Mégane Coupé-Cabriolet and Scénic have just been unveiled; the radical Vel Satis has earned respect for daring to

THIERCELIN 91.

*Above:*

Fourth-generation Espace is the
outcome of Renault's desire to move
the spacious people-carrier concept
into the luxury segment and project a
more masculine and sporty image

*Left:*

Design sketch for production Vel
Satis already shows clear Renault
frontal identity; le Quément wanted
to form a distinctive French
personality rather than imitate
German executive-sector
competitors

challenge Mercedes-Benz and BMW in the luxury segment, and the fourth-generation Espace has once again redefined the shape of sophisticated high-speed passenger carrying and versatility. These are substantial achievements, for sure, but again the real reasons for the close focus on le Quément go much deeper – deeper than any individual products, any commercial success and any transient moods or fashionable themes within the automotive industry.

For where le Quément has arguably gone one step further than his peers is in the scale of what he has achieved, especially within Renault – but, again, this is not something that's as straightforward as a crude numerical tally of commercially successful designs or a roll-call of highly regarded concept cars. Instead, le Quément's claim to fame is one that's likely to outlive even his most critically acclaimed designs: that he has taken design out of the studio and placed it firmly in the boardroom – and at the top of the agenda, too.

This is the real revolution he has brought about: to promote design as a key strategic tool central to long-term business planning rather than a short-term tactical fix to dress up products in the hope of cashing in on a possibly transient styling whim. For le Quément, design is more than just the shape of a fender, a headlight or an instrument pack – though these are undeniably important too; for him, design is key to the identity of the whole company as well as that of its vehicles. It is only through considered and consistent design, he argues, that a company can bring about a permanent shift in its market position, the way it is perceived by customers, both current and potential; the way it communicates its message as well as the content of that message.

In short, le Quément has taken the art of the design professional and extended it that crucial step further, elevating it to the status of a powerful strategic mechanism. It is a planning tool able to achieve fundamental transformations in brand perceptions and thus exert a positive influence on marketing metrics such as consumer desirability and, as a result, improve vital business ratios like profitability and retained value.

The le Quément record at Renault says it all. When he joined the company in 1987 it was in one of its all-too-regular depressed phases, with an odd and inconsistent range of family cars whose only shared attribute appeared to be a poor reputation in the marketplace stemming from indifferent design and cheap, shoddy execution. Historical highlights such as the Dauphine, the trend-setting R16 and the chic R5 were just that: clear sparks of inspiration that served only to stress the dullness of the company's mid-80s offerings.

The transformation of Renault has been complete. It was led by the highly original Twingo in 1992 and the Laguna and Scénic in the mid-90s, followed by the consistent flow of innovative and dramatic concept cars that placed the Renault 'lozenge' on everything

*Left:* Ambitious second-generation Mégane programme represents everything Le Quément has worked towards since his arrival at Renault in the late 1980s

from exotic luxury sedans to smart off-roaders and back-to-basics sports cars. Renault has extended its design language to almost every shape, size and format of four – or even six – wheeled vehicle. Sometimes that language has been softly spoken and subtle – as in the pioneering and profoundly influential Scénic concept – while at other times it has been strident and even shocking, with the large Vel Satis, Initiale and Avantime concepts being cases in point. But always, whatever the format or the form of the concept, it has always set tongues wagging, sparking debate among other designers, stirring arguments among motor show crowds and prompting often furious correspondence in magazine letters pages.

Few moves have proved more provocative than the one that in early 2002 saw Renault extend its confident, design-led approach into the hallowed territory of BMW and Mercedes-Benz. Stung by the failure of the technically competent but bland Safrane in the early 1990s, le Quément had vowed never to repeat the mistake of trying to beat the Germans with a car that aped German design values. Instead, he reasoned, not all customers in this high-prestige class necessarily wanted a German-style car; a 'majority of the minority' could be drawn to an alternative which matched German technical standards but which offered a distinct and clearly French style. Thus the idea of the Vel Satis was born. Many commentators found the thought of a Renault challenge to the BMW-Mercedes hegemony somewhat implausible. These sceptics had all the ammunition they required when the production Vel Satis was

revealed as a forceful, powerful and openly avant garde design, as likely to antagonise the notoriously conservative luxury customer as it was to tempt the courageous few who could afford to make such a bold design statement.

The Vel Satis had a predictably rough ride among the less open-minded elements of the automotive press, and indeed continues to draw criticism; only those more favourably disposed to moving the design game on seem prompted to draw helpful comparisons with the individualistic role of, say, Apple Macintosh in the computer industry or Bang and Olufsen in home audio.

Patrick le Quément, for his part, is unfazed by the jibes and the taunts that tend to accompany the presentation of these often ground breaking new shapes. After all, explorers, pioneers and those pushing the frontiers in any area of endeavour rarely have an easy time. Mindful of Carl Jung's observation that to be in advance of others is always to invite a flogging, le Quément is patient and understanding in the face of the critical comments often flung his way when new designs are unveiled. 'It is quite normal that it should not necessarily be instantly likeable,' he said of the Mégane II at its press preview in summer 2002. 'There was the same feeling with the first Golf, and also the Mercedes 190, which was highly debated when first launched.

'If you don't want to do an anonymous car, you have to take a certain risk,' he adds. 'In the final analysis, our CEO Louis Schweitzer takes the decisions, but I make the recommendations. And this [the Mégane II] is the right design for our company.'

And it is in this acute sense of what is right for Renault that le Quément truly distinguishes himself. Yes, there have been others in the past – notably Sir William Lyons at Jaguar – who have carried an intuitive consciousness of what a brand is all about and who have stamped an unmistakeable marque identity on every model emanating from the factory. But though the

Lyons heritage is not to be underestimated – his designs have once again become the inspiration for today's generations of Jaguars – he did by comparison have it rather easy. His three principal products all fell into a narrow market segment with a single, clearly defined type of buyer, and as the unquestionable boss of the company his instincts would have held sway with the board even had they been wide of the mark.

For le Quément it must have been more of a battle. By the time he joined Renault in 1987 he had already worked for several major carmakers, including Ford and Volkswagen, and was thus wise to the way the auto industry decision-making processes operated. So when he was approached by the then Renault chairman Raymond Lévy to lead the increasingly directionless company's design team, he agreed to join on the express condition that design would be accountable direct to the very top of the company's management rather than reporting in through the traditional engineering channels. In this way, recalls le Quément, he hoped to make design a fundamental rather than an afterthought; to make it responsive to outside influences rather then internal engineering constraints.

It was a gamble for both men. Le Quément had halved his salary to move to Renault, while the Renault chairman had introduced a wild card into the company pack at a very high level and with virtual carte blanche to do whatever it took to establish a strong design identity for Renault. However, the two immediately found a rapport and, remembers le Quément, other senior figures who had been at Renault for 20 years or more were shocked to hear him and the deputy managing director Aimé Jardon conversing in the familiar 'tu' form after little more than two months. A later shock was to be top management's agreement to substantial spending on new design studios at Boulogne-Billancourt – at a time when cutbacks were affecting the rest of the company at every level.

Of course, this was the opportunity le Quément had been awaiting for many years; the chance to build on the extensive but often bitter experience he had built up in the highly structured environments of large multinational corporations. It was a passion that had taken hold nearly three decades earlier when, as a 15-year-old school student who had been drawing cars, planes, ships and locomotives for longer than anyone could remember, he read a book that mentioned Pininfarina.

'It hadn't occurred to me that there was a job called design,' he remembers. 'It was then that I realised there was a profession in automobile design – that there were companies that did design, not just engineering and manufacturing.'

At school in England le Quément had been fortunate in having an art teacher who was also a professional illustrator: this helped his artistic skills considerably, and he soon resolved to embark on a career in car design. However, when it came to the next step he was disappointed to find no auto design courses in Europe; the nearest

*Left:* **Espace sketches show a desire to make the luxury minivan sportier, and to distance it from from van-like associations**

was at Art Center in Pasadena, clearly out of the question in terms of distance and cost.

'So I went to art college in Birmingham to study product design: I was one of three students interested in car design – one of the others was Trevor Creed, who's now in charge of design at Chrysler,' he recalls.

The problem with the course, le Quément felt, was that it was too industrially based and not aesthetic or artistic enough. Nevertheless, it did not deter him from approaching the legendary industrial designer Raymond Loewy, whom he knew indirectly through family connections, for a job upon graduation. Meeting in Paris, the two disappointingly failed to click and no suitable job offer was forthcoming – merely one which, in his words, 'gave me just enough to pay my rent or eat, but not both.'

Ironically, it was much later – in 2002, in fact – that le Quément was presented with the coveted Lucky Strike Designer Award by the Raymond Loewy Foundation. He is only the second automobile designer to receive the award, previous recipients having included design notables such as Richard Sapper, Donna Karan and Karl Lagerfeld.

After having applied to several companies, the young le Quément was eventually taken on by Simca at a salary that was enough to pay for an apartment and keep hunger at bay. Equally importantly, Simca was one of the few firms at that time to have a proper design centre. It was to prove the perfect first job in more ways than one, as le Quément recalls:

'It was a great education. When I got to Simca I began working alongside John Pinko, who was famous for his association with the Ford Mustang. I learnt a tremendous lot from him, and very quickly too: it was like being paid a salary to have the best teacher give you the best training.

'At college I had found it hard to develop a style [of drawing] that was my own. But working with John Pinko I soon found myself able to draw without thinking – a crucial ability for any designer. The ideas simply appear to flow onto the paper – it's something that comes gradually with experience.'

Those ideas have powered him through a long and continuing career of ever-expanding and steadily more influential roles in the auto industry – but there is a clear sense that the Renault he has done so much to shape is very much his spiritual home. At Renault he has created a structure that gives design equal top billing in the vehicle development process alongside engineering and product planning. Most vitally, this creates the stability and the consistency to enable the building up of a strong brand and, equally vitally in Renault's case, to track quality from the very first concept stage to the final vehicle assembly on the production line.

When asked about the best and the worst things about his job, le Quément immediately beams with satisfaction. 'The best thing is that I'm doing what I best like doing – I don't consider it as a job: it's what I would do as a hobby in any case.

'As for the worst aspects, I suppose it must be the tremendous pressure I'm under to maintain the course I have given myself. It's a bit like the ancient Gauls: they went round terrified the sky was about to fall on their head. For me, the fear is mediocrity. This self-imposed task is a very demanding one, but I suppose my biggest struggle is trying not to go mad whilst still maintaining the faith and ensuring we resist going for short-term goals.'

The le Quément crusade against mediocrity has taken many weird and wonderful forms over the past decade and a half, but its four-wheeled expressions are always radical and thought-provoking, and invariably involve a strong cultural content. The latter is an especially significant strand in the Renault design philosophy, for as vehicles become steadily more equal in performance, specification and quality, the cultural context of the design will become an increasingly important differentiator

'THERE'S NO OTHER AREA WHERE YOU HAVE TO MIX THINGS LIKE TECHNOLOGY AND AESTHETICS, EGO, CULTURE AND POPULAR TASTE'

between brands. Le Quément will happily talk about the differences between French and English garden design, the distinct nuances of Italian as opposed to French haute couture, or the relative merits of Finnish versus Danish furniture. All these elements can be manipulated to feed into the perceived national identity of a product, be it a lamp, a table, a building or a car: for le Quément and his team there is no greater compliment than for someone to remark that a design comes across as clearly French in character.

Naturally, none of this happens merely by accident. Designing and building a car in France is no guarantee whatsoever that it will come across to the consumer as French, just as a UK-built Honda is hardly British in character and is subjectively no less Japanese than a Toyota built across the channel in eastern France. Indeed, in past eras Renault has been especially guilty of producing models with near-Japanese levels of blandness – but, sadly, failing at the same time to remotely approach Japanese levels of technical integrity.

The best guarantee of that strong sense of national identity is to have a wide range of nationalities in the design team, maintains le Quément. Non-French people often have a better idea of what constitutes the French character, he reasons: the current tally of different nationalities in his team stands at 25, and with the recruitment of Japan's Nissan and Korea's Samsung into the Renault fold the span is set to become broader still.

Culture is about more than nationality, however, and many of the more rapidly evolving trends cut right across national barriers. Lifestyle, entertainment, shopping patterns, fashion, family and other influences can be felt more or less simultaneously across continents or round the world: the sudden global explosion in mobile phone use is a case in point. Yet in each part of the world the impact of such changes is subtly different, and for this reason Renault regularly sends teams of designers on carefully structured trend missions to gauge developments in other fields, to see how people respond to their

environments and to watch how they interact with different forms of technology.

So the three well-dressed 20-somethings making notes and taking in the ambience of an English pub on a Friday evening could well be a team from Renault design – as could a couple outside a German kindergarten or the four-man delegation to the Milan furniture fair or the Las Vegas consumer electronics show. As well as feeding in visual ideas into the design process, these missions also serve to establish how people use their products and how this is likely to evolve in the future. It was just such a perceptive anticipation of evolving consumer demand that led Renault, almost a decade ago, to spot the need for a medium-sized multi-purpose vehicle and launch the segment-busting Scénic – which of course went on to become a phenomenal success and a powerful cash-earner for the company.

In the build-up to the new X84 Mégane programme, le Quément has intensified Renault's dialogue with car owners and potential customers – but not in the way that's typical of many large corporations in search of easy design answers. 'We haven't done an average type design here, clinicked down to the last detail,' he explains. 'We do a lot of market research work on our customer base, but we don't ask them to choose the design.

'There's some merit in always listening to customers,' he continues, 'looking at how they live and what they do. But don't ask them to design your product, because then it will be yesterday's product.

'Automobile design is one of the last renaissance-type occupations,' observes le Quément, philosophically defining the breadth of his brief. 'There's no other area where you have to mix things like technology and aesthetics, ego, culture and popular taste, while also taking into account costs, investment, manufacturing and much, much more.'

All this philosophy and more has fed into the new Mégane programme, of which – in mid-2003 – four of the eventual seven distinct body shapes have been revealed. It's a huge and highly visible undertaking, competing in Europe's biggest market

*Below:* **As much thought goes into details as into the overall shape of a vehicle. This column assembly is from the Koleos concept vehicle**

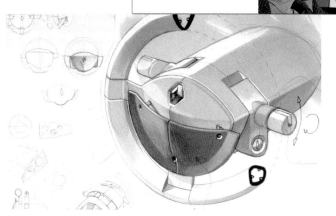

and selling upwards of 800,000 units a year. But for le Quément is represents more than just an important and ambitious new model range: in many ways, it is the culmination of all he has been striving for at Renault for so long.

'This car has had a design book written for it,' he explains. 'We have circulated 600 copies within engineering and product planning: we had to design all seven versions of the car at the same time – and they were all approved on a moving line basis.'

The Mégane programme design manual isn't the only book on the designers' shelves. So firm is le Quément's vision of how Renault should present itself that he has also drawn up an internal guide to the fundamentals of good car design, a closely guarded volume which incorporates Renault Design's latest thinking not only on aesthetic issues such as the stance of the vehicle and the relationship between the wheels and the body, but also the more recent policy that places much more emphasis on presenting a recognisable front-end identity across model ranges.

'In recent years we have had a major rethink in our car design strategy,' explains le Quément. 'In the late 1990s we were strongly influenced by a brand survey we carried out in Western Europe. It emerged that our models were much stronger than our brand: people's appreciation of our models was much more positive than that of the Renault brand. This had a large influence on the company, and one of the

recommendations I made was that we should introduce a more recognisable front-end identity – each model should appear as a link. For instance, the next Twingo should be a Renault Twingo. We also elected to put the accent on the logo, not the word Renault – rather like Nike and its swoosh.'

All these moves are typical of someone who thinks strategically rather than tactically, who is committed to bringing audacious design into the volume markets – and who has built up a powerful shared vision of this with the company president.

Le Quément is quick to wield the famous remark of France's First World War prime minister Georges Clémenceau that 'war is too important a business to be left to the generals', clearly implying that the latter are the technical people and that designers and top management are better placed to see the broader picture and are thus integral to all aspects of strategy. But at the same time he won't let anyone forget the downstream responsibilities of the designer, either – firstly to wage war on mediocrity and the 'me-too' culture, and underlying it all, to remember the 1920s dictum of Bauhaus founder Walter Gropius which, roughly translated, says that the mission of the designer is to instil a soul in the product still-born from the machine.

In essence, this means that the cars on our streets can gain an artistic integrity that goes beyond the fundamental consumer requirements for technical integrity – and renders entirely obsolete the dreaded 'dressing-up for selling' philosophy embodied in traditional car-styling processes. If the new wave of design-conscious Renaults succeeds in truly capturing the buyers' imagination, le Quément will have succeeded in raising the game of mass production from something habitually mundane to something altogether more inspirational and exciting. And there can be no higher accolade for an industrial designer than that.

# RENAULT DESIGN

RENAULT IS UNUSUAL IN MANY WAYS, NOT JUST IN THE WAY IT GIVES SUCH PROMINENCE TO DESIGN. THE FACT THAT DESIGN ENJOYS SUCH A HIGH PROFILE AND IS ANSWERABLE TO THE VERY TOP LEVELS OF MANAGEMENT HAS A LOT TO DO WITH THE WAY THE REST OF THE COMPANY'S DECISION-MAKING PROCESSES ARE STRUCTURED.

The company's *'Créateur d'automobiles'* advertising tag-line is, for once, no hollow slogan – and the massive Technocentre near Versailles gives credence to the claim. This is a deeply impressive place where cars really are created – and, what is more, the physical layout of the complex mimics the sequence of the creative process behind the development of a vehicle. >

*Left:* Rear window and trunk design of Vel Satis concept proved influential within Renault

*Below left:* Working on scale clay model of Mégane showing Vel Satis concept influence

*Below:* Full-size clay model is used for minute detailing work

> The front of the building is the more public area, where visitors are received, where ideas flow in, and where information is exchanged. Further back, ideas begin to crystallise into potential programmes and may even take shape in the design studios; next, modelling and engineering areas have the ability to put these ideas into three dimensions, even going as far as full build of prototypes. Also included are product planning and purchasing, testing, validation, training and even the developing of manufacturing systems. The aim is to develop a car that is absolutely ready to be volume-built – in fact, all that's missing is the production line itself.

The exact processes by which designs eventually reach production are clearly confidential within the Technocentre. However, Patrick le Quément, senior vice president of corporate design, is proud of the fact that there are only three tiers of management between a designer on the studio floor and the Renault president, Louis Schweitzer. New initiatives can develop in several different ways: there can be the mainstream programmes that are part of the cycle of renewal and replacement of existing models (the Mégane II was one of those). There can be programmes for concept cars simply to explore new ideas or targeted at specific motor shows, and there is a design initiative scheme where new and radical ideas – not necessarily with any particular goal in mind – can be developed, not necessarily attached to any project, and taken forward if they look promising. This can even lead to a full concept car, says le Quément. A further important strand is the acceptance of outside commissions for the design of non-automotive items: one such example is a special TAG Heuer F1 watch, not for high-street retail sale but marketed at Formula One circuits. 'Doing this kind of work enables us to unwind,' says le Quément.

Individual designers are free to contribute ideas to any project and, to a large extent, designers can ask to be assigned to particular programmes. The Technocentre is just one of four Renault design studios worldwide: the others are in central Paris, in Barcelona and at Renault-Samsung in Korea. Nissan in Tokyo employs more than 400 designers; there is, however, no horizontal link with the Renault teams: at the top of the pyramid Patrick le Quément is responsible for co-ordinating the design effort and ensuring the brands retain separate identities. The design staff in the Technocentre is 350 strong,

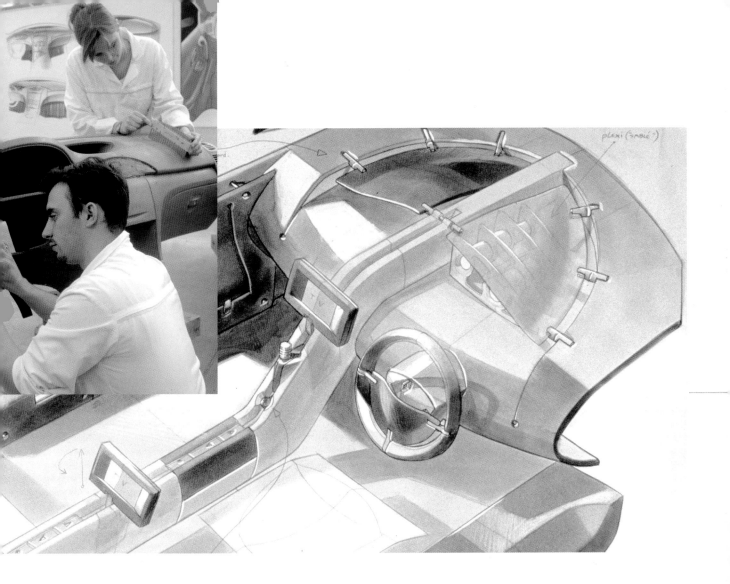

including just over 100 designers. Design staff in other locations account for another 50.

The normal practice in major programmes such as the Mégane is for each studio to submit one or more proposals and for senior management to decide which one to go with. The Mégane II hatchbacks were conceived in the Technocentre, for instance, while the new Scénic was based on an original proposal from the Barcelona design studio.

An important central principle of the Renault design process is that everyone owns the whole of it: designers, for instance, are responsible for ensuring the quality and performance of their creations right through to the final production vehicle – and indeed for in-service problems, too.

There are few rules within Renault Design, says le Quément, save for his mantra that it is 'forbidden to forbid'. Nevertheless, with the wholesale adoption of the Alias computer design software he is beginning to feel that designers are designing on too small a scale. He is now trying to encourage his staff to use paper a lot more and to draw very large, even life-size.

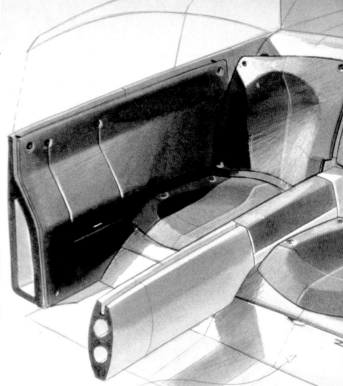

## HOW THEY WORK

### PATRICK LE QUÉMENT

'I DO SPEND A LOT OF TIME
THINKING ABOUT DESIGN
STRATEGY, AND QUITE OFTEN I
WILL COME IN ON A MONDAY
MORNING WITH SOME THEMES
THAT WE COULD TAKE FORWARD'

Renault's head of design (who says he doesn't design cars any more and that he has an excellent staff doing an outstanding job) has a blue notebook on his desk, which regularly fills up with sketches.

'I do spend a lot of time thinking about design strategy,' he confesses, 'and quite often I will come in on a Monday morning with some themes that we could take forward – for Dacia or Samsung, for instance. However, I don't want to impose ideas on anyone – these are merely thoughts, possibilities, ideas up for discussion along with everyone else's.'

In terms of technique le Quément likes to work on small pads and with his favourite brand of ballpoint, SENSA, much favoured by designers for its weight, good balance and firm, definite lines.

'When I'm doing an exterior I will start with one side elevation. I will do the two wheels, then the rocker panel, then the front. I will then develop the overall shape and move over to the back. After that, it could be another elevation and maybe a view in perspective – but I don't often need to go that far.'

Fascinated by design and architecture in all their forms – he has designed his own house – le Quément cites the atmospheric lights of Ingo Mauer and the interior designs of Andrée Putman as particular passions. Among automotive artefacts he takes pleasure in any Ferrari designed by Pininfarina, especially the 250 GTO, the '63 GT Lusso and the 328 GTB, while in terms of vehicle detailing the shape of the windshield and the relationship of the wheels to the body are important areas to get right. Audi is good at getting the wheel/body relationship right, he says, while in the new Espace he has tried to emulate the higher, more open feeling of the GT Lusso windshield – 'I didn't want it to be like a hat sat on your head,' he observes.

**ANTHONY GRADE** vice president, exterior design

Right-hand man to Patrick le Quément, UK-born Antony Grade began sketching cars from an early age, his passion increasing dramatically after a visit to the 1968 London Motor Show – his first. With his family in the movie business, there were always lots of exotic cars around: it was the era of the Lamborghini Miura and TV series such as *Thunderbirds* and *Stingray*, all of which helped fuel his determination to become a car designer.

After he had finished school he approached the Royal College of Art and then Rover about sponsorship, but received little encouragement. However, David Bache, designer of the award-winning Rover SD1, suggested he try Ford, which was known to be open to students. Grade's interviewer at Ford proved to be none other than Patrick le Quément, at that time a young design executive; le Quément agreed to sponsor Grade through four years at Coventry, after which he joined Ford.

At Renault, where he insists that management is hands-off, allowing designers considerable freedom, one of Grade's main responsibilities is transmitting his experience to others and, as he puts it, 'getting what we've drawn into production'. As the architect of the whole process he admits to moments of frustration when his own creativity has to take second place to organising, managing and allocating resources. The toughest challenge he has faced to date was the simultaneous development of four key products: Laguna, Vel Satis, new Espace and Avantime. Nevertheless, the most satisfying reward is to see new models such as the Mégane and Vel Satis on the streets.

Contemporary cars he admires include the Audi A6 and VW Phaeton, but one senses some of his strongest influences come from the 1960s with designs like the 'simple, efficient and elegant' Lotus Elite, the Miura and the Citroen DS ('I was brought up in one,' he says). The Tizio lamp by Richard Sapper, the Bang and Olufsen hi-fi with the famous sliding doors, and Alessi products with their sense of humour are among his design icons – and among his unfulfilled ambitions is to design a powerboat, sculptural curves and all.

'THE BIGGEST CHANGE OVER THE LAST FEW YEARS HAS BEEN THE INTRODUCTION OF FULLY CAD-BASED DESIGN METHODS. IT MAKES IT POSSIBLE TO DO MANY MORE ALTERNATIVE PROPOSALS'

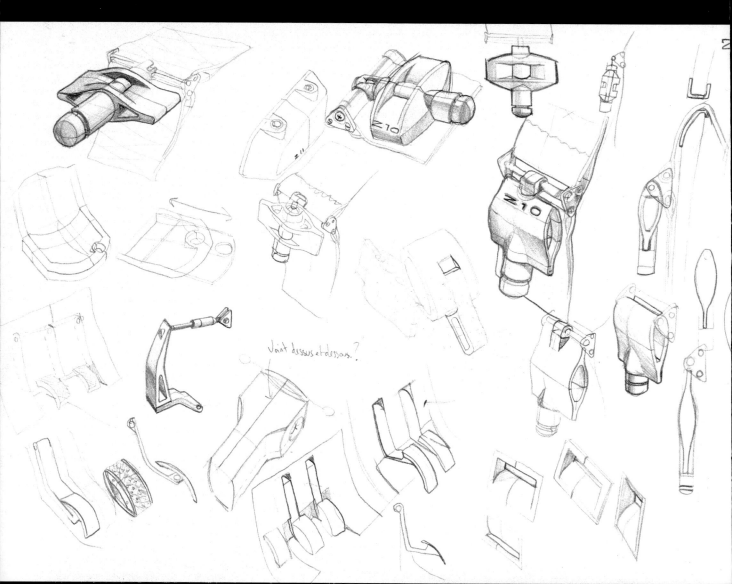

J'ai dessus et dessous ?

**KEN MELVILLE** design director, medium cars and Dacia

Officially listed as a designer specialising in medium cars, Edinburgh-born Ken Melville is in fact working on other projects too confidential to talk about. For him it all began with a visit to the Jackie Stewart Speed Show, which prompted the young, keen artist Melville to begin collecting brochures, reading *Autocar* and writing to car firms. All this eventually led to his enrolment on a four-year degree course in industrial design, supported by Talbot, which later merged into PSA.

Next it was down to London for the post graduate vehicle design course at the Royal College of Art where he received offers from Rover, Audi, Opel and PSA. 'I chose PSA,' says Melville, 'and ended up doing the exterior design on the replacement for the Citroen BX.'

'Ideas don't come in a flash,' he says: 'Ideas also come from product planning or purchasing – for us it's better to have a problem to solve. Concept cars, on the other hand, are essential to our work, too – they free up the imagination.' In terms of technique Melville tends to start with lots of small sketches, lots of interesting design ideas. 'First I do the wheels, how it sits on the road – and I then build upwards from that.'

Unlike many other designers, his initial sketches tend to be perspectives rather than geometrical elevations. Favoured materials are pen and pencil an A4-sized paper, slightly transparent, even tracing paper to allow areas to be copied across. The vehicle's proportions and packaging come with experience, he says. 'Computer-aided design techniques can be quite a help,' he explains. 'Before CAD we used to do the side, the plan, the front, the rear. Now, computers do it instantaneously. It makes the job much faster: it hasn't made people more creative but it has given them more options – you can get more ideas down, and it's good for timing.'

There is room for all techniques, he believes: the art of drawing is not endangered, especially as one of the problems with CAD is that the proportions of a design don't seem the same on a small screen.

# 01.08 DESIGNER DIARY: A WORKING WEEK

MARK PHILLIPS IS A PRINCIPAL DESIGNER AT JAGUAR CARS ADVANCED DESIGN STUDIO IN COVENTRY, ENGLAND. DURING HIS CAREER MARK HAS BEEN INVOLVED IN MANY PRODUCTION AND CONCEPTUAL DESIGN PROGRAMMES AND DESIGNED THE INTERIOR OF THE JAGUAR R-COUPÉ CONCEPT CAR SHOWN AT THE 2001 FRANKFURT MOTOR SHOW.

MARK IS CURRENTLY WORKING ON A TWO-YEAR SECONDMENT AT FORD'S INGENI DESIGN STUDIO IN SOHO, LONDON.

## MONDAY

| 08.00 | 10.00 | 12.00 | 14.00 | 16.00 | 18.00 |

*Walked into work today, the sun is out – summer's here! Got a coffee and after a lot of debate and self-justification – an egg muffin breakfast to take to the office – a good start to any week.*

**8.00** Sat down at desk with breakfast and had a quick discussion with some of the guys about the weekend's highlight: England's rugby team's victory over Ireland in Dublin, their Six Nations Championship success!

**8.30** Went through e-mails and plans for the day and week (I always try to plan my week on a Sunday and at the end of each day).

**9:00** Set up presentation to start the second phase of an internal automotive design project – a virtual concept car. Designers mounted research and support work on presentation boards. Set up plasma screen – for supportive marketing presentation.

**12:45** Popped out for lunch . Discussed an article in Wallpaper magazine about a new restaurant called Sketch in Conduit street. Should visit this week.

**1.30** Presented to the project chief the initial completed research which will be used to explore the car's overall personality and focus the design direction.

**3:30** Reviewed presentation with chief, agreed next steps and amended timing plan with deadlines and reviews.

**5:00** Reviewed emails.

**8.00** Finished work. Caught up with friends at The Alphabet bar in Soho for bar food and a drink. Cool Ron Arad car-style seating and abstract map of Soho on floor.

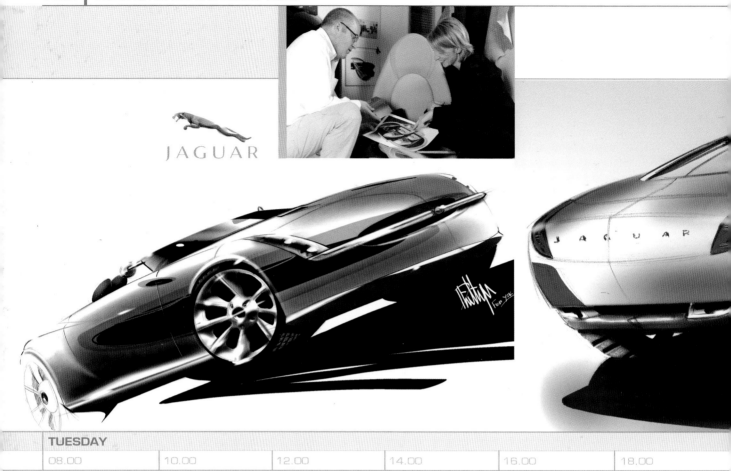

**TUESDAY**

| 08.00 | 10.00 | 12.00 | 14.00 | 16.00 | 18.00 |
| --- | --- | --- | --- | --- | --- |

*Went to work by Tube today ...
guess the summer isn't quite
here then?*

**8:00** Went straight into office and reviewed my e-mails. Received e-mail of vehicle engineering package data file name and location.

**9:30** Went through the presentation boards that the designers have been putting together - forgotten how much we did! Few adjustments needed.

**11:00** Met with designers and discussed how to use brainstormed research in order to start defining the brand and reflect the car's identity. Set the brief for next sketching phase of personality themes.

**1:00** Lunch

**1:45 – 5:00** Brainstormed brand evolution. Highlighted what the product needs to say and feel like
  – Need to explore potential of the existing brand
  – Reflect aspirations and values of a future market

**6:00** E-mails then finished work. Walked home.

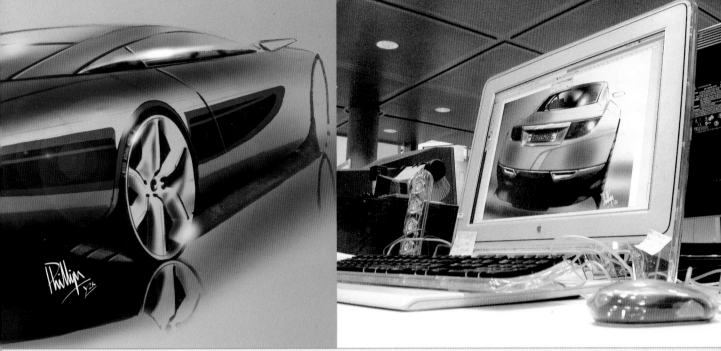

## WEDNESDAY

| 08.00 | 10.00 | 12.00 | 14.00 | 16.00 | 18.00 |
|-------|-------|-------|-------|-------|-------|

**8.30** Went through e- mails. Reviewed the day's work plan.

**9:00** Meeting with the team of four car designers and two colour and trim designers.

**11:00** Started Designers developing sketches to express aspects of the car's identities through different architectures. The initial sketches are intuitive and free - developed quickly to generate ideas and explore face graphics, proportion and form language.

**2:00** Colour and trim are to develop mood boards, colour palettes, interesting textures and materials to support five themes. They will use research on London street influences – fashion/interiors/graphics – flyers/cool magazines, photos of shops/restaurants to inspire visuals for mood boards.

**7.00** Finished work. On the way home went with a few of the designers to Sketch – what a place. This is contemporary luxury at its best !... loved the Newson egg-shaped loos - totally mad... The decor: full of surprise – Georgian elegance with a twist - colour, materials and dramatic lighting.

## THURSDAY

| 08.00 | 10.00 | 12.00 | 14.00 | 16.00 | 18.00 |
|-------|-------|-------|-------|-------|-------|

**8.30** Went through e-mails and reviewed the day's tasks.

**9:00** I started sketching exteriors today - I enjoy drawing and mixing rendering mediums.
It is a great and fun challenge drawing a car that is not what I'm used to.

**12:45** Lunch

**1:30** Merchandise meeting - one of my responsibilities is to manage and guide licensee design work and ensure that the values are consistent to the Jaguar brand. Must call Jaguar to give a progress feedback.

**3.00** Management meeting. Discussed all projects with our chief and project design managers to coordinate headcount and ensure maximum possible efficiency. Two designers temporarily lent to another team in order to support an important external client project.

**6.30** Left work for a gallery opening of a Beatles/Bob Dylan exhibition at The Proud Gallery off the Strand. The work was of the two photographed on tour in India, during the late sixties – great exhibition. Must visit the gallery's next exhibition – always presents interesting shows.

On my way over I saw an Aston Martin Vanquish parked up – the first I've seen out on the street. Stunning from ALL angles, sexy, modern and very BRITISH – think Sophie Anderton in a Savile Row Suit!

**FRIDAY**

| 08.00 | 10.00 | 12.00 | 14.00 | 16.00 | 18.00 |

**8.30** Started the day reviewing my e-mails and the usual day's objectives. Set up a meeting with The chief designer at The Volvo Design Centre in Barcelona, Spain whilst I'm on holiday there at the end of the month. Think the studio's proven expertise and experience operating as a true virtual studio will be of huge help to this project and Ingeni.

**9.00** Meeting to discuss and plan for Alias 3D modelling resource – will need two Alias modellers for the first two chosen theme sketches.

**10.30** Took a look at the sketches – a variety of very creative ideas – looking good so far.

**1:00** Visited the RCA (Royal College of Art) to see the work of a talented Jaguar sponsored design student. Also, had a good look around the college studios at other students' work and an interior design and jewellery design exhibition – this place is always a source of inspiration.

**5.00** Went over to the Queens Arms for a beer and a bite to eat. The Queens Arms is set in a cobbled street mews and overlooks every 'car nuts sweet shop': Coys (auction house). What can I say…? This place never fails to impress me – what beautiful old cars…. Reminds me – must get tickets for the forthcoming Goodwood weekend!

# 02

## 02 | HOW TO DO IT

### CONTENTS

Andy Entwhistle, Coventry

Joey Lam, Coventry

## 02.01 | WHAT MAKES A GOOD DESIGN?

**WE HAVE ALREADY CAUGHT A GLIMPSE OF THE HIGH-PRESSURE WORLD OF THE PROFESSIONAL CAR DESIGNER AND SEEN SOME OF THE TREMENDOUS VARIETY OF SHAPES AND FORMS HE OR SHE PRODUCES, ALONG WITH THE DAUNTING LIST OF CHALLENGES EACH OF THE PRINCIPAL VEHICLE TYPES PRESENTS.**

But what of the actual creative processes involved? Where does the designer start, and, perhaps more importantly still, how does he or she build that long-nurtured pet idea into a vision which can be clearly communicated to others so that it can become a production reality?

In this part of the book we move the focus away from the finished product and go back to the very basics. In series of tutorials compiled by leading professional and practising designers we learn the fundamentals of perspective drawing, of sketching and of colour rendering for maximum presentation impact; we learn the value of brand-building through consistent design, and look at the most useful techniques and tools of the trade – including clever software shortcuts – that can give your work an invaluable boost.

First, however, we go to one of the world's leading automotive design schools – Coventry University in England – whose graduates have gone on to design many of the most attractive and best-respected cars in current production. Here, in attempting to answer the rhetorical question 'what makes a good design?', we learn an important but simple-sounding lesson – that a design, however clever, attractive and appealing it may superficially seem, can only be counted a success if it fulfils the brief set out for it.

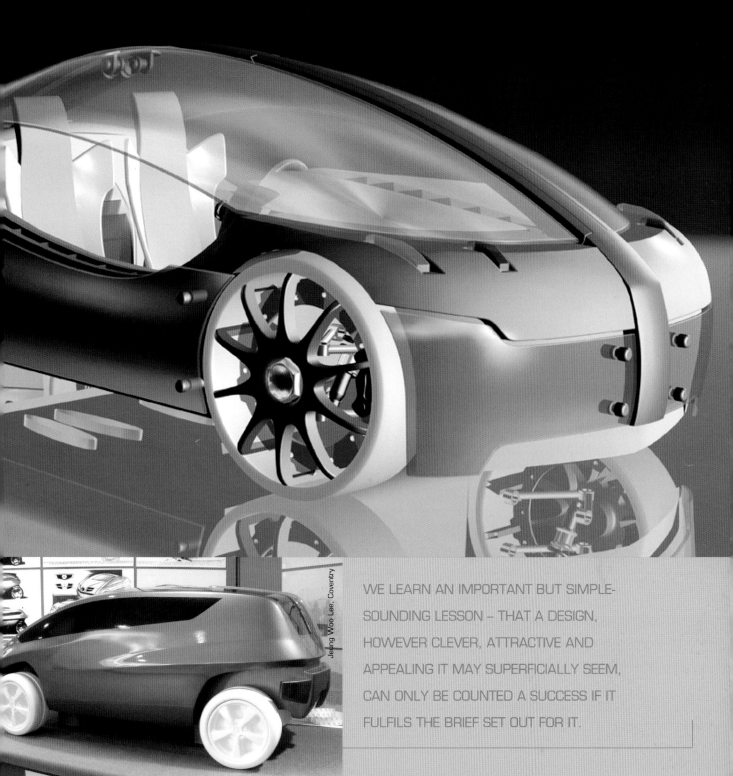

Jeung Woo Lee, Coventry

WE LEARN AN IMPORTANT BUT SIMPLE-
SOUNDING LESSON – THAT A DESIGN,
HOWEVER CLEVER, ATTRACTIVE AND
APPEALING IT MAY SUPERFICIALLY SEEM,
CAN ONLY BE COUNTED A SUCCESS IF IT
FULFILS THE BRIEF SET OUT FOR IT.

Fulfilling the design brief is an absolutely vital first step to decide between profit and loss, success and failure in real-life car building, but the maxim also provides an important discipline for design students. And as the many highly imaginative student designs so eloquently testify, discipline in the design process need be no barrier to creativity or freedom of expression. In fact, for anyone contemplating taking up car design as a career there could be no better inspiration than the designs from students from Coventry as well as London's Royal College of Art we reproduce in the pages that follow.

## WHAT MAKES A GOOD DESIGN?

THIS IS OFTEN REGARDED AS AN IMPOSSIBLE QUESTION TO ANSWER, BUT JENNY HANN, HEAD OF INDUSTRIAL DESIGN AT COVENTRY SCHOOL OF ART AND DESIGN, COVENTRY UNIVERSITY, MAKES SURE HER STUDENTS' DESIGNS FIT THE BRIEF BEFORE ANY AESTHETIC JUDGEMENTS ARE APPLIED.

To answer the question 'what makes a good design?' we need to know the context in which the design was undertaken. What is the proposed function and purpose of the product? Who is the intended user? Does the product meet the needs of the intended user? How does the new design fit into the proposed manufacturer's product range? Is it better than competing models? And, most importantly, is it desirable? The latter is the trickiest question of all, but is seen as the holy grail: self-evidently, it is desirability at the right price that sells products.

Unless we know the function and purpose of a proposed design identified in the designer's brief then we cannot say with objectivity whether it is a good solution or not – after all, how do you know that you have arrived if you do not know what your destination is?

So, we can look at the original design brief and evaluate a concept or a final design solution against the set of criteria identified within the brief. In short, only then can we say whether the design has met the brief. However there is a paradox – a design solution can meet the requirements of the design brief but still not be a good design solution. It could still be a product that people don't like and therefore won't buy; it could be the brief itself that is at fault.

Visual characteristics are the most difficult to quantify on a scale – the little matter of taste enters into the equation. Whilst we can identify that one person's meat is another person's poison and that there is no accounting for taste, there are some visual rules in design.

CER

Sunraycer study. Adam Hopwood

RIOR RENDERINGS

Key criteria include the following: Does the vehicle have a coherent and resolved overall form – does it hang together with balance and harmony in terms of its proportions? Are there any parts that look as if they have been added on as an afterthought – or do all the parts look purposeful and deliberate? Does anything look out of place or odd? Is there harmony to the lines – do they flow, or are there uncomfortable interruptions in the lines?

'Busy-ness' is a frequent problem – the 'less is more' axiom is usually appropriate. This rule also applies to use of colour, with the additional requirement that the colour must be appropriate to the context of use and to the overall form of the vehicle. We often wonder why some cars look well in one colour and abhorrent in another, and why some models always look

right – and others always wrong – whatever the colour. Colour and tone are powerful – colour can advance or recede, make things look heavier or lighter, bigger or smaller.

The ability to manipulate the perception of form through the use of line and colour is a key feature of the designer's activity. Making a large form look smaller or vice versa, or a squat form appear lighter, longer or otherwise more elegant – these are common design tasks. This manipulation or visual manoeuvre (visual cheating) can be applied with the knowledge and application of a few simple rules.

For example, emphasising the horizontal lines in a vehicle can be achieved by reducing the impact of any upright forms. Blacking out the pillars or even the edges of the pillars is a

Ian Bunting

Brand inspired roadster study: Peter Bladesnixon

common trick. This has the effect of giving a sleeker appearance and suggests speed. A darker (either in recess, or through darker colouration) lower section of an object has the effect of making it appear to float; it also reduces the visual mass of a plane.

Framing a form – it's helpful to think of a painting – contains an area and stops your eye from wandering off. Conversely, the eye continues lines that do not butt up against another or do not come to a deliberate end; likewise, the eye tends to mentally complete forms that are not fully there. The brain wants to make sense of an incomplete form by completing it.

Designers need to understand the phenomena of optical illusions because the eye can play all kinds of tricks on the viewer – tricks which can be used to good effect in car design. Most people are familiar with optical illusions in which lines of equal length look longer or shorter depending on lines that surround them. Similarly, the amount of space around a form can affect the way you perceive its size. Thus a door handle on a large expanse of surface area will look smaller than the same size handle on a smaller door. There are hundreds of optical illusions, many of which crop up unexpectedly. A clued-up designer will be able to

make the most of them – or, where the illusion causes a problem, he will be able to stop it from happening

## DOES THE DESIGN LOOK RIGHT?

There is a school of thought that suggests that if a design looks right, then it is right. Harmonious and balanced forms, which have continuous flowing lines defining the overall shape, tend not to jar or disturb the viewer. Interrupted forms, and forms made up of a variety of different elements, cause the eye to jump about haphazardly from one bit to the other and can be less visually appealing – but there is something else...

Does the design look like it will do what it is supposed to do?

Does anything look as if it wouldn't do what it is supposed to do? For example, do any parts look flimsy or as if they may break? Does the safety cage or roll bar look as if it would indeed protect its occupants? On a more general level, if it is a sports car, does it look as if it will hold the road well? Or, for an SUV, does it project the ruggedness required to cross rough terrain?

Does the design remind you of something else? This is usually detrimental to product acceptance. A station wagon that is reminiscent of a hearse, for example, is unlikely to be

MANY STUDENTS NOW GRAPPLE WITH THE TASK

OF DESIGNING A COMPACT CAR WITH THE

DESIRABILITY OF A LARGER ONE. CARS LIKE THE MCC

SMART HAVE CHANGED THIS. THIS IS A VEHICLE THAT

DOESN'T TRY TO BE BIGGER AND MORE SOPHISTICATED

THAN IT IS. ITS APPEAL IS JUST THAT.

appealing, and once so compared it is difficult to rid oneself of the associated image.

There is a big difference between visual cleverness and visual sensitivity. Clever design can be intriguing and interesting but unappealing – we can admire the thought behind the form – but that does not necessarily mean that we respond to it favourably on an emotional level. The Fiat Multipla is a classic example of functional cleverness getting the better of aesthetic balance. While the six-seater accommodation provided by the top-hat silhouette of Fiat's design drew almost universal praise, the strange looks of the external form were equally widely derided.

## HOW HAVE PROPORTIONS CHANGED?

There have been really significant developments in the last twenty years or so. At one time the only desirable car was a car of large and luxurious proportions. This was usually low and sleek. Concern for the environment caused us all to aim for compact and efficient vehicles. But habits die hard – many people still associate size with status. Many students now grapple with the task of designing a compact car with the desirability of a larger one

Cars like the MCC Smart have changed this. This is a vehicle that doesn't try to be bigger and more sophisticated than it is. Its appeal is just that. Its sophistication comes from

thorough attention to the detail of the product, inside and out, from the thinking behind the product and the system of support for Smart owners.

Attention to the practical aspects of a vehicle are now high priority – this has led to technological developments giving smaller cars larger and more flexible interiors whilst maintaining relatively compact overall dimensions.

The one-box Mercedes A-class (designed by Coventry graduate Steve Mattin, now chief designer at Mercedes) had very different proportions, a surprising departure for Mercedes, and was widely perceived as something of a breakthrough. As well as the fresh proportions made possible through its double floor construction, it exhibits an unusual reverse sweeping C pillar.

Traditional distinctions between vehicle types are no longer so rigid – terms like saloon car, coupé, sports convertible, van and pick-up truck have lost their rigidly stereotyped profiles. So-called crossovers have become the name of the game as manufacturers rush to combine the appeal of two or more niche products into a single design, thus drawing on two potential sets of customers. An excellent example is the Volvo XC90, which does duty as both a station wagon and a four-wheel drive off-road vehicle, yet which also has the seven-seater passenger-carrying ability of a minivan.

**THE PROCESS**

PRODUCT PLANNING

Before any work begins on design and manufacture of a new car, the company planning to produce it generally undertakes market research to make sure that the product is needed and wanted. The company also has to make sure that factory capacity appropriate to the vehicle is available – for instance, a switch to aluminium as a structural material will require a complete rethink of the manufacturing process and equipment, which in turn will impact on how the vehicle itself is designed.

All aspects of vehicle design and manufacture require careful planning and, following this research stage, the company will produce a brief for the designer.

THE BRIEF

All designers work to a design brief. The brief sets out all aspects of the design task. The brief will state who the car is for, what type it shall be, how much it is expected to cost. The brief identifies the position of the new vehicle in the range of vehicles produced by the company. Getting the brief right is very important to the success of the product.

CONCEPT GENERATION

When designers receive the brief they will begin a process of concept generation. In a sketch programme the designers will put ideas for the exterior and the interior of the new vehicle on paper. Ideas for the outside of the vehicle usually come before interior concepts, though sometimes ideas for the interior of the car will affect the exterior shape. In the early stages designers will produce many sketch ideas.

THEMES SELECTION

Following concept generation the sketched ideas are evaluated and a design theme for the project is selected. Drawings are chosen which most closely match the needs identified in the design brief and which look the most interesting. Sometimes several style directions are chosen for taking on to the next stage. When the theme or themes have been selected the designers have a style direction for further development of ideas for the inside and outside of the new car.

3D AND COMPUTER MODEL DEVELOPMENT

After further drawing development it will be time to see what the car looks like in three dimensions. A scale model, generally in clay, is built to evaluate the vehicle shape in the round. From 2D drawings it can be difficult to imagine what the design will look like when it is turned into a model. Computers can help designers to do this. Measurements of the vehicle are put into the computer and the design can be manipulated by the computer to show different views of the vehicle.

Although computers are very useful to help visualise the design, nothing beats creating actual scale and full-size models. Model makers use special styling clay to create scale and full-size models. Sometimes computer data is sent to a machine which can cut material directly to produce a model.

## DESIGN EVALUATION

Full-size exterior and interior models and drawings are used to evaluate the vehicle's appearance and ergonomics. These will be compared with competitors' cars.

When the company believes it has a potentially successful design proposal it may choose to gauge customer reaction by inviting typical users to a so-called customer clinic. Some carmakers use this process to help decide between themes; others use it at a later stage to fine-tune design details or equipment provision in relation to reference vehicles from competing companies.

## STYLING FREEZE

The so-called styling freeze is the point at which the proposal becomes a programme proper. Many companies will have a 'gateway' at this point where the financial viability of the programme is assessed once again in the light of what has been learned so far. The body style and mechanical specification are finalised, the launch date is set and the countdown to 'job 1' – the first production unit – begins. Major changes to exterior sheet metal or significant mechanical elements are very expensive beyond this stage and are likely to lead to delays in the start of production.

## PROTOTYPE DEVELOPMENT/PRODUCT TESTING

Hand-built prototypes, usually with heavily disguised bodywork, are tested under normal and extreme driving conditions. Crash test performance is evaluated on computer. Eventually real cars will be tested to meet strict crash and safety requirements.

## PRODUCT LAUNCH

The product will be unveiled at a major international motor show in a blaze of well-organised publicity. The ultimate success of the new car will be judged not just on the.reception the vehicle receives at launch, but primarily on the strength of sales and the return on the investment during the model's production lifespan.

# 02.02 | BUILDING BRAND VALUES

WHAT MAKES A BMW A BMW OR A FORD A FORD? WHY CAN A MERCEDES BE RECOGNISED AT THE FAR END OF THE STREET, WHILE YOU MIGHT STRUGGLE TO KNOW A DAEWOO OR A DAIHATSU EVEN IF IT WERE PARKED RIGHT NEXT TO YOU? AND WHY DO OFF-ROADERS LOOK TOUGH AND RUGGED CRAWLING ROUND CITY CENTRES, JUST AS SUPERCARS SEEM TO BE DOING 200 MPH EVEN WHEN STANDING STILL?

LOOK CLOSER AND YOU CAN TELL AN AUDI JUST BY THE SHAPE OF A WHEELARCH OPENING OR TAIL-LIGHT LENS; A SAAB IS GIVEN AWAY BY THE SILHOUETTE OF ITS WINDSCREEN, A CORVETTE BY ITS PARED ROUND REAR LIGHTS. THE MEREST LIFT IN THE REAR FENDER LINE MEANS IT'S A JAGUAR, A KINK IN THE REAR PILLAR MAKES IT A BMW, WHILE SLANTING HEADLIGHTS SIGNAL A PEUGEOT.

None of these details carry any logo or emblem, still less any overt badging. But while these features might be meaningless in structural or engineering terms, their emotional symbolism is highly significant: each is imbued with powerful visual coding that straightaway triggers pre-programmed brand messages in the observer's brain.

Sales and marketing divisions like nothing better than a strong identity for a brand, signalled by the ability of consumers to instantly recognise the product and, hopefully, identify with the other members of the brand and the values shared by the broader brand family.

Of course, brand identity such as that enjoyed by BMW and Mercedes is no accident: it is a prodigiously valuable corporate asset that has been painstakingly built up over many years, honed and polished to keep it at the top of the pile. And, needless to say, designers are right up there when it comes to creating, projecting and controlling the visual message the company's products put out. These are the people who develop the visual cues that we as consumers interpret as brand identity; these are the people who build personas for their products, adding the emotional content that ordinary people will recognise and respond to.

Here, leading designer Paul Wraith trains his professional eye on three distinctive automotive brands – Rolls Royce, Renault and BMW – to show step by step how their visual identities are built up. First, however, he takes a look at three different market segments to identify the crucial characteristics – and a few clever designer's tricks – that ensure that city cars look small, funky and friendly, sports cars come across as irresistibly fast and powerful, and 4x4s promise adventure and go-anywhere indestructibility even on a trip to the local supermarket.

# CITY STYLE

HERE, COMPACTNESS IS EVERYTHING: THE PROPORTIONAL CRITERIA OF THE DESIGN ARE DEFINED BY THE VERY SHORT PACKAGE.

SO I BEGIN (TOP) WITH A SHORT WHEELBASE AND SLOT IN THE DRIVER: THE SITTING POSITION HAS TO BE QUITE HIGH BECAUSE OF THE SHORT WHEELBASE, MAKING THE DRIVER'S EYELINE HIGHER TOO – A USEFUL BONUS IN CROWDED TOWN TRAFFIC. THE 'BOX' SURROUNDING THIS CAR THUS ENDS UP BEING VERY TALL, NARROW AND SHORT – THE PRECISE OPPOSITE OF THAT ENCLOSING A SUPERCAR.

THERE IS NOT MUCH DESIGN HISTORY IN THIS SEGMENT – EVEN THE SMART IS STILL SOMETHING OF A NOVELTY, BUT IT DOES ITS JOB VERY WELL. IN THIS EXAMPLE I HAVE GONE FOR A MORE EXPRESSIVE DESIGN LANGUAGE, WITH A CLEAR WEDGE SHAPE TO THE WINDOW LINE EXPANDING TOWARDS THE FRONT TO ADD MOVEMENT AND HELP DISGUISE THE PACKAGE. WHEN YOU GO AS SMALL AS THIS IT ALL HAS TO BE VERY TIGHT AND DISCIPLINED: THERE IS FAR LESS ROOM FOR MANOEUVRE THAN WITH A LARGER CAR.

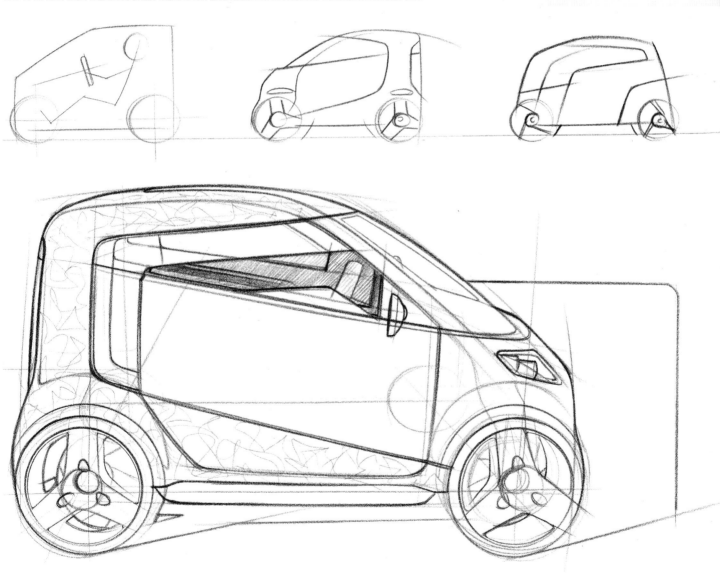

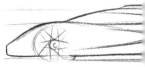

# SPORTS STYLE

THERE'S A RICH BACK CATALOGUE OF SPORTS CAR ICONS THAT GIVES EVERYONE A STRONG AND CLEAR IDEA OF WHAT A SPORTS CAR SHOULD LOOK LIKE: NOT JUST LONG, LOW AND WIDE, BUT ALSO WITH FAST, SMOOTH CURVES TO ITS SHAPE AND A CHARACTERISTIC STANCE THAT HAS IT CLINGING TO THE ROAD.

THE PROPORTIONS IN FRONT OF AND BEHIND THE PASSENGER COMPARTMENT ARE ONE OF THE MOST IMPORTANT THINGS: CLASSIC PRE-WAR SPORTS CARS WERE ALWAYS CHARACTERISED BY VERY LONG BONNETS, SIGNIFYING A BIG AND POWERFUL ENGINE – THINGS LIKE THE SQUIRE FROM THE '20S AND '30S. THERE WAS EVEN A HEALEY WHERE THE DRIVER WAS PUSHED RIGHT TO THE VERY BACK.

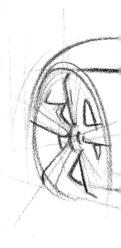

ON MORE MODERN MID-ENGINED SPORTS CARS THE WINDOW AREA HAS MOVED FORWARD, SOMETIMES FURTHER FORWARD THAN THE MIDDLE OF THE CAR, TO ACCOMMODATE THE LARGE ENGINE BAY. THE WHEELARCH LINE IS KEY, TOO: OFTEN, IT DIPS DOWN BETWEEN THE FRONT AND REAR ARCHES, EMPHASISING HOW LOW THE BUILD OF THE CAR IS, ESPECIALLY IN THE COCKPIT AREA. LIKEWISE, A RISING TAIL AREA PROVIDES A LINK WITH THE DIFFUSER AERODYNAMIC FEATURE OF RACING CARS AND ALSO EXPOSES ENGINEERING ELEMENTS SUCH AS SUSPENSION AND EXHAUSTS THAT SIGNIFY PERFORMANCE.

THIS IS SIMILAR TO A PORSCHE CARRERA GT, A SUPERCAR WITH A LOT OF HERITAGE ASSOCIATED WITH IT. LIKE MANY SUPERCARS, IT HAS THE PHYSIQUE OF AN ATHLETE, A SMOOTH SKIN STRETCHED TAUT OVER THE MUSCLES AND BONES. IT'S FORM ALLUDING TO FUNCTION ONCE MORE, THOUGH IN WHAT HAS COME TO BE A FAIRLY CLASSICAL INTERPRETATION: SOMETHING LIKE A LAMBORGHINI IS MORE EXTREME, SEEKING TO JUMP AHEAD OF THE CONVENTION AND CHALLENGE THE ESTABLISHED FORMS.

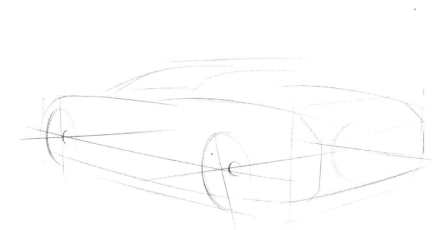

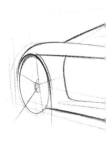

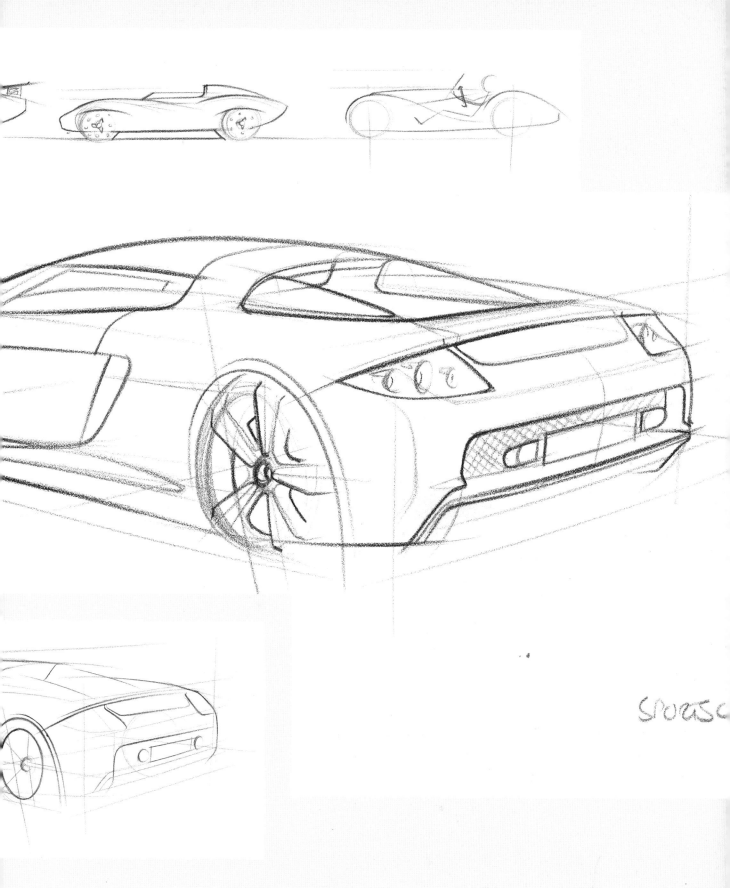

Sroasc

# SUV STYLE

THE BASIS HERE DERIVES FROM THE GENERIC TWO- OR THREE-BOX SHAPE, AS TYPIFIED BY THE ORIGINAL LAND ROVER AND JEEP. IT IS SHORT AND CHUNKY, SITS HIGH OFF THE GROUND ON LARGE WHEELS, AND HAS VERY SHORT OVERHANGS FRONT AND REAR TO ENABLE IT TO TACKLE THE APPROACHES TO STEEP SLOPES WITHOUT THE BODYWORK DIGGING INTO THE GROUND.

I'VE GRADUALLY REFINED THE GENERIC SHAPE, MAKING IT LONGER AND ADDING A BIT OF SPEED TO THE LOOK, BUT STILL KEEPING THE WHEELS CLOSE TO EACH END. IN THE THIRD THUMBNAIL I'VE ADDED MORE SURFACING, TOO, AND THE WHEELS GAIN STILL MORE EMPHASIS. HISTORICALLY, OFF-ROADERS HAVE ALWAYS HAD BIG WHEELS, BUT NOW THIS HAS TAKEN AN EVEN MORE EXTREME TURN. THE FOCAL AREA FOR THESE VEHICLES IS NOW THE STREET, RATHER THAN OFF-ROAD: IT'S IRONIC AND DOESN'T HAVE A GOOD RATIONALE, BUT TO MAKE THEM DRIVE DECENTLY ON THE ROAD THEY HAVE BEEN GIVEN STIFFER SUSPENSION AND LOWER-PROFILE TYRES, WHICH HAS LED TO EVEN BIGGER WHEELS.

THIS GIVES A CUSTOM ELEMENT TO SOME OF THE DESIGNS – THE BMW X5 IS A GOOD EXAMPLE. IT IS TALL AND IMPOSING BUT DISGUISES ITS HEIGHT CLEVERLY WITH A COLOUR BREAK AND A SILL BREAK – A SACRIFICIAL AREA THAT'S PAINTED DARK OR BLACK SO THAT IF EFFECTIVELY DISAPPEARS FROM THE MASS THAT YOU SEE.

PEOPLE PREFER THE TALLER SEATING POSITION OF THESE VEHICLES: IT MAKES THEM FEEL SAFER, WHICH IS WHY THEY ARE POPULAR WITH WOMEN AND CHILDREN ON THE SCHOOL RUN. TO THE DESIGNER, IT'S A CHALLENGE TO ACHIEVE A BALANCE BETWEEN PRESENCE AND AGGRESSIVENESS, AND BETWEEN A STYLE THAT CONVEYS SPEED AND STABILITY YET WHICH STILL PERFORMS ADEQUATELY ON THE RARE OCCASIONS THE VEHICLE IS DRIVEN ON THE ROUGH.

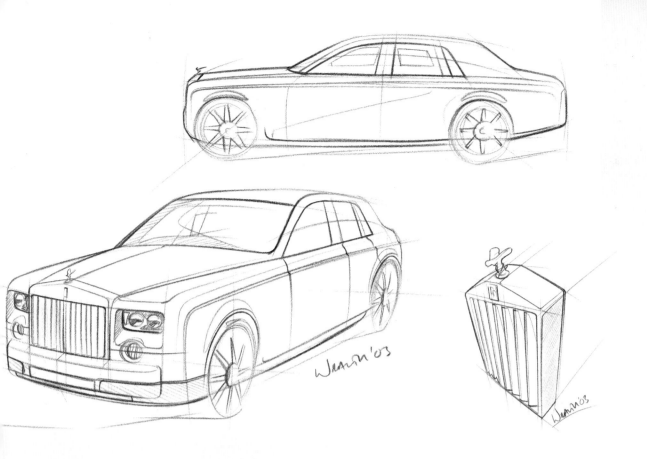

## LUXURY STYLE

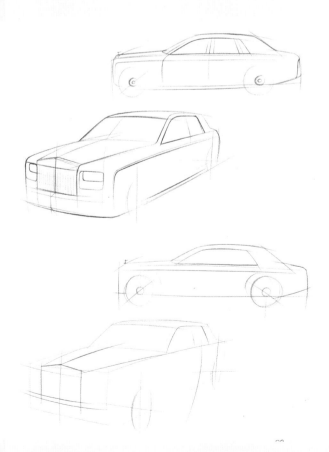

WITH A SUPER-LUXURY CAR LIKE A ROLLS-ROYCE THE PROPORTIONS ARE AGAIN EXAGGERATED, BUT IN A DIFFERENT WAY.

A CAR IN THIS CLASS HAS TO BE VERY LONG, WEIGHTY AND IMPOSING – THAT'S THE KEY. IT HAS TO BE HEAVILY BRANDED, TOO: THE RADIATOR DOMINATES THE FRONT AND DICTATES THE PROPORTIONS OF THE REST OF THE CAR.

IN PROFILE, THE SHORT FRONT OVERHANG AND THE LONG REAR ARE THE OPPOSITES OF THE RACING-CAR PROPORTIONS. THE LONG BONNET IS SUGGESTIVE OF POWER, HERITAGE AND HISTORY, WHILE THE CABIN AREA IS ESPECIALLY INTERESTING. THE EMPHASIS IN THE GLASSHOUSE IS 100 PERCENT TOWARDS THE REAR, WITH EXTREMELY DEEP REAR PILLARS OFFERING PRIVACY AND PROTECTION TO THE OCCUPANTS. THERE'S MUCH LESS EMPHASIS ON THE FRONT PORTION OF THE PASSENGER COMPARTMENT: IT'S LIKE THE OLD HORSELESS CARRIAGES, WHERE THE IMPORTANT PEOPLE SAT IN THE BACK AND THE CHAUFFEUR COULD EVEN BE EXPOSED TO THE ELEMENTS MUCH FURTHER FORWARD.

THE LONG BOOT IS VERY VISUAL, TOO: ITS SHEER SIZE SUGGESTS THE ABILITY TO TRAVEL VERY LONG DISTANCES IN UTTER LUXURY, PERHAPS EVEN WITH SERVANTS ON CALL. THE CAR HAS A MASSIVE CONFIDENCE TO IT AND ITS DETAILS CAN AFFORD TO MAKE BIG STATEMENTS TOO. THE ROLLS-ROYCE EMBLEM, FOR INSTANCE, IS COMPLEX AND POWERFUL.

THIS CAR MAKES AN INTERESTING COMPARISON WITH THE MAYBACH FROM MERCEDES. THE MAYBACH IS WIDE BUT LOW, AND ITS GRILLE LACKS PRESENCE. IT'S MORE LEAR JET, WHILE THE ROLLS-ROYCE COULD BE BLENHEIM PALACE.

BMW 01

## BMW STYLE

BMW IS IN THE THROES OF SOMETHING OF A STYLE UPHEAVAL AT PRESENT, BUT THE MODELS WITH WHICH IT HAS BUILT UP ITS POWERFUL IMAGE AND REPUTATION DISPLAY A REMARKABLE COHERENCE AND CONSISTENCY ACROSS EACH OF THE MODEL LINES.

THE PROPORTIONS MAY BE SUBTLY DIFFERENT BETWEEN THE SERIES, BUT EACH IS FUNDAMENTALLY ORTHODOX IN SHAPE, RELYING ON SUPERB DETAILING TO GENERATE THE STRONG BRAND IDENTITY. KEY TO ALL MODELS IS A SHORT FRONT OVERHANG, GIVING A FORWARD MOTION TO THE SHAPE; ON THE 3-SERIES HERE, THERE IS A SUBTLE WEDGE TO THE SIDE PROFILE, WITH A LOW NOSE ACCENTUATED BY LARGE WHEELARCH CUT-OUTS WITH LITTLE MASS ABOVE THEM. BIG WHEELS COMFORTABLY FILL THESE ARCHES, GIVING A LOW, GRIPPY STANCE ON THE ROAD.

A STRONG SWAGE LINE RUNS THE FULL LENGTH OF THE CAR, DIRECTING THE EMPHASIS TO THE KEY BRAND MARKERS AT THE FRONT – THE QUADRUPLE LIGHTS, NOW FAIRED IN UNDER SMOOTH COVERS, AND THE CHARACTERISTIC BMW GRILLE. THE GRILLE IS GIVEN ADDED PROMINENCE BY THE CONTOURS OF THE BONNET, WHICH SWEEPS DOWN BETWEEN THE LIGHTS TO MEET THE FRONT BUMPER. EACH OF THE LIGHTS HAS ITS OWN RECESS IN THE BUMPER, HINTING AT THE FOUR-LIGHT LOOK WHICH BUILT THE BRAND'S PRESENT-DAY IDENTITY.

THE GLASSHOUSE IS AGAIN CHARACTERISTIC, WELL BALANCED IN TERMS OF MASS AND PROPORTION, AND WITH THE FAMILIAR KINK TO THE C-POST THAT HAS BEEN A FEATURE OF BMWS FOR SEVERAL GENERATIONS.

# RENAULT STYLE

HERE WE SEE A VEHICLE WITH QUITE STRIKING DETAILING, AND ONE WHICH ALSO TRIES NEW PROPORTIONS IN A CLASS WHERE THE NEED FOR PRACTICALITY HAS FORCED A PRETTY UNIFORM OVERALL LOOK.

ASIDE FROM THE DRAMATIC, NEAR-VERTICAL TREATMENT OF THE REAR WINDOW, WHICH NEVERTHELESS CURVES PANORAMICALLY WHEN VIEWED FROM ABOVE, THE MÉGANE CONVEYS A FEELING OF ROOMINESS THROUGH THE USE OF A VERY LOW BELTLINE. THE EFFECT OF THIS IS TO DRAW ATTENTION TO THE GLASSHOUSE, WHICH ITSELF IS VERY UNUSUAL – ESPECIALLY ON THIS THREE-DOOR VERSION. HERE, THE SIDE WINDOW SILHOUETTE IS ALMOST SEMI-CIRCULAR, GIVING THE FEELING OF THE SWEEPING CURVES OF A COUPÉ. YET THIS IS A VISUAL TRICK, FOR THE ACTUAL ROOFLINE IS DRAWN STRAIGHT BACK FROM THE B-PILLARS TO PROVIDE REAR HEADROOM AND A LOT OF MASS HIGH UP AT THE REAR OF THE CAR. THIS IN TURN GIVES A PROPULSIVE EFFECT TO THE CAR'S PROFILE, WHILE FROM THE REAR THE COMBINATION OF THE VERTICAL, ALMOST SEMI-CIRCULAR BACKLIGHT AND THE BUTT-LIKE BOOT EVOKE HUMAN CONNOTATIONS AS WELL AS SENTIMENTS OF GLAMOROUS VINTAGE LUXURY CARS.

THE LOW, NEAT FRONT USES AN INTERESTING MIX OF LINES, PLANES AND CURVES TO DRAW THE VIEWER'S ATTENTION TO THE RENAULT LOGO IN THE CENTRE – THOUGH THE OVERALL SHAPE IS SUFFICIENTLY DISTINCTIVE FOR THE MODEL'S BRANDING TO BE OBVIOUS EVEN WITHOUT CORPORATE BADGING.

RENAULT 03

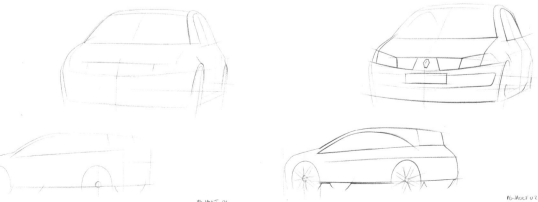

RENAULT 01

RENAULT 02

## 02.03 | STUDENT DESIGN WORK

ON THE SIX PAGES THAT FOLLOW WE PRESENT DESIGN WORK BY STUDENTS AT TWO OF THE UK'S FINEST AUTOMOTIVE DESIGN ESTABLISHMENTS, LONDON'S ROYAL COLLEGE OF ART AND COVENTRY SCHOOL OF ART AND DESIGN. ALL ROUND THE WORLD, MANY THOUSANDS OF STUDENTS ARE PRODUCING CREATIVE AND IMAGINATIVE DESIGNS AND HAVE THEIR EYES SET ON WORKING WITH A BIG-NAME CARMAKER. THESE PAGES GIVE A CLEAR PICTURE OF THE HIGH STANDARDS OF PROFESSIONALISM NOW BEING ACHIEVED.

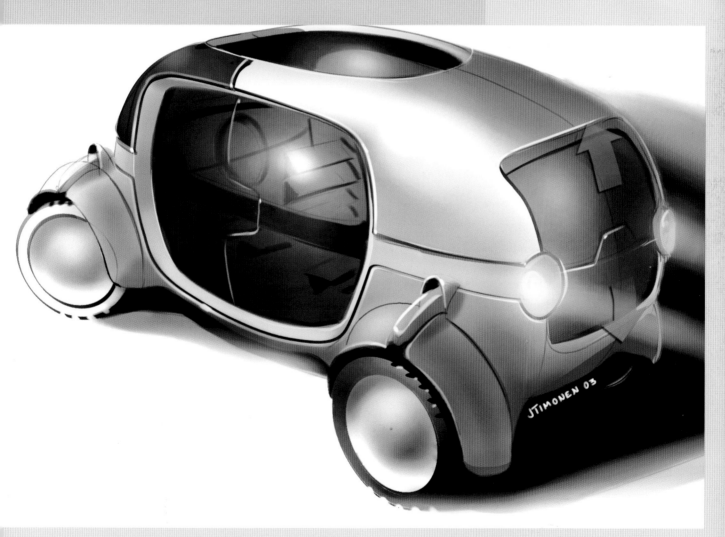

# JUSSI TIMONEN
## ROYAL COLLEGE OF ART

TOYOTA PROJECT ENTITLED: *VIBRANT/CLARITY – WHY SUV FOR THE Y GENERATION?* 2003

# NORAYATI CHE DAUD
## COVENTRY SCHOOL OF ART AND DESIGN

BRAND-INSPIRED COMPACT CITY CAR

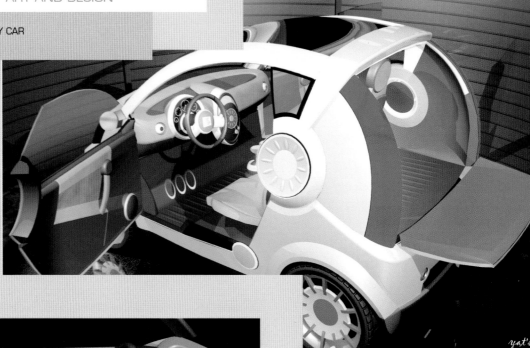

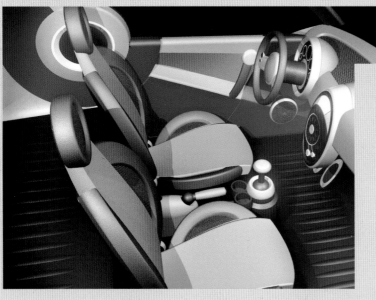

# IVAN WEIGHTMAN
COVENTRY SCHOOL OF ART AND DESIGN

MAYBACH STUDY

# MATTHEW SWANN
## ROYAL COLLEGE OF ART

SPORTS CAR CALLED HOME, 2002

The sketches show more ornamentation on the
of the vehicle. There are more light catchi
and the panels are now more recessed

Swann

P_13

suggests many components
ought together to create a
t, as items in a house do.

anks recall
chines.

P_16

# GETTING STARTED 1: PERSPECTIVES

A GOOD SKETCHING TECHNIQUE IS THE FOUNDATION STONE ON WHICH ANY DESIGNER'S PROFESSIONAL SKILLS ARE BUILT: AS A PRACTISING DESIGNER YOU WILL BE REQUIRED TO CREATE MANY AND VARIED IDEAS IN A SHORT SPACE OF TIME, AND TO COMMUNICATE THESE IDEAS IN A WAY THAT ENABLES OTHER TO SEE AND UNDERSTAND YOUR THINKING.  ESSENTIAL TO THE ABILITY TO SKETCH QUICKLY AND CONFIDENTLY IS A CLEAR UNDERSTANDING OF THE RULES OF PERSPECTIVE. HERE, IN THE FIRST OF OUR THREE TUTORIALS, PROFESSIONAL AUTOMOTIVE DESIGNER ALLAN MACDONALD TAKES US FROM THE KEY STARTING POINTS TO THE THREE PRINCIPAL PERSPECTIVE TYPES THAT WILL ALLOW YOU TO PRODUCE DRAWINGS WITH SPEED, EFFECTIVENESS AND IMPACT.

Although we all like to see and admire well-crafted illustrations, as a professional designer you will find that these constitute only a small percentage of the work you will produce. As a designer your job is to create many and varied ideas in a short space of time, and to do so in a way that others can see and understand your thinking. A good sketching technique is important for both of these. When practising sketching it can be very hard at first to know when to stop: this can lead to every drawing becoming a time-consuming rendering. It is important to learn not to be overly precious when sketching. By doing so you will produce more and improve much faster.  Over the next few pages we aim to show a good technique for working out ideas in both a fast and a readable manner. To be able to produce sketches which read as 3D objects, a basic understanding of perspective is required.  For this reason our tutorial begins by giving a brief overview of the rules of one- and two-point perspective, including ellipses. It then talks through three examples, all using different perspective viewpoints. Each one shows how to build a sketch from a blank page, through the rough line work, and finally simple colouring methods.

### PERSPECTIVE

When drawing, a basic understanding of the rules of perspective is essential if you are to achieve a realistic effect.  Only once you have learned these rules can you begin to distort or exaggerate them in order to accentuate elements of your design. There are three basic forms of perspective (one, two and three point). There are also three main elements present in each of these (the vanishing point, convergence lines and horizon line). This tutorial shows the basics behind one- and two-point perspective only: three-point perspective is not required in automotive sketching.

*Allan Macdonald is a professional automotive designer and graduate of Coventry University's MDes Transportation Design Course. He has worked for Arup Design Research, MG-Rover and Volvo Trucks.*

## HORIZON LINE

THIS LINE, AS ITS NAME SUGGESTS, DESCRIBES THE HORIZON, WHICH IS ALWAYS CONSIDERED TO BE AT EYE LEVEL. FOR INSTANCE, AN OBJECT SITED ABOVE THE HORIZON LINE IS ABOVE THE VIEWER'S EYE LEVEL AND WILL THEREFORE SHOW ITS UNDERSIDE.

## VANISHING POINTS

SITED ON THE HORIZON LINE, THESE ARE THE POINTS WHERE ALL CONVERGENCE LINES MEET. ALTHOUGH ALWAYS ON THE HORIZON, THEIR POSITION DEPENDS ON THE VIEWER'S ANGLE.

## CONVERGENCE LINES

ALL PARALLEL LINES IN A SCENE WILL ALWAYS APPEAR TO CONVERGE TO A SINGLE POINT (THE VANISHING POINT). THE EXCEPTION TO THIS RULE IS THAT LINES VIEWED IN PARALLEL OR PERPENDICULAR TO THE VIEWER WILL NOT CONVERGE. FOR INSTANCE THE LINES RUNNING LENGTHWAYS THROUGH THE VEHICLE IN PICTURE ONE. IN ONE- AND TWO-POINT PERSPECTIVE YOU CAN ALSO CONSIDER ALL VERTICAL LINES AS NON-CONVERGING LINES.

## ONE-POINT PERSPECTIVE

ONE-POINT PERSPECTIVE IS EVIDENT WHEN THE OBJECT BEING VIEWED LIES PARALLEL OR PERPENDICULAR TO THE VIEWER. THIS MEANS THAT ONLY LINES TRAVELLING TOWARDS OR AWAY FROM THE VIEWER APPEAR TO CONVERGE TO A SINGLE VANISHING POINT ON THE HORIZON. PICTURE ONE SHOWS HOW THIS MAKES FOR A VERY SIMPLE VERSION OF PERSPECTIVE, WHICH IS ESPECIALLY USEFUL FOR SKETCHING QUICK SIDE VIEWS OF A VEHICLE.

## TWO-POINT PERSPECTIVE

WHEN THE OBJECT BEING VIEWED LIES AT AN ANGLE TO THE VIEWER, AS IN PICTURE TWO, ALL THE HORIZONTAL LINES APPEAR TO CONVERGE. THIS THEREFORE INTRODUCES A SECOND VANISHING POINT ON THE HORIZON. WHERE THE VANISHING POINTS FALL ON THE HORIZON LINE DEPENDS ON THE ANGLE OF THE OBJECT TO THE VIEWER. LOOKING AT PICTURE TWO YOU CAN SEE THAT IF THE VEHICLE WERE TURNED SO THAT MORE OF THE SIDE WAS VISIBLE, THEN THE RIGHT VANISHING POINT WOULD MOVE TO THE RIGHT AND OUT OF THE IMAGE.

## ELLIPSES

GETTING CORRECT ELLIPSES WHEN DRAWING A CAR IS PROBABLY THE HARDEST PART OF PERSPECTIVE. IF YOU LOOK AT A CIRCLE STRAIGHT ON AT AN ANGLE OF 90 DEGREES, WHAT YOU SEE IS INDEED A CIRCLE. BUT ONCE YOU START TO REDUCE THE ANGLE YOU VIEW THE CIRCLE FROM, IT STARTS TO APPEAR TO BE AN ELLIPSE. AN ELLIPSE CONSISTS OF A MAJOR AXIS AND A MINOR AXIS. IN PICTURE THREE YOU CAN SEE WHERE THESE ARE SITUATED ON AN ELLIPSE. THE MAJOR AXIS DIVIDES THE ELLIPSE INTO TWO EQUAL HALVES ALONG THE LONGEST DIMENSION, WHILST THE MINOR AXIS DIVIDES THE ELLIPSE INTO TWO EQUAL HALVES ALONG ITS SHORTEST DIMENSION. A GOOD RULE OF THUMB IS THAT YOU SHOULD ALWAYS ALIGN THE MINOR AXIS WITH THE AXLE OF YOUR VEHICLE. THE MAJOR AXIS, AND THEREFORE THE LONGEST DIMENSION OF THE ELLIPSES SHOULD THEREFORE RUN PERPENDICULAR TO YOUR AXLE LINE. FINALLY, HOW DO YOU ENSURE THAT THE ANGLE OF YOUR ELLIPSE IS CORRECT?

## ONE POINT PERSPECTIVE

KEY:
- VANISHING POINTS
- CONVERGENCE LINES
- HORIZON LINE

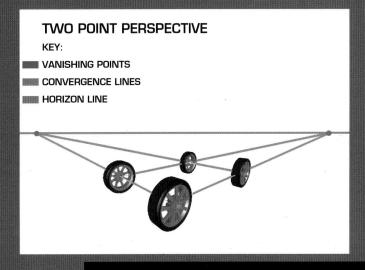

## TWO POINT PERSPECTIVE

KEY:
- VANISHING POINTS
- CONVERGENCE LINES
- HORIZON LINE

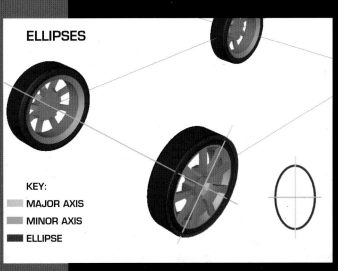

## ELLIPSES

KEY:
- MAJOR AXIS
- MINOR AXIS
- ELLIPSE

## ONE-POINT PERSPECTIVE

WHEN I BEGIN A SKETCHING PROGRAMME I ALMOST ALWAYS START BY DRAWING ONLY IN SIDE VIEWS. THE POINT OF EARLY SKETCH WORK IS FOR THE DESIGNER TO FIND MANY IDEAS IN A SHORT SPACE OF TIME. BY SKETCHING IN SIDE VIEW (AND USUALLY REASONABLY SMALL), I CAN GENERATE MANY PAGES OF IDEAS VERY QUICKLY. THIS IS MOSTLY DOWN TO THE FACT THAT YOU NEED TO THINK ABOUT PERSPECTIVE VERY LITTLE, AND CAN THEREFORE CONCENTRATE ON THINKING ABOUT IDEAS. ALMOST THE ONLY ELEMENT OF PERSPECTIVE VISIBLE IN THESE DRAWINGS IS THE WAY THAT YOU CAN SEE THE FAR SIDE WHEELS. THIS IS DUE TO THE FACT THAT IN ONE-POINT PERSPECTIVE THE ONLY CONVERGENCE LINES THAT CONVERGE ARE THOSE MOVING TOWARDS OR AWAY FROM THE VIEWER.

**01**

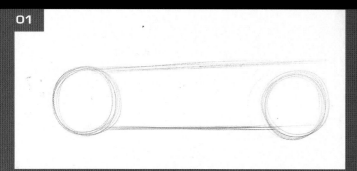

You can see here that I have started by gently roughing in a ground line and two wheel positions. I have also lined in a shoulder height for the vehicle. The important thing to remember here is to keep your line work fast and light. This way you can change and move things around as the sketch progresses. A common mistake when learning to sketch is starting a new drawing when you realise something is out of place. Don't! Continue with the drawing, using the mistake as a guide to sorting out the problem.

**02**

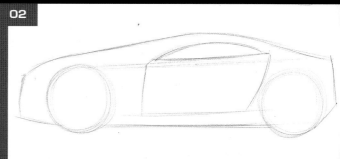

Here I have lightly marked in the rough proportions of the vehicle, using a centre line and the window opening. When putting in the centre line try to avoid the temptation to shorten the overhangs too much by bringing the front and the rear very close to the wheels. Look at a photograph of a car in side view and you will see that the corner of the vehicle falls somewhere in the space you are leaving. If your vehicle has a lot of plan shape at the front or the rear then you will have to leave even more space.

**03**

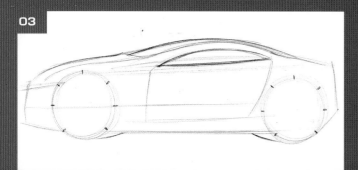

I have now defined the top edge of the bodywork from the rear window, over the roof and down to the front bumper. Remember when drawing this line that it denotes the curvature over the roof and through the two screens (when looking directly from in front or behind the vehicle). For instance you can see that the rear screen has a little curvature, which flattens out into the roof (although not completely flat) and then as the corner surface travels into the windscreen the curvature increases. You can see that the closer the edge line is to the centre line, the less curvature is implied for the surface between.

**04**

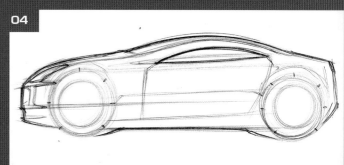

Once you are happy with the general shape and proportion you can begin to firm up some of the details (remembering of course that it is only a sketch). I have added some light reflection lines in the side window and down the body side. I have also defined the front corner. Again the same rule applies here as when drawing the roof. The further the corner is from the centre line of the front end, the more curvature you are giving the front bumper in plan view (viewing from above).

**05**

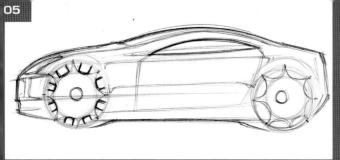

This is the final stage before applying colour. Here you can see I have firmed up all the details I am happy with and added some detail to the wheels. It is always worth putting a little bit of effort into getting the spacing reasonably correct on the wheel details since it will lift the look of your sketch a lot. Also important to note is that the sketch is still very loose and fast in its line work. This will only come through perseverance and practice.

**06**

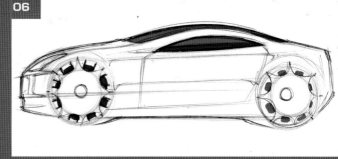

When you are happy with the general design and proportions you can begin to add colour. Here I have simply shaded the windows and wheels using a dark grey marker five or six. Note that this does not have to be super-accurate. I have then further darkened the lower area of the windows and the front wheels, by letting the marker dry and going over the area again. The reason I have only darkened the front wheels further, and not the rears, is to help give the drawing a sense of movement. If you give all areas of your sketch the same weight and level of work, the final result can look very flat on the page.

**07**

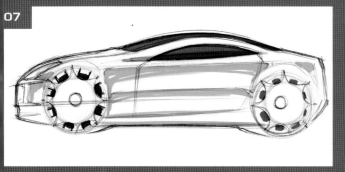

This is the stage where you will have to force yourself to not become precious about your sketch. Hopefully you will now have a nice drawing on the paper, and to attack it in a loose and fast manner with a marker pen is not easy. These lines represent the scenery reflecting in the body side. You can see that I have continued the reflection in the window onto the bodywork and darkened down just beneath the shoulder. The area I have lightly marked halfway up the body side represents the horizon line, which is reflecting from behind the viewer. The important thing here is to be very loose and to keep your choice of marker very light.

**08**

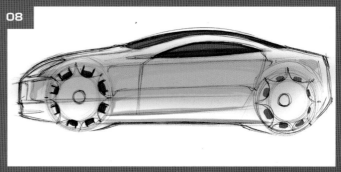

This is probably the simplest part of the drawing, yet the one where you really see your sketch coming to life. Just choose a colour of pastel similar in colour to the previous marker work and apply it along the length of the bodywork, centring just beneath the shoulder line. Do not worry about going over the edges of the drawing.

**09**

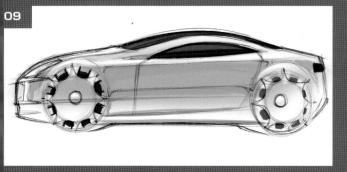

You are now in the final stage of the sketch and really just finishing off. Using an eraser and gently rubbing out all the areas where pastel has fallen on upwards-facing surfaces, you can really bring out the 3D form of your vehicle. This is the point you could stop. The drawing is now complete enough that anybody can look at it and get a good idea of the 3D form you are trying to describe. For a little bit of extra sparkle to the drawing, however, you will probably want to add the smallest hint of highlights.

**10**

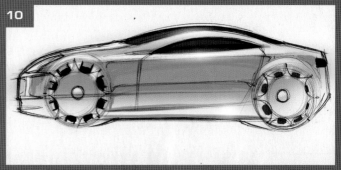

By using an airbrush (this is easiest to do in Photoshop) you can brush a very quick faint line down through the bodywork. Then, on all the upward facing surfaces it falls on, you can spray a light halo of white. Remember to be subtle here since you don't want to lose the definition of your surfaces – you only want to add that final bit of sparkle.

# FLAT TWO-POINT PERSPECTIVE

## FLAT TWO-POINT PERSPECTIVE

WHILE YOU ARE PRODUCING THE SIDE VIEWS WE'VE JUST BEEN DESCRIBING, YOU WILL WANT TO WORK OUT WHAT IS HAPPENING AT THE FRONT AND REAR OF THE VEHICLE. TO DO THIS WITHOUT RESORTING TO A SIMPLE FRONT OR REAR VIEW, YOU WILL NOW HAVE TO BEGIN SKETCHING IN TWO-POINT PERSPECTIVE. FOR THESE EARLY SKETCHES, HOWEVER, YOU WILL NOT WANT TO GET TOO LOST IN TRYING TO DRAW GOOD PERSPECTIVE. BECAUSE OF THIS I LIKE TO SKETCH IN A VIEW I CALL FLAT PERSPECTIVE. ESSENTIALLY THIS IS A CAR VIEWED AT AN ANGLE BUT FROM DOWN LOW SO THAT ALL THE CONVERGENCE LINES FALL ON THE HORIZON LINE AND THROUGH THE CENTRE OF THE VEHICLE.

**01**

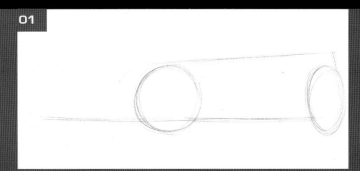

You start this drawing in a similar fashion to the side view, by sketching in a ground line and two wheels. You can see however that this time the rear wheel is at an angle. The more you want to see the front of the vehicle the thinner this ellipse will be. Remember to sketch lightly, since you are now more likely to want to adjust things than when drawing a simple side view.

**02**

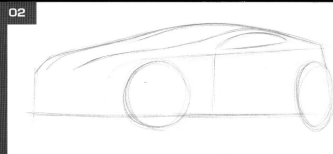

I have now added the profile of the vehicle. During this stage I am lightly working out the rough proportions and theme of the vehicle. If at this point I want to adjust something such as the position of the wheels in order to fine-tune the proportion of the vehicle, then I can. By sketching lightly at this stage you can make these adjustments without fear of spoiling your sketch. Take note of the way the centre line is most visible on the more vertical surfaces.

**03**

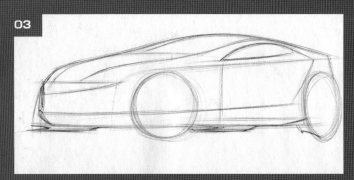

Here you can see that I have added the wheels from the far side of the car. A trick usually employed by designers is to exaggerate the position of the front wheel, putting it out in front of the car. This gives a dark background against which to emphasise the body shape of the bumper. At this stage I am still working things out and sketching lightly, making changes where necessary.

**04**

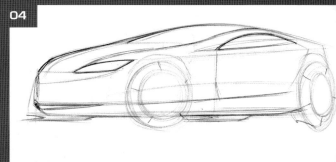

Once you are happy with your design and its proportions you can begin to firm up the lines you want to emphasise. These are usually the lines that represent a strong graphic element of your design. Other lines, which represent changes in the body surface should be left lighter, since you can emphasise these better with the use of colour and shading.

**05**

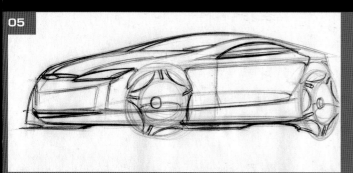

In this final stage before adding colour you can see that I have drawn the final details, and added some more light line work defining my surfaces a little better. Take note of things like how the shoulder highlight runs through the front wheel and down, becoming the corner of the bumper.

**06**

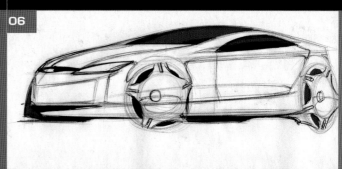

Now that you can begin to add colour to the design, the process is very similar to a side view sketch. You can see that I have used a dark grey marker, in a similar manner as with the side views, to colour all of the windows. The reason for using such a dark colour on these elements and a light colour on the bodywork is that it makes the sketch easier to read. At a glance you can get a feel for the shape and graphic of the vehicle, because of the strong contrast.

**07**

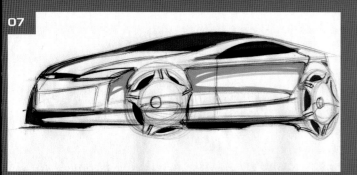

Following the same rules as in the side view sketch, you can now add a little light marker work representing reflections in the body side. Keep these simple and loose without adding too much marker. You can see that I have also shaded everything on the far side of the centre line (with the exception of the upward-facing surface on the bumper). This helps to emphasise the curvature of these surfaces and the general 3D feeling of the sketch.

**08**

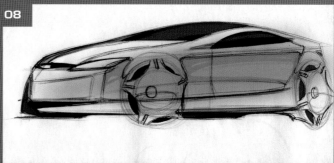

This, as in the previous example, is the easiest part of the sketch. Just apply a quick brush of pastel along the body side of the vehicle.

**09**

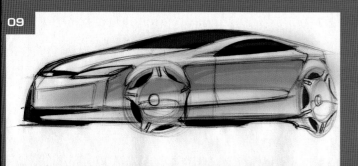

Using an eraser I have now picked out all the upward facing surfaces on the vehicle. This includes the surfaces of the spokes on the wheels. Try to be gentle when erasing against a line that represents a soft change in the body surface, since a sharply erased edge will obviously signify a sharp angle in the body.

**10**

Finally you can if you wish add some gentle highlighting.

# FULL TWO-POINT PERSPECTIVE

**FULL TWO-POINT PERSPECTIVE**

PROPER TWO-POINT PERSPECTIVE IS THE HARDEST OF THE THREE EXAMPLES HERE TO GET CORRECT. FOR THIS REASON I USUALLY WAIT UNTIL I HAVE A ROUGH IDEA OF MY DESIGN BEFORE MOVING TO THIS KIND OF VIEW. IT IS HOWEVER ESSENTIAL THAT YOU DO LEARN TO SKETCH USING FULL TWO-POINT PERSPECTIVE, SINCE SKETCHING WITH SIMPLIFIED VIEWPOINTS DOES NOT ALLOW YOU TO FULLY RESOLVE ALL THE SURFACES IN A DESIGN. YOU CAN SEE IN THE GRAPHIC (BELOW LEFT) THAT USING THIS KIND OF PERSPECTIVE MEANS THAT ALL PARALLEL LINES RUNNING BOTH DOWN THE BODY SIDE AND ACROSS THE FRONT OR THE REAR OF THE VEHICLE WILL CONVERGE. THIS CAN MAKE IT HARD TO FIGURE OUT HOW TO DRAW THINGS SUCH AS SLOPING SHOULDER LINES. A GOOD WAY TO PRACTISE TO BEGIN WITH IS BY SKETCHING A SIMPLE CUBE OR RECTANGLE IN PERSPECTIVE, AND THEN BY ADDING WHEELS AT EACH CORNER. ONCE YOU ARE CONFIDENT AT THIS YOU CAN BEGIN TO ADD SIMPLE FORMS TO THIS BOX, BUILDING THE DRAWING INTO A MORE CAR-LIKE IMAGE. FROM THERE YOU CAN BEGIN TO DISREGARD THE BOX AND ONLY USE THE GUIDELINES YOU FEEL WILL HELP YOU SKETCH YOUR DESIGN.

## 01

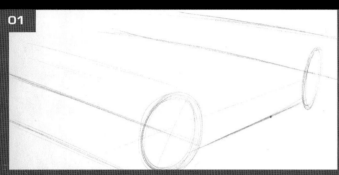

I have started this sketch by drawing some simple guide lines, all showing the convergence of the parallel lines. Onto this I have sketched the wheels. You can see that, as explained earlier, the major axes of the ellipses are at right angles to the axle lines on the vehicle. Remember to sketch lightly here as it is almost certain you will want to adjust your ellipses as the sketch progresses.

## 02

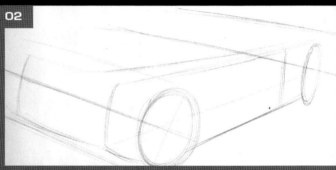

In the second step I have built up a simple side surface for the vehicle. You can see how the shoulder line of the vehicle also creates the rear corner, creating a single surface down the side of the vehicle. It is usually easier to work in this way, working out the major surfaces before adding the smaller surface details such as wheelarches. You can see I have also added the front shut-line from the door to help me define this side surface.

## 03

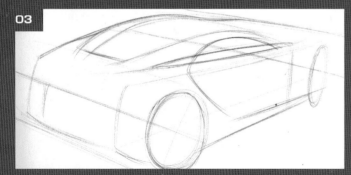

This stage is the hardest part of drawing in perspective. You must now work out how the surfaces you have drawn on the near side of the vehicle will appear on the far side. The important thing is that you understand the general rules and principles of perspective. From there you should practise sketching using only simple guidelines which will ensure that the sketches remain fast, fluid and spontaneous. It is usually helpful at this point to have some pictures of similar vehicles at the same angle of view on your desk that you can look at. As in the previous step, you can see that I have worked out all the major surfaces first. Also of note is the way the tumble-home (leaning inwards) of the side windows flattens out the far edge of the vehicle.

## 04

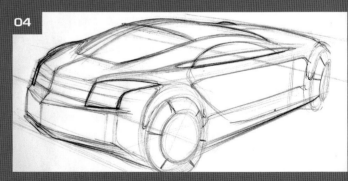

Once you are happy with the rough proportions and are confident you have got the major elements of the perspective correct, you can add the rest of the detail surfaces. Note how the centre line of the vehicle can be used to emphasise the treatment of the surfaces. You can also see that I have exaggerated the plan curve of the rear by putting the far side lamp almost out of sight around the corner of the body.

05

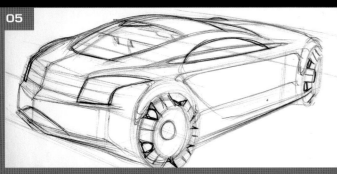

The final ballpoint stage is to add some interior and alloy wheel details to the drawing. When adding the interior details you don't have to spend a lot of time, since all you want to do is give a suggestion of the shapes inside.

06

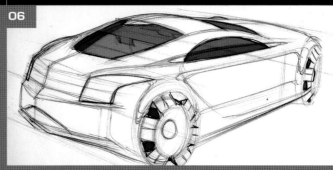

To shade the inside of the vehicle I have used two grades of marker. With these two markers you can achieve four tones of colour. By using only two grades of dark grey you can help keep the change in shades very subtle. If you half shut your eyes and look at the sketch, you should read the whole window, and not each separate shade. The same should be true after you have applied the colour to the bodywork, which is why you should choose a reasonably dark colour for your windows and a light one for the bodywork (or vice versa).

07

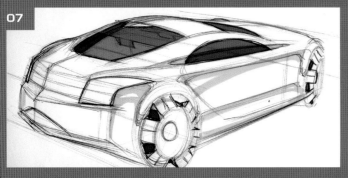

Remembering to keep things simple, you can now add a light-coloured marker to the bodywork. You can see that I have also added a little marker at the furthest edge of the vehicle. You could also try blocking in every surface on the far side of the centre line except the upwards-facing ones, as shown in the flat two-point perspective sketch.

08

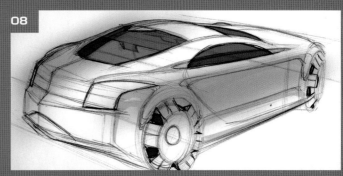

It can be easy to over-complicate the pastel work when shading a two-point perspective sketch, since you try to correctly shade every surface. I always try to resist this temptation, and try to use only two dominant areas of colour. The first one passes down the body side of your vehicle just as in the side view sketch, whilst the second goes on the far surfaces. This leaves a core of brightness running through the surfaces closest to the viewer, which helps give the sketch a strong 3D feel.

09

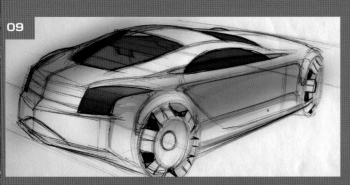

The last two stages are quick and simple. Add a quick bit of red marker or pencil to the rear lights and erase the pastel from the up-facing surfaces just as in both previous examples...

10

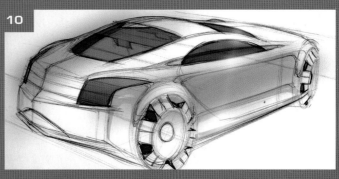

.....and finally add the little bit of airbrush shine.

| # GETTING STARTED 2: QUICK SKETCH

SPEED IS OF THE ESSENCE IN THE HIGH-PRESSURE ENVIRONMENT OF THE DESIGN STUDIO, WHERE A SUCCESSION OF IDEAS MAY NEED TO BE COMMUNICATED RAPIDLY AND CLEARLY, AND WITH MAXIMUM EFFECTIVENESS. IN THE SECOND OF OUR TUTORIALS, CALIFORNIA-BASED PROFESSIONAL DESIGNER JOHN FRYE TAKES US THROUGH THE SEVEN SIMPLE STEPS OF HIS QUICK SKETCH TECHNIQUE THAT CAN YIELD AN IMPRESSIVE RESULT IN LESS THAN TEN MINUTES.

**01**

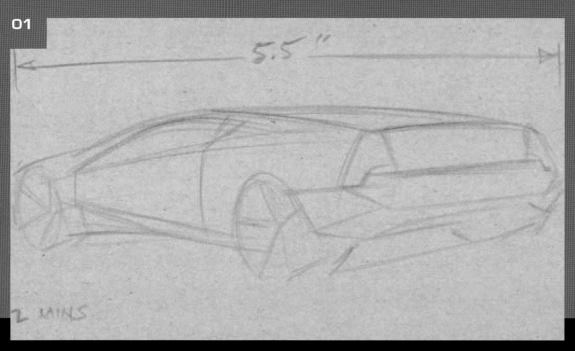

I start out with an 8.5"x11" piece of cover stock weight (takes marker well and holds up to abuse over time) recycled style paper. I buy this in large packages at the office paper supply store (much cheaper than getting a similar paper at an art store). The paper here is Neneh brand Desert Storm. I start out with an erasable blue or regular lead pencil and quickly put the idea down on paper, simultaneously considering the product I am designing, the purpose, its buyer, current trends, future trends, styling theme, dynamic perspective, realism versus excitement (cheating proportions) and other sketches from the project that this sketch will play off of or create new design directions. These early sketches need to be free and spontaneous – too much thought, care, and precision at this point only stifle new ideas and restrict free thinking. Good things can happen by accident if you let things go. As a habit, I tend to draw with too much precision, too much care, so I find it helps to loosen up by drawing very small which increases the looseness proportion versus the size of the sketch (if that makes any sense.) Since I have a computer and printer at my disposal to resize and manipulate a series of sketches into the same format later, I do not concern myself over the placement on the page or notations or studies around the sketch – this is an extension of the proverbial 'napkin sketch' only with better paper and art supplies – but the idea of spontaneity is the same. You could easily crank out a series of

**02**

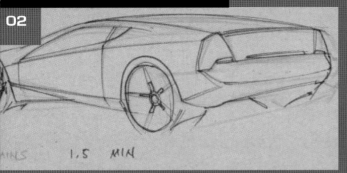

AINS    1.5    MIN

**03**

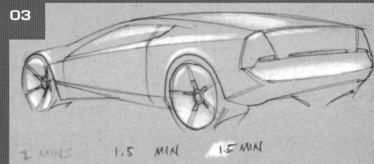

2 MINS    1.5   MIN        1.5 MIN

The line work above took less than two minutes and is intentionally rough just to lay in general perspective and proportion. Make sure the line work is light on the paper so that you can erase most of it later. BE SPONTANEOUS! Listen to good music, that always helps me. If you are getting stuck for ideas, it helps to alter an element of the process – maybe sketch with a different tool, try a completely different perspective, different paper, or even go to a different location and sketch. If you do the same thing repeatedly, your mind sometimes learns the process too well and things become automatic – new designs won't come to you unless you throw your brain something new to deal with. This is just my theory, but it seems to work for me. If you are drawing the same car over and over again, quit and move to a different company!

In the next step I have moved to a razorpoint fineline black ink pen and put down more deliberate lines to clarify the design. I use the pencil lines underneath as a rough guide and look to see what is working and what is not – for example, I decided to fix the right rear corner perspective a bit. This step might take longer than the first step of sketching in lines with pencil because you have to take a little more care to get the lines right as there is no erasing from this point forward.

**04**

AINS       1.5    MIN       1.5 MIN     .5MIN

GREY#4
.5MIN

The next step is to begin adding highlight areas with white prismacolor (if you are drawing on white paper, you can't do this). But first, I make sure to erase the original pencil lines as they will only get in the way and contaminate the colours that go over them– notice how a little bit of pencil work remaining on the rear decklid has given the white prisma in this area a bluish tint. Where you put highlights is very simple – areas facing up are lighter than those facing down. Don't use too much white pencil – there is often a tendency to try to 'finish' the sketch with every step; it doesn't look done NOT because it needs more white pencil, but because there are steps remaining – if you put down more white pencil, there won't be any room for marker and other colours.

This is a continuation of the marker work with a slightly darker grey – in this case a 7. The marker is of a different brand so it is almost the same value as the previous at its darkest, and the hue is slightly more purple, but it is good enough.

This step adds black with a common Sharpie marker, getting tighter areas may require a finer pen. Now that we have both white and black on the paper, we can see the car much clearer as the complete range in values is now represented. Unless the car paint itself is supposed to look black, I only apply black ink to shadow, tyre, and glass areas. The sharp contrast of black butted up against white on the glass helps the mind read the surface as something that is very shiny and different from the material of the paint and body. The eye naturally is attracted to areas where value contrast is the greatest so the viewer tends to look at the glass and tyre. Look at the image above quickly and try to be aware of where your eye goes – does it start at the rear wheel then quickly move up and to the left, landing on the glass, perhaps continuing to the front wheel? Careful control of this phenomenon is key in drawing the viewer in and selling your design. On a large presentation, the path of the eye can be controlled to keep the viewer looking at certain elements of your design. On a quick sketch like this, being conscious of this process while sketching will only slow things down, but once you have learned a few dynamic perspectives that work, it becomes automatic.

Once again, I have picked up the Prismacolor pencils to finish things up, adding areas of detail colour to show different materials or finishes. I have also revisited some of the media I used before to tighten up certain aspects of the sketch. I add a couple of swipes of black marker to push the background behind the car where it should be, and help define the silhouette of the vehicle. I am done on paper at this point and it has taken less than eight minutes in theory (in actuality it has taken much longer, having had to scan the picture into the computer at every step!). You can see, though, how at this pace, you can get a lot of ideas out very quickly.

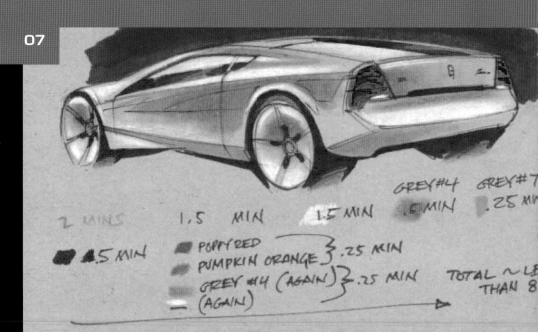

The next step for me is to take the sketch (usually I do several sketches on paper first, then do all of the scanning and computer manipulation at the same time) and scan it at about 200-300 dpi and import the image into Photoshop. I usually punch up the contrast, saturation, and may adjust hue and brightness. In this case, I went with: brightness +10, contrast +10, saturation +40. The image may look better on your monitor, but you have to keep in mind how it looks when it prints. It might take some time to get familiar with your printer and how it changes the image. Keep your original image on file in case you need to manipulate some of the aspects and do some tests. The flood fill/paint bucket tool is helpful for making the sketch especially punchy. I grabbed the tyre orange colour with eyedropper first then flood the entire background area. I also went in with the airbrush tool and pulled out some softer white, red and orange highlights.

That's it! Print it and save it to disk for prosperity. Time to move on, there are 20 more sketches to finish by midnight

# GETTING SERIOUS: RENDERING TECHNIQUES

WITH A SECURE GROUNDING IN THE BASICS OF PERSPECTIVE AND THE ART OF PRODUCING QUICK-FIRE SKETCHES AT THE DROP OF A HAT, YOU WILL ALREADY BE ABLE TO COMMUNICATE YOUR OWN DESIGN IDEAS ON PAPER OR COMPUTER SCREEN WITH BOTH CONFIDENCE AND ACCURACY. NOW IT IS TIME TO BRING YOUR CHOSEN DESIGN TO LIFE AND GIVE IT THE TRUE PROFESSIONAL LOOK THAT COMES WITH REALISTIC RENDERING OF PAINT SURFACES, HIGHLIGHTS AND KEY DETAILS. ONCE, THE PROCESS OF ADDING COLOUR, DEPTH, LIGHT AND SHADE USED TO BE THE MOST INTIMIDATING AND TIME-CONSUMING STAGE OF ALL, BUT NOW – UNDER THE EXPERT GUIDANCE OF ALLAN MACDONALD – RENDERING IS STRAIGHTFORWARD, FAST, AND, MOST IMPORTANT OF ALL, FAIL-SAFE

With this tutorial I am going to guide you, stage by stage, through the methods I use to produce a rendering. I have developed this style over the past couple of years and find it the simplest and most efficient way to produce a good drawing. Just remember, however, that there is no right or wrong way to render. This tutorial aims only to inspire, not to instruct…

## MATERIALS USED

- MARKER PAPER – REDUCES THE BLEEDING OF INK WHEN USING MARKER PENS
- BLACK BIRO PEN – FOR MOST LINE WORK AND PRELIMINARY SHADING
- CHARTPAK MARKERS - FOR BLOCKING IN THE LARGEST SOLID AREAS OF COLOUR
- AIRBRUSH – USED TO CREATE SMOOTH COLOUR GRADIENTS
- COLOURED PENCILS – FOR FINAL DETAIL FINISHING WORK

Bear in mind that this is only a guide – so if you feel that you can achieve a suitable result using a different method, then do so. For instance, I have substituted using a real airbrush and coloured pencils for similar tools in Photoshop and a sketch tablet. Using this I am able to achieve very similar results but in a more versatile way. I also find it faster and, dare I say it, less stressful – it's a lot easier to remove mistakes on the computer.

Nevertheless, whatever media you end up using, the principles are very similar and throughout the tutorial I will point out how the varying methods compare.

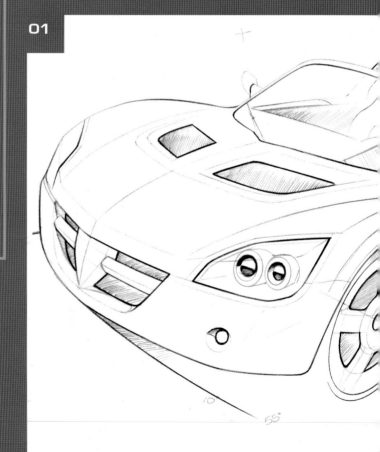

01

With a normal black biro I have drawn this on marker paper, using a photo as an underlay. At this stage I find it important to think how I am going to colour the vehicle, as this dictates the thickness of the lines. For instance on the body side, where the varying darkness of the colour work will show the body creases, I use lighter lines that will be invisible in the final piece. However, around areas like the headlamps and grille – where I know that there will be a high contrast in colour darkness – I have really darkened and thickened my lines. The most important thing is not to trace your lines with no thought. You should try to get what is usually referred to as 'quality in your lines'. It's a very hard thing to explain, but the more you draw, the more you will get a feeling for what this is.

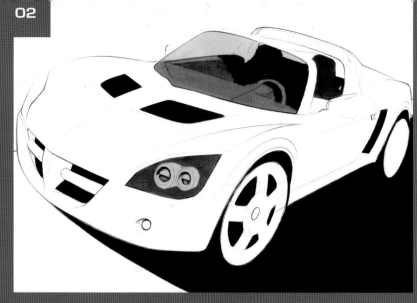

Before starting this stage it is important to decide where you want your light source to be: it is the light source which dictates where you are putting down the colours. I have decided to use a light source that is just above the horizon at the top left of the page. This means that a long shadow will be cast, and the visible side of the vehicle will be in shade. Using marker pens, I have blocked in the areas I know to be darkest. When colouring I try to aim for a very graphic final look. To achieve this I usually colour the ground, lamps and details darker than the bodywork. I have used Extra Black on the ground and vents, then Cool Grey 6 and 7 along with Ruby Red in the interior. Note that on areas of the interior behind the shadowed part of the screen I have used colour shades slightly darker than on the lighter side of the screen. I did this by going over these parts with the same marker again after the page had fully dried. In theory you can reach three shades of the same colour using this method. The effect that you should be trying to achieve is that glass reflecting a bright light (the sky) is harder to see through than when it is in shade.

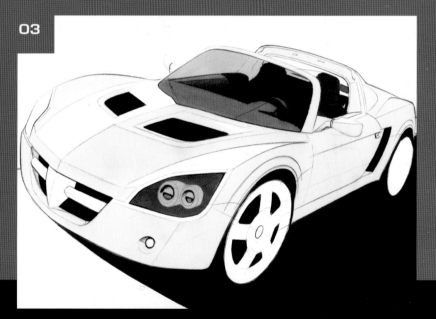

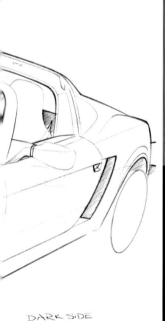

DARK SIDE

Still using the marker pens, I have now blocked in the bodywork using the Cream Chartpak Marker. Note that I have left the surfaces facing in the direction of the light source white. Apart from those two small areas, however, the rest of the body is coloured. When choosing a colour for this stage, remember that it will represent the lightest areas of your bodywork (except the white areas), so it is probably wise not to choose too dark a colour. When using marker pens to block in such large areas of colour it is also important not to work too slowly. If you let a part of the page dry then have to go over it again you will be left with a patchy block of colour.

**04**

**05**

It's at this stage I always feel the drawing coming to life. Using a Warm Grey 7, I have darkened down the areas of the vehicle most in the shade, then used a Warm Grey 2 to darken the front slightly. The reason for using grey for the shaded areas is that colour will lose some of its saturation when in the shade. Something to note here is that most other base colours will look better if you use Cool Greys to darken the shaded areas, although you should feel free to experiment. Remember to shade the small detailed areas too, for instance in the grille and spot lamps.

At this point I usually feel the need to work some of the details back in using a biro. I have sharpened up the details in the lamps for instance. Remember, however, that as in stage one it is best to avoid building up lines that represent folds in the bodywork. Also try to avoid all lines being of the same thickness. Remember that by adding weight to some lines and keeping others fainter, the drawing has more character.

Now that I have blocked in the basic light and dark areas of the body I am ready to move on to airbrush work. At this stage I generally move to Photoshop: however, the principle is the same whether you are going to use airbrush, pastels or the equivalent tools in Photoshop. The idea is to put smooth gradients onto the paper without being hindered by having to work around areas like the wheelarches, lamps or windows. To do this you will need to have a method of removing areas of overspray. If you are using a real airbrush you will need to mask off all the non-bodywork areas of the vehicle as shown. If you are using pastel, or like me, Photoshop, then you can use the eraser to remove areas of overspray. It is worth taking care at this point, as it is very easy to forget to mask smaller items, such as the spot lamps. Here I am aiming to further darken down the bodywork on the shaded side of the vehicle. I have therefore masked off all areas of non-bodywork.

**06**

Here you can see exactly how masking around areas that you don't want to colour enables you to put a smoother gradient down. I have chosen the colour red because as you move away from the light into the shade, colours tend to get colder as well as darker and less saturated. At the rear of the vehicle you can see I have even moved into a shade of purple. When spraying this area, the idea is to have as smooth and steady a gradient as possible. In Photoshop this meant using a large, soft brush, which covered about half the vehicle; with an actual airbrush it would mean holding the spray relatively high. What you don't want to do is have blotches of colour.

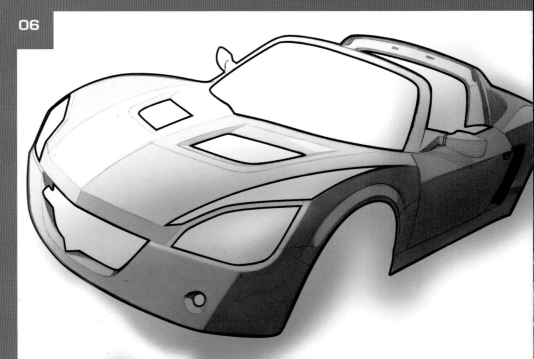

07

Once you remove the masking (or use the eraser) you can see that the vehicle now has a real sense of depth. You can see at the rear of the vehicle I have also darkened down the bodywork until it is almost as dark as the ground. This helps make the drawing more dramatic, although you must take care not to completely lose the details in this area.

## 08

As in stage 5 I have now masked off the windscreen, although I ignored masking the wiper arm. This is such a small detail that it is probably best left until the end, when you can add it back in with coloured pencils. If the car you are rendering has side windows, then you might want to include them here. Doing the front and side windows at the same time will help ensure you have continuity in your shading.

When spraying the windscreen I have used a very dark shade on the left of the vehicle, but on the right have gone for a very light shade of blue. Windscreens are clearly very reflective, and by using the light blue I have given the impression of the screen reflecting the sky. Take care not to go too dark at this stage as you do not want to lose the interior details.

## 09

With the mask removed you can now see that the screen has a stronger glass like feel. Later we are going to lighten up the area that is the reflection of the sky with white airbrush in order to achieve a truly shiny look. Next, repeat the process for the headlamp – just a quick spray of a very dark blue.

10

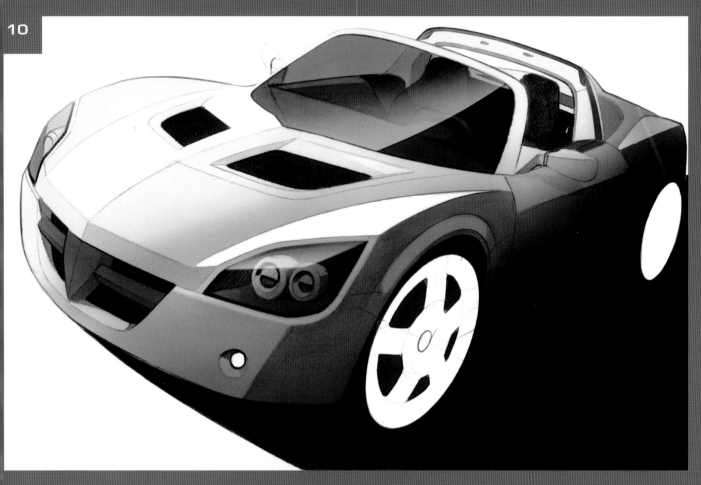

Here you can see that I have again masked the lamp and windscreen but this time stopped where the shadows begin. I have then applied a touch of white airbrush. Again, as when applying the darker colours, take care not to completely white out these areas.

Having looked at the drawing at this stage I have decided that the body side at the rear probably needs a little more darkening. I have added just a little colour to aid the dramatic contrast of the light and shade. This was done, as before, with some masking and airbrushing.

11

Since it is hard to tell exactly what the drawing is going to look like when you remove the masking, you may find that you need to repeat the masking and spraying stage a couple of times. Here I have decided that my wheel arches are a little too dark and not prominent enough. I have therefore done another quick mask and lightened them up with a touch of yellow.

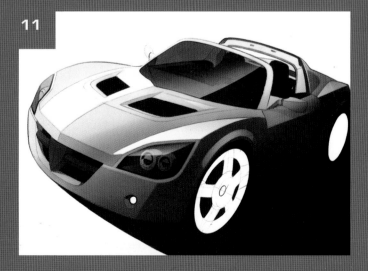

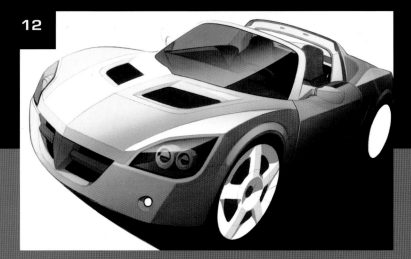

## 12

When you feel that you have completed all your marker and airbrush work it is time to move on to one of the final stages – bringing out some shut-lines and highlights. On this drawing I felt I wanted to keep this to a minimum to avoid cluttering an already very complex shape. Nevertheless, the idea is that a shut-line compromises two coloured lines. A dark line on the edge facing away from the light source, and a lighter line on the edge facing towards the light source. Try and avoid using black and white for these lines, and instead try to use lighter or darker tones of the colour which you have used on the body panels that the line cuts through.

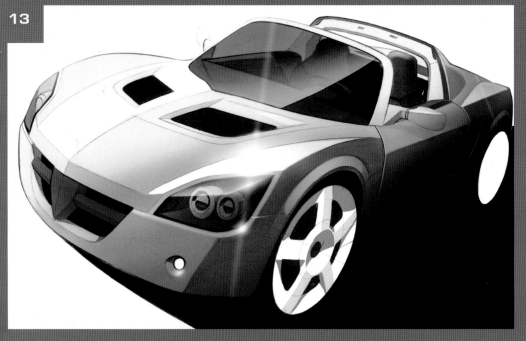

In order to add highlights to the vehicle I have begun by drawing a very faint white line through the body. Onto this line will fall the brightest highlights. The further you move from this line the less intense the highlights will be. Try and place the line so that it does not pass through areas that will be awkward to highlight. Having drawn this line I have then used a white airbrush to really punch out the areas that are reflecting the light. If you are using a real airbrush as opposed to working on Photoshop, this is the stage in which you should really take care: mistakes from here on will be very, very hard to remedy.

Since I am working in Photoshop I have used the airbrush tool for the rest of the smaller highlights. If you are working on paper you can try using white gouache or white pencil. If using gouache, squeeze a little onto a saucer with a little water. Mix some gouache with the water to get a thick but usable consistency, then, using a paintbrush, pick out areas where the light would catch on things like shut-ines. There is no need to make all your highlights obvious as even the smallest pinprick of white on a dark surface will have the desired effect. You may also want to spray a faint halo of white using an airbrush over some of your highlights to give them a very bright, shiny look.

Finally, you may have noticed that I have thus far ignored the rear wheel. I tend to do this at the end because using Photoshop it is a simple task for me to copy, cut and paste the rear wheel with a little bit of resizing. I have also darkened it down just to put it a little more into the distance.

## CONCLUSION

Hopefully you will now have learned some of the basic methods I use in my renderings. Simply being able to see the drawing at each stage is something I find very useful. What is now important is that you mix what you have learned here with things you have learned elsewhere – and then give yourself plenty of practice.

By doing this you will soon develop your own style and your own ways of doing things. In the competitive world of automotive design, having your own distinctive style that will genuinely stand out from the crowd is an asset you should not underestimate.

IF YOU HAVE FOLLOWED THE TUTORIALS IN THE PREVIOUS THREE CHAPTERS YOU WILL HAVE BUILT UP SOME IMPORTANT FOUNDATION SKILLS THAT WILL STAND YOU IN GOOD STEAD WHEN IT COMES TO PRODUCING PROFESSIONAL-LOOKING SKETCHES AND RENDERINGS OF YOUR DESIGNS. HOWEVER, VERY FEW SUCCESSFUL DESIGNS RESULT SOLELY FROM THE SYSTEMATIC FOLLOWING OF EVERY STEP OF A PRESCRIBED APPROACH OR A LONG LIST OF INSTRUCTIONS. INVARIABLY, INSPIRATION IS AS IMPORTANT – IF NOT MORE IMPORTANT – THAN PERSPIRATION IN THE TRANSFERRING OF GRAPHICAL IDEAS FROM THE BRAIN TO THE PAPER OR COMPUTER SCREEN.

YOU MAY BE MAKING YOUR FIRST FEW HESITANT PENCIL STROKES ON A CLEAN SHEET OF PAPER OR PUTTING THE FINISHING TOUCHES TO A COMPLEX DIGITAL MODEL IN ALIASWAVEFRONT AUTO STUDIO. NO MATTER THE LEVEL OF YOUR EXPERTISE, THERE ARE MANY HELPFUL TECHNIQUES AND SHORTCUTS THAT WILL GET YOU TO THE DESIRED RESULT FASTER AND MORE EFFECTIVELY, BUT WITHOUT CUTTING CORNERS EN ROUTE OR COMPROMISING THE QUALITY OF THE FINAL PRODUCT.

*Above:* DESPITE THE ADVANCE OF COMPUTER TECHNIQUES, SKETCHING IS STILL A VITAL SKILL. CLAY-MODELLING IS A KEY PROCESS TOO

*Right:* COMPUTER PROGRAMS SUCH AS ALIAS ARE ABLE TO RESOLVE COMPLEX SHAPES AND PRODUCE IMPRESSIVELY REALISTIC RENDERINGS

Clearly, having the right materials helps a lot. But sometimes the right materials aren't necessarily the most obvious ones: designers, contradicting the advice given out by generations of art teachers in schools, often choose to do their sketches in ballpoint pen, preferring its accuracy of line and ability to provide variety in texture. Nor is it immediately obvious why designers should wish to work on such thin, almost transparent paper. But once you have had a few failures, scrunched them up and thrown them frustratedly into the trash as a waste of time, you will understand that thin paper allows you to make mistakes without having to go back to square one for a complete restart each time. Simply place a fresh sheet on top of the failed one, trace through the parts of the design that were OK, and you are back up to speed without having to spend time on getting the basics right yet again.

The same approach can be used if, midway through your design process, you are unsure which of two (or more, even) options to pursue. Each solution can be worked on a separate overlay placed on top of the base sheet where you have laid down the basic structural hardpoints of the design. As there is no

doodles where the initial sparks of inspiration so often lie.

'I will always sketch something on paper first,' says Ron Saunders, visiting lecturer at London's Royal College of Art. 'You need to get a feel for the package of the vehicle. The sketch is still the most spontaneous way of getting what you want. I generally sketch on A3 – it's a big enough scale. A4 is a bit too small, but I do tend to use it for a whole page of doodles, which I can pick up from later on.'

If you are in any way serious about designing on a professional level, there is no question that you will have to go digital at some stage in the process: the whole of the manufacturing industry is geared towards computer-aided design. However even for design hopefuls with limited resources many of the advantageous features and much of the professional appearance of top-level programs are now available at accessible prices and through the intelligent use of familiar suites such as Photoshop and Illustrator.

The big step in any design process is the move from 2D to 3D. This, say the staff in top teaching establishments such as the RCA, is where students are most likely to come unstuck.

Conventionally, students would go from sketches to formal side, front and rear elevations and from there to larger – often quarter-scale – tape drawings. Measurements taken from these flat tape drawings would yield the section profiles that would be used to shape the solid clay model. Inevitably, there would be many areas unresolved by the 2D drawings which could only be interpreted at the clay model stage, lending some uncertainty to the whole process.

The advent of computer-based design techniques has made many of these often laborious steps either optional or obsolete: in particular, the computer can ease the tricky transition from 2D to 3D and give the designer a very good idea at an early stage of what their product will look like in solid form. In some programmes, adjustments to the 3D shape can be made and viewed on screen, long before any solid model is constructed.

The generally accepted standard design programmes is known in the auto industry as Alias, though

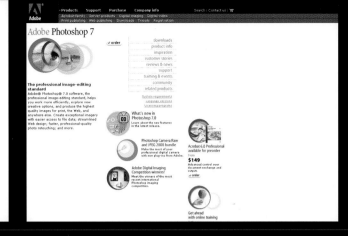

its proper title is Auto Studio. Auto Studio is the top-end product of a suite of design programmes developed by AliasWavefront, an independent Toronto-based software company now owned by Silicon Graphics. Alias first came to public notice when it was used to animate the movie Jurassic Park; more recently, AliasWavefront has launched Maya, an even more sophisticated animation programme. In the auto industry it is used by Renault, among others, to create highly realistic movie action sequences of designs that exist only in the computer database.

As a professional tool, Auto Studio is quite naturally very expensive, selling for upwards of $70,000 for a single node-locked seat licence. The AliasWavefront website (www.aliaswavefront.com) carries regular reports on how customers such as General Motors have used particular elements of Auto Studio to good effect in particular model programmes. AliasWavefront's simpler Design Studio programme costs only about one-tenth as much, but the good news for aspiring designers is that student access to Auto Studio is available for around $650 a year. Colleges and universities often have special arrangements with software publishers that can also provide other beneficial terms.

Not every student finds it easy to get comfortable with Auto Studio: some find Rhino (www.rhino3d.com) a more approachable solution. It is certainly a lot less expensive, costing $895 for a professional version and $195 for students and teachers. It has the advantage of also being able to run on a Mac with System X and Virtual PC: Alias is Windows only and requires a special graphics card.

All these programs are subject to regular upgrades, some of which are included in the basic licence fee. These fees can vary from one year to the next, too, as well as from country to country – so for precise details, and the all-important hardware requirements, it is essential to get the latest information from each publisher's website before deciding which programme to go for.

A third option is 3D MAX (www.3dmax.com), another animation suite favoured in the movie business. Car designers appreciate its animation and rendering abilities, but maintain Rhino and Alias

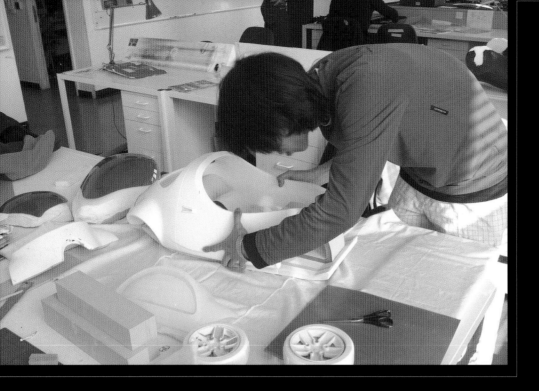

are better for modelling.

All these programs will enable the magical transformation from flat elevations to a solid, realistic-looking model that can be turned and swivelled on screen to be viewed from any angle. This, more than anything else, has accelerated the process of giving a design depth, contours and reflective surfaces for the light to play on – in other words, adding that professional dimension.

However, as RCA student Linda Andersson is quick to point out, even the computer-assisted transformation to 3D is not without its challenges. She was able to scan her sketches into Alias to produce the underlays for her model: 'You have to have it in your head what you want to end up with – you can't just have a top view and side view and go into Alias. You have to think 3D all the time you are sketching. Alias is a big and complex programme. Once you are good, you can change a lot of things, and it gives a good feeling for the volumes, too.'

By having her model developed in Alias, Linda was able to enjoy another big bonus of working in a semi-professional design environment. By feeding in the model's data into the RCA's numerically-controlled milling machine, Linda was able to have her design cut from a solid block of foam, ready for surface finishing, detailing and painting.

Clearly, a computer-controlled multi-axis milling machine is a luxury that few people will be able to afford at home. Nevertheless, there are several intelligent shortcuts to both model-making and that other time-consuming task, rendering, that can be accomplished using the familiar Adobe Photoshop (www.adobe.com), which retails for around $675 and which is found in almost every school and college art department.

The principle is simple: paper sketches can be scanned in to the computer and worked on in

Photoshop, where the programme's many effects can be used to adjust lines, shapes and textures as well as to add professional-looking surface finishes and backgrounds. Later on, when you have perhaps progressed to a clay model, you can use a digital camera to photograph the model, take the image back into Photoshop and manipulate it once again before applying the changes to the clay. While this is clearly not true 3D computer-modelling and the images cannot be rotated or viewed from different angles on screen, it is a helpful step forward.

'There is no substitute for the quick pen sketch at the beginning,' says Royal College of Art visiting lecturer Ron Saunders, 'but once you've got the basic lines and got a feel for the package you can go into Photoshop and colour up the sketch, which effectively makes it as good as a rendering. Photoshop can be very realistic.'

Photoshop can produce airbrush-like effects that can enhance renderings without any risk to the original artwork, as would be the case when doing masks and cutouts on a paint-and-paper drawing. 'It's much quicker with Photoshop,' says Saunders, 'and the great thing is that if you don't like what you have done you can simply take it away again.

'Photoshop doesn't stop you playing with the forms. For me, the manifestation of the form is the way it reflects light, and once you've got the basic lines, the shape of the car and the package, you can begin to refine the surfaces. You can do this much more quickly and easily using the Photoshop route. You can print things off and compare them as hard copy and make little changes, or you can view them on screen.'

What Photoshop cannot do is to calculate things like light and shade, highlights and reflections. Ron Saunders: 'With Photoshop you are building up a picture, applying paint, so you are in a way assuming a light source when you render it or sketch it. But with a full 3D design program like Alias you are creating surfaces that are neutral – there is no light until you pick a light source to examine the form.'

Still more technical innovations are continuing to break down the boundaries between paper design and its digital counterpart. Some designers like to work on graphic tablets, in essence an electronic paper pad that mimics the effects and feel of conventional tools like pencils, markers, erasers and brushes. Most are sensitive to pressure, angle and tilt, too, and in each case the result is seen on the main computer screen. HP even has the Compac Tablet PC which combines the functions of a touch-sensitive screen with a drawing tablet: it is a pricey business tool at present, but a possible indicator of the way products for the creative industries will evolve in the near future.

One way or another, however, one observation remains abundantly clear. Software, hardware, scanners, printers and pricey electronic gadgets are no more than useful tools that will enable you to get the job done more quickly and, sometimes, more effectively. At the end of the day it will be your inspiration, your imagination and your perseverance that will really determine the quality of the results you get.

# 03

03 | **TEN DECADES OF DESIGN**

## CONTENTS

| **PININFARINA:** INVENTOR OF AUTOMOTIVE DESIGN

IF ANY SINGLE COMPANY COULD BE SAID TO HAVE INVENTED CAR DESIGN, IT MUST BE PININFARINA. THE ITALIAN STUDIO HAS PENNED ALMOST EVERY FERRARI, MOST POST-WAR ALFA ROMEOS AND MANY HIGHLY SUCCESSFUL PEUGEOTS, ESTABLISHING AESTHETIC DESIGN STANDARDS THAT SET THE GLOBAL AGENDA FOR AUTOMOTIVE STYLE. HERE, WE TRACE THE ROOTS OF THIS POWERFUL ARTISTIC DYNASTY AND SHOW HOW IT HAS STEERED THE EVOLUTION OF CAR DESIGN.

*Above:*
Battista Farina, brother of founder Giovanni, took the firm on to greatness

*Right:*
The lithe Ferrari Dino Berlinetta Speciale stunned the design world in 1965

*Top right:*
Farina's mass-market designs such as the Austin A40 won a wide audience

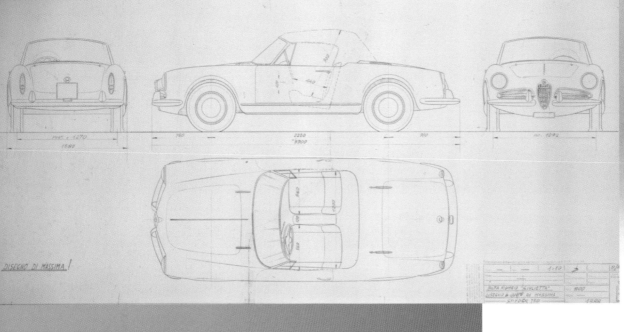

DISEGNO DI MASSIMA !

The fortunes of Pininfarina, one of Italy's towering giants of car design, sprang from the design of a simple radiator grille.

The Italian automobile's early days were as starkly industrial and engineering-led as any experienced in tough places like America's Detroit or Britain's West Midlands. The simultaneous rush to build new industrial complexes and also to perfect the unsteady technology of the internal combustion engine left little time for such niceties as aesthetics.

Early carmakers were concerned with the oily, greasy, metallic business of hammering out basic car platforms called chassis. The first models had rudimentary fittings like seats and mudguards but, if you wanted to travel in the rain, a substantial overcoat was essential.

To satisfy the need for motoring luxury, even if that meant basic weather protection, companies that previously built horse-drawn vehicles turned to providing the 'motor carriage' owners with a choice of body styles. But there were also new entrants in this business, canny enough to realise that here was a nascent technology they could cash in on. One of these was Giovanni Farina, who set up shop in Turin in 1906 expressly to 'coachbuild' wood-framed, metal-panelled bodies for the rapidly evolving automobile.

Patronage of the right sort was vital for success, and Farina was fortunate to attract the attention of Giovanni Agnelli, the august, cigar-chomping founder of Fabbrica Italiana Automobili Torino – FIAT. Most of Fiat's first cars had been playthings and racing cars for the idle rich but, in 1911, Agnelli and his co-directors decided – no doubt spurred on by Henry Ford's phenomenal success – they

were going to become proper manufacturers with a new model called the Zero.

For identity, this car needed a distinctive radiator grille 'face' and Farina was happy to oblige with a dozen alternative proposals. One was the work of his 18-year-old brother Battista, usually known by his family nickname Pinin, who'd just joined Giovanni Farina as a factory boy. It was this one that Agnelli, through his haze of cigar smoke, liked the best, and it led to much lucrative work, including the Zero's entire bodywork. It was the making of Stabilimenti Farina.

It was also the making of Pinin Farina. With his keen eye and client-pleasing manner, he quickly became head of the company's design office. There must, however, have been friction between the brothers over a share in the profits Stabilimenti Farina generated – enough to see Battista up sticks and, on June 30, 1930, set up Carrozzeria Pinin Farina at Corso Trapani 107, Turin: an exact rival to his brother's coachbuilding enterprise. He did this with just one million lire of capital and a coterie of 90 staff. After a year, they'd built 42 car bodies. Still, with Pinin's limitless chutzpah, business gathered pace. To the undoubted chagrin of his brother, in 1931 came Pinin Farina's first Fiat, a snappy two-tone 525SS coupé that amply demonstrated the new company's knack of creating car bodies that really stood out from the crowd.

*Right:*
Pininfarina's 1978 XJ Spyder proposal for a Jaguar E-Type replacement plays clear homage to the original

*Far right:*
1961 Ferrari 250GT was one of countless Ferraris designed by Pininfarina

By 1939, Pinin Farina employed 500 workers building 800 car bodies a year, a mixture of bespoke models and small series. The company fast garnered a reputation for smooth, sleek but usually very elegant styling, radiator grilles raked back, headlights faired in, rear ends tapering gently to a pointed, streamlined finish. Quality was a watchword, and chassis employed ranged from humble Fiats to the most expensive Lancias, Alfa Romeos and Hispano Suizas. Occasionally, Pinin Farina produced a really surprising car, like the highly aerodynamic Lancia Aprilia coupé it built for the race track in 1937, but mostly they were discreet and assured touring cars.

The Second World War changed everything for Pinin Farina, as the company was forced to build aircraft seats and ambulances. Afterwards, the market was grim. The costly luxury cars of the pre-war period were mostly obsolete, and customers were more concerned with basic mobility than ostentatious style. Pinin Farina realised the days of the one-off, individually coachbuilt car were numbered: it was adapt or die, and the events of the next few years formed the turning point for his company.

First, by 1947, the factory floor was humming again with production of small series of designs, Fiat 1100 cabriolets, Maserati roadsters. Then Pinin Farina unveiled the Cisitalia 202, a two-seater GT coupé penned by a young designer called Giovanni Sovonuzzi. The car's stunningly modern lines, clutter-free contours and ground-hugging stance made it an instant design classic. Endorsement by New York's Museum of Modern Art helped bring Pinin Farina to the fore as a design-led organisation and not a parochial metal-basher. Two companies, in particular, were impressed.

First, Alfa Romeo. It not only approved Pinin Farina's design for a two-seater roadster version of its Giulietta, but signed a deal with Pinin Farina to build it too. Battista Farina then set about creating a factory environment where, in the end, 27,000 examples were built; a large new factory at nearby Grugliasco, opened in 1958, turned Pinin Farina from essentially a craft-based company into a fully fledged production line manufacturer. And secondly, Peugeot. A resolutely conservative French, family-owned car manufacturer, it called in Pinin Farina to add a touch of much-needed style to its products. They began collaborating in 1951 and the first public result was the practical yet tasteful 403 saloon four years later.

Both relationships were highly significant because they endure unbroken to this day. As, of course, does the close co-operation with Ferrari. That association started in

1952 with a convertible body on the 212 Inter chassis and, with the debut of the 250 series of road cars two years later, almost every Ferrari sold to the public for road use has been designed at Grugliasco.

Completing Farina's frenzy of activity in the early 1950s was a contract with Lancia that saw the Gran Turismo theme of the Cisitalia 202 (a commercial flop) made real. The Aurelia B20 GT was an essay in fastback design simplicity that, aided by a wonderful engine and a successful motor sport career, was a popular choice for monied enthusiasts. Only Battista Farina knew that its bodywork was constructed in time-honoured fashion from over 100 hand-beaten metal panels.

On a smaller scale was Pinin Farina's first American deal, producing handsomely rugged bodies for the Nash Healey sports car; and its first British one, to add the final beautifying touches to the Bentley R-type Continental.

If this seems like a bewildering list of wildly contrasting projects, then that's precisely what it was. Carrozzeria Pinin Farina's output was amazingly prolific, its design offices, fabrication shops and production lines white-hot with activity. Battista Farina even got into car retailing: he gave his son Sergio the job of marketing a line of special-bodied Fiat 1100 TV coupés between 1954 and 1957 through a dedicated dealer network across Italy. In stark contrast was Stabilimenti Farina. In 1951, Pinin's brother Giovanni Farina closed its doors after 45 years. He simply could not or would not adapt to the changing world of specialist car design and production.

The unveiling of Pinin Farina's 1955 Lancia-based Florida show car was a defining moment for the company. It was long, low, exotic and not a little American in its pillarless flavour. A tamed, four-door version hit the streets as the Lancia Flaminia in

1958, and Battista used it as his everyday car; but it was the car that alerted several European car manufacturers to their own design shortcomings, and to the fact that Pinin Farina's carefully nurtured stable of designers and artists were available for hire. The UK's British Motor Corporation was probably the most frequent customer, beginning with the uncommonly neat Austin A40 in 1958 and progressing through the 1.5-litre and 3-litre saloon ranges a year later, the 1100 and 1800 cars, and even the MGB GT. Prototypes for aerodynamic BMC 1100 and 1800 cars, created by Pininfarina's Leonardo Fioravanti in the late 1960s, were never built but still exerted an extraordinarily powerful influence over the profiles of many 'two-box' family cars throughout the 1970s.

You will notice, in the previous paragraph, Pinin Farina changes to

*Right:*
**Honda-badged Argento Vivo concept of
1995 paved the way for the S2000
sports car**

*Far right:*
**1998 Alfa Romeo Dardo study will be
one of several influences on the
forthcoming Spyder replacement**

Pininfarina. In 1961, Italian president Giovanni Gronchi decreed Battista Farina's nickname and surname could be joined to form a new family surname and business trademark. It was a favour that recognised the founder's gathering industrial importance and reputation in Italy and beyond. But it must have taken some getting used to by Battista's son Sergio, the mastermind of the company's industrialisation, if not his brother-in-law Renzo Carli. The two men took command of Pininfarina five years later when, in April 1966, Battista died in Lausanne, aged 60.

It rapidly became a very different sort of Pininfarina. Ferrari styling – we think of the many contrasting 250s and 500s, the Dino 246, Daytona and later 512BB and 400i – became its signature, although such labour-intensive and small-scale production work was often performed elsewhere. The Grugliasco factory was a sports car sausage

machine, squeezing out a Fiat 124 Spider, Alfa Romeo Duetto or Peugeot 504 convertible every few minutes. Sergio's expansion was focused on Pininfarina as a design hotbed.

The work spoke for itself, with one glamorous and/or technically innovative design following another, and often bearing the names of Pininfarina's most loyal 'gang of five' customers: Fiat, Lancia, Alfa Romeo, Ferrari, Peugeot and General Motors. Behind them was a brand new Design Centre, opened in 1967: it eventually spawned a separate design 'thinktank' in 1982, the 'Centro Studi e Ricerche'. In 1972, Pininfarina opened its own wind tunnel, the first in Italy and big enough to accommodate full-size cars and designs.

The Pininfarina 'brand' became vital to the company. Individual designers were seldom credited; only when they left, as with

Fioravanti and also Paolo Martin – the stylist of the incredible Modulo show car of 1970 and later the Pininfarina-accredited Rolls-Royce Camargue, Peugeot 604 and Fiat 130 Coupé – was the individual responsible finally revealed.

The company weathered the turbulent times of the 1970s and '80s thanks, in large part, to the industrial benevolence of Fiat. A portfolio of design-hungry clients was one thing: keeping the company's industrial apparatus rolling was another. From the Lancia Montecarlo to the Ferrari Testarossa, the Lancia Gamma coupé to the Fiat 124 Spider, Grugliasco's body assembly halls were never idle. 'They have helped us a lot, and we too, by which I mean all of us coachbuilders, have represented a significant added value,' said Sergio Pininfarina at Fiat's centenary celebrations in 1999. There have been over 130 Fiat-Pininfarina joint projects.

Other milestones were Pininfarina's accession to full car manufacturer status in 1981 when it began contract-production of the Fiat Campagnolo off-road vehicle, and the company's 1986 debut on the Italian stock market. By then, it had also broadened its design horizon to encompass research for Italy's National Research Council, leading to the formation of Pininfarina Extra in 1986, an in-house design bureau devoted to non-automotive design. Over the ensuing 16 years, Pininfarina Extra has designed a high-speed locomotive for the Italian railways, trams for cities including San Francisco and Zurich, an interactive helmet, a Lavazza coffee maker, the Casio G Cool Type I watch, and sports shoes for Fila.

The list of Pininfarina car designs of the last three decades is dauntingly enormous. Under the harsh motor show spotlights we have had the Jaguar XJS Spyder in 1980,

the Honda HP-X in 1984, the Ferrari Mythos in 1989 and the Peugeot Nautilus in 1997. Under what is perhaps the even more critical scrutiny of actual car buyers, Pininfarina's designs for the Peugeot 205 of 1982, the 1986 Cadillac Allante, the 1992 Ferrari 456GT, the 1994 Fiat Coupé, the 1999 Peugeot 406 and the 2001 Hyundai Matrix have taken to the streets in droves. Listing the others would bring this section to a romping close; get a reference book or surf the web if you want to recall them all.

Rather, it's Pininfarina's recent strategic changes that give an idea of the 73-year-old company's future direction. The manufacturing side continues, bolstered by useful contracts to assemble off-road vehicles for Mitsubishi and estate cars for Lancia. But on the design front, there is little room for growth among Pininfarina's traditional European customer base –

especially with Fiat's parlous financial state. So Pininfarina changed the name of its Studi e Ricerche (Design and Research) division to Pininfarina Ricerca e Sviluppo (Pininfarina Research and Development) to reflect the still family-controlled group's move to become a 'full service partner' in styling and niche production in automotive engineering. It's a shift from traditional design-and-manufacturing towards design, engineering and development.

This has attracted new clients; like Ford, which has contracted Pininfarina to design, engineer and build its StreetKa budget two-seater sports car; like Hafei, a Chinese start-up whose new Lobo city car (and total brand identity for a European debut) is being brought from concept to mass-produced item by the company; like Volvo, with whom Pininfarina has undertaken the complete engineering genesis of a totally new car that

has, in fact, already been styled by the Swedish automaker; and like GM-Daewoo, with the Nubira saloon, an even more commercially important car than the Pininfarina-penned Tacuma mini-MPV of 2000. In addition, a new joint venture with Webasto, the German-domiciled Open Air Systems, cements Pininfarina's reputation as a folding roof specialist on cars as diverse as the Peugeot 206CC and Bentley Azure.

Achieving all this is done in a very different style to the sheer hard graft Battista Farina poured into the growth of the firm in the early 1950s.

Pininfarina spends an annual €17 million ($19 million) on research into design, aerodynamics, new technologies and materials, safety, and environmental protection. In October 2002, Pininfarina inaugurated its new, 12,000 sq m Engineering Centre, where 500 design and engineering staff now work.

Still, what about sheer automotive beauty – that intangible quality on which the entire, thriving, industrial edifice that is today's Pininfarina was founded by 'Pinin' Farina 73 years ago? A stream of new Ferraris sees that is maintained, from the extraordinary Enzo supercar and the thrusting yet sybaritic

550 Maranello series. And Battista Farina himself doesn't need to be around to keep on accumulating accolades. When alive, he received the Italian equivalent of a knighthood, honorary membership of London's Royal Society of Arts and Turin's Society of Engineers & Architects, and plaudits from the Turin Polytechnic that included 'constantly renewed inventiveness' and 'superb artistic talent'. In 2000, 34 years after he died, he entered the Automotive News European Automotive Hall of Fame. So if you decide to become a car designer yourself, remember to pour everything you have into that first radiator grille.

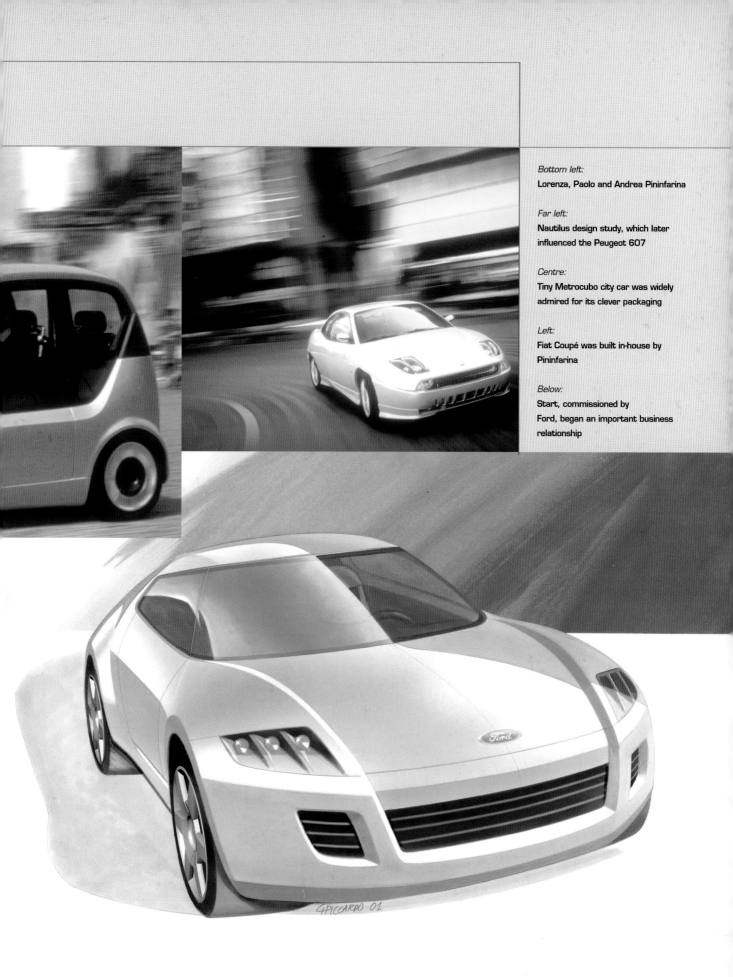

*Bottom left:*
**Lorenza, Paolo and Andrea Pininfarina**

*Far left:*
**Nautilus design study, which later influenced the Peugeot 607**

*Centre:*
**Tiny Metrocubo city car was widely admired for its clever packaging**

*Left:*
**Fiat Coupé was built in-house by Pininfarina**

*Below:*
**Start, commissioned by Ford, began an important business relationship**

GPICCARDO 01

# THE MEN WHO SHAPED CAR DESIGN

AUTOMOTIVE DESIGN HAS A RICH AND VIBRANT HISTORY, JUST LIKE FINE ART, SCULPTURE AND ARCHITECTURE. AND, JUST LIKE ARCHITECTURE, ITS PRODUCTS – BOTH OLD AND NEW, GOOD AND NOT SO GOOD – POPULATE OUR EVERYDAY ENVIRONMENT TO GIVE US A MOBILE SHOWCASE OF OLD MASTERS, NEW UPSTARTS AND FAST-EVOLVING ART ON WHEELS. HERE WE CELEBRATE THE AUTOMOTIVE ARCHITECTS AND ENGINEERS WHOSE WORK HAS DONE SO MUCH TO SHAPE THE WORLD WE LIVE AND TRAVEL IN – AND WE PAY TRIBUTE TO THE OFTEN HARD-FOUGHT STRUGGLES OF CREATIVE DESIGNERS TO GET THEIR TALENTS RECOGNISED AND THEIR DESIGNS INTO PRODUCTION.

Until Harley Earl came along, 'car design' had been little more than window-dressing for automotive engineering. What mattered to the pioneering car companies of the early part of the 20th century was perfecting the internal combustion engine and transferring its amazingly efficient power output to the road. How the car looked was an entirely secondary issue, and it was left to the cart- and carriage-building industries, used to providing vehicles to be drawn by beasts, to make the faltering and uneasy transformation to building bodywork for automobiles.

With the simultaneous arrival of Henry Ford's Model T and the mass production process in 1908, the democratisation of the car took a giant leap forward. It was now a consumer object that many more people could buy, own and enjoy. Rivals scrambled to compete, but it was the shrewd recruiting of Earl by General Motors architect Alfred Sloan that truly kick-started the battle for the hearts of car buyers.

Harley Earl had run a workshop in Hollywood, where he created movie props and customised cars for the wealthy but predictably fickle local clientele. He knew exactly what needed to be done to a car to make his customers part with large sums of money and, while performance was important to them, an individual and glamorous look to the car's surface was what they really craved.

Initially, Earl was appointed to GM's Paint and Enamel Committee, whose brief was to 'study the question of art and color combinations in General Motors products'. Then in 1926 he was hired full-time to establish an Art and Color Department at the corporation, and car design as we know it was born. Ten years later Earl re-christened the department the Styling Division. Car design had, belatedly, come of age.

By the late 1930s, Earl's flourishes were seen on Chevrolets, Cadillacs and La Salles as the separate units of engine cowling, passenger cabin, roof, wheel covers and luggage locker began to be

integrated. But General Motors' rivals were anxious not to be left behind.

Ford took on a talented yacht designer called Eugene 'Bob' Gregorie and, under the wing of the aesthetically literate Edsel Ford (Henry's son), he defined the look of a generation of Ford cars, including the first model designed in the USA specifically for Europe, the 1931 Model Y, and the later Lincoln Zephyr and Continental luxury cars.

In Britain, a provincial sidecar and bodywork manufacturer called William Lyons showed an uncommon intuition for what would excite customers with his 1931 SS1, a rakish two-seater sports car with a long bonnet and skilfully detailed features. It was the first of a series of SS cars, which in 1935 adopted the model name Jaguar for the first time. Lyons then went on to instigate and supervise the styling of the Jaguar XK, E-type, MkII and XJ6, design classics one and all. Even the 1975 XJS was his and arguably, since his death in 1985,

every Jaguar has been derived from his ethos.

Ferdinand Porsche was a giant of 20th-century car design, although he was primarily an engineer with an instinctive feeling for concepts – working from his Austrian design bureau, he was as inspired to design a speed-record car as a tractor. The Volkswagen Beetle, with its twisted and politically charged genesis, owes its phenomenal reputation to Porsche's thinking, not least for its iconic, aerodynamic shape, an exercise in efficient minimalism. Using the same mechanical underpinnings, Porsche did it again in 1948 with the first of the sports cars that, ultimately, made his family name a household one.

But it is back to the US that we move for three more important influences on the image of post-war cars. Raymond Loewy was an industrial designer of fearsome repute. He started his career by creating an attractive housing for a copying machine, and ended it

THE MINI WAS AN EXAMPLE
OF ANTI-STYLING: ITS CREATOR,
ALEC ISSIGONIS, ALWAYS HATED
THE NOTION THAT WHAT HE DID
WAS CAR STYLING.

*Above:*

**Sir Alec Issigonis, creator of the
Mini, shunned notions of car styling
and reduced his design to the bare
practical minimum. Even so, the Mini
was to have a profound effect on all
aspects of car design**

by designing the interior of NASA's Skylab. In between came the Lucky Strike cigarette packet, Coca Cola's voluptuous bottle (in part), and a series of designs for Studebaker which were the first to hitch the wind-cheating visual language of aircraft to cars. Some 1950 Studebakers even featured a propeller on their noses, but they were all startlingly up-to-the-minute. As a consultant, he also worked on British cars for Hillman and Humber, imbuing them with some much-needed transatlantic style.

Loewy's industry peers Howard Darrin and Brooks Stevens made different contributions to the language of car design. Darrin was the first to create the 'straight-through' wingline that finally consigned the notion of separate forms for front and wheel mudguards or wings to the wastepaper basket of history. His 1946 Kaiser Frazer sedan featuring this may not have been the most elegant motor car in the world but it inspired a slew of 1950s saloons from the Ford Consul to the Fiat 1400 and the Borgward Hansa to the Alfa Romeo 1900. Brooks Stevens, meanwhile, helped Willys to sell the Jeep to the public after the Second World War by turning this light military vehicle into a hybrid 'sports car': the 1950 Jeepster. It seemed weird at the time but it was, of course, the first-ever sports-utility vehicle. Stevens' 1963 Jeep Wagoneer set the style for everything from the Range Rover to the Mitsubishi Shogun.

Carlo Anderloni was neither rich nor famous but his influence is enormous. He was the in-house stylist at Italian coachbuilder Carrozzeria Touring, and his simple 1947 rendering for the Ferrari 166 Barchetta has helped define the profile of small sports cars ever since; its sculpted contours and clever swage (breaking up the 'little boat' side profile), really were the last word in simple beauty.

Pininfarina's Giovanni Sovunuzzi is, likewise, an unsung hero – the creator of the modern GT car after his revolutionary design for the 1100cc Cisitalia 202, also of 1947. Stunningly beautiful for its day, the New York Museum of Modern Art acquired one for its permanent collection, while Pininfarina refined the fastback coupé concept further for the Lancia B20 Aurelia.

While many of the designers touched upon so far devoted their working lives to making car design more egalitarian, one man, in his way, was charged with maintaining its formality. John Blatchley was a young man who, thanks to the Second World War, found himself working for Rolls-Royce after a short career as a talented graphic artist for a traditional London coachbuilder. Rolls-Royce had decided it would now build its own bodies (until that point, it had built merely rolling chassis), and Blatchley had to work his skills on the company's first, rather mediocre design to create the Silver Dawn and Bentley MkVI. Left to his own devices, however, he created both the Silver Cloud and the Silver Shadow, accomplished examples of design that seamlessly carried Rolls-Royce's fastidious virtues into newer, more informal times.

We have covered Italian design genius already, but Chrysler's Virgil Exner was the first to introduce it to an American audience. A combination of his eye for visual drama and the skills of the Ghia artisans he hired brought some astonishing concept cars to US motor shows during the 1950s, with some of the ideas working their way into Chrysler's production cars.

No list of the design greats is complete without mention of Alec Issigonis, although he always hated the notion that what he did was car styling. The Mini, indeed, was an example of anti-styling, a car so stripped of unnecessary things that its very starkness was its beauty. The British economy car began a trend towards unadorned, clean lines that put car design in the 1960s in sharp contrast to the chrome-laden excess of much of the previous decade. Much of that had been down to William Mitchell, Harley Earl's successor at General Motors and a happy proponent of outside influences on cars' designs, whether it was aeroplanes or sharks. He's usually recalled for his work on the Chevrolet Corvette sports car in its various guises, the compact Corvair, and several of GM's concept cars of the late 1950s and early 1960s.

The 1955 Citroen DS stood car design on its head, and it was Flaminio Bertoni who threw away the rulebook to create its shark-like shape and space-age design touches like a single-spoke steering wheel. Oddly, however, it remained an influence primarily on future Citroens, whereas the Renault 16 of ten years later made a seismic difference to the design of a whole spectrum of family cars. It was the first five-door family hatchback in the modern idiom, and was created for Renault by an extremely talented outside design consultant called Philippe Charbonneaux. One of his fellow countrymen, Michel Boué defined another market sector that, today, is part of car industry fabric: the 'supermini'. His Renault 5 of 1972, while not absolutely the first design of its type, was by far the most progressive. Sadly, he died at 35, before the 5 was launched.

The work of Giorgetto Giugiaro alone could fill a large book. As a young man, he built up a phenomenal reputation at Italian design house Bertone for his assured and dramatic interpretation of the 1960s sports and GT cars like the Fiat 850 Spider and Maserati

Below:
Ferdinand Porsche was a giant of 20th-century design: passionate about everything from racing cars to tractors, he is best known for the Volkswagen (below) and the sports car company that carries his name

UNTIL HARLEY EARL CAME ALONG IN 1926, CAR STYLING HAD BEEN LITTLE MORE THAN WINDOW-DRESSING FOR AUTOMOBILE ENGINEERING.

Ghibli. Then, after establishing Ital Design in 1968, he co-created some of the seminal family cars of the following two decades, including the Alfa Romeo Alfasud, the Volkswagen Golf, the Lancia Delta and the Fiat Panda and Uno.

A lesser-known Italian is Ercole Spada. Where Giugiaro has rarely turned out a design that wasn't smoothly acceptable to just about everyone who saw it, Spada, who worked for coachbuilder Zagato throughout the 1960s, was one of the few designers who liked to break moulds. Spiky, daring, sometimes counter-intuitive, his designs seemed to say that it was fine to go against the grain and come up with something that, at first, would shock and, in contemplation, delight. If it wasn't for figures like him, car designers today would be afraid to do anything but clone.

We edge closer to modern times in our look at the most influential designers, while trying to avoid focus on the developers of established themes or the accomplished plunderers of the past for the modern-day 'retro look'. Fergus Pollock is someone you're unlikely to have heard of but who has been hugely important in changing the popular perception of family cars. As a young designer he worked at Chrysler UK, where an obsession with old delivery vans sparked the initial drawings and ideas for what became, through many corporate convulsions, the Renault Espace in 1984. American and Japanese firms can possibly lay claim to devising the Multi-Purpose Vehicle, or MPV, first but nothing from Chrysler Corporation or Nissan could match the ground-breaking style and profound design legacy of the Espace.

At any international motor show today, you will see products that encapsulate the design philosophies and aspirations of their manufacturers with hair-splitting accuracy. Volkswagens are assuredly Volkswagens, a Saab says everything a Saab should, and Toyotas clearly communicate the appropriate brand values. This stuff, though, is clever fettling. The most influential man of recent times is not even a car designer himself but a Swiss entrepreneur called Nicolas Hayek. His daring plan for the Swatch watch phenomenon saved the Swiss watch industry; then, his scheme to interest Europe in tiny city cars resulted in the MCC Smart. It took the manufacturing and marketing might of Mercedes-Benz to make it a reality but there is no doubt that, in the year congestion charging took hold in the first major world city (London), the arrival and acceptance of the Smart is timely. Persuading what were previously thought to be conservative car buyers to switch to it in droves has been one of the key car design achievements of the early 21st century.

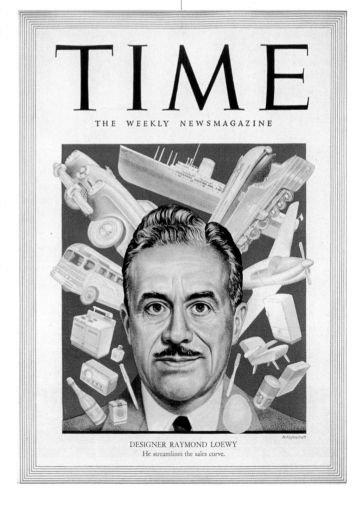

TIME

THE WEEKLY NEWSMAGAZINE

DESIGNER RAYMOND LOEWY
He streamlines the sales curve.

## 03.03 | CONCEPT CARS: THE TEN MOST INFLUENTIAL

CONCEPT CARS HAVE MANY IMPORTANT ROLES WITHIN THE AUTOMOTIVE INDUSTRY: TO GIVE SHAPE TO NEW CONFIGURATIONS AND NEW STYLES; TO FLOAT NEW ENGINEERING IDEAS; TO SIGNAL COMPANY INTENTIONS FOR THE FUTURE, AND TO TEST PUBLIC REACTION TO THOSE NEW IDEAS AND STYLES. THE BEST CONCEPT CARS WILL ACHIEVE ALL THESE – AND THESE ARE THE DESIGNS TAKING SUCH BOLD AND INNOVATIVE STRIDES FORWARD THAT THEY EXERT A POWERFUL INFLUENCE NOT JUST ON DESIGNERS, BUT ALSO ON THE WHOLE COURSE OF VEHICLE DESIGN.

THE ANCESTRY OF MANY OF TODAY'S CARS CAN BE TRACED BACK TO THE SEMINAL CONCEPTS OF THE LAST 30 YEARS, SUCH AS GIUGIARO'S LANCIA MEGAGAMMA WHICH PREVIEWED THE MODERN PEOPLE CARRIER A GENERATION AGO. HERE WE SELECT TEN OF THE VERY BEST – THOUGH THE LIST COULD EASILY RUN TO DOUBLE THAT NUMBER – AND ADD A WILDCARD FROM THE 21ST CENTURY THAT MIGHT PROVE THE MOST PROFOUNDLY INFLUENTIAL DESIGN OF ALL.

THE 1986 CHEVROLET CORVETTE INDY LAUNCHED THE SWOOPING, SPORTY CAB-FORWARD LOOK THAT WOULD BE SEEN ALMOST A DECADE LATER IN JAGUAR'S XJ220 AND THE MCLAREN F1 SUPERCARS

# CHEVROLET INDY, 1986

The economic boom of the late 1980s and early 1990s was characterised by a new breed of supercars, many with huge price tags catering for buoyant demand from the newly affluent super-rich.

To a large extent, the Bugatti EB110, Jaguar XJ220, McLaren F1 and the more affordable Honda NSX all share their design genes with the sensational 1986 Chevrolet Corvette Indy, which beat them all to public appearance by at least two years. Key designers, now in senior positions in the industry, often name the Indy as a powerful influence when they were aspiring designers in the mid-1980s.

At a time when production vehicles — both supercars and bread-and-butter sedans — were characterised by angular edges, the Indy was a revelation, its sexy shape characterised by flowing body curves and an aircraft-like glasshouse. In fact the shape was influenced by mid-1980s endurance racing cars, hence the raked-back and sweeping windshield, aerodynamic nose and distinctive side-intakes to feed air to the mid-mounted engine.

The narrow, glazed cockpit even sat, race-car like, on the broad-shouldered, low slung bodywork. But the dramatic nose treatment had a practical foundation. The driver was positioned far forward in the cabin, demanding a large front overhang to accommodate outstretched legs, pedals, steering gear and radiators.

To hide the huge front overhang that resulted, the nose curved towards the Indy's centre, giving the impression of less visual mass ahead of the front wheels.

Unfortunately Chevrolet's parent company, General Motors, failed to see the merit in the design, which was the work of Tom Peters and Julian Carter. At the time GM had just bought Lotus and the Indy could have carried a Lotus badge. The concept was even developed as a technology demonstrator by Lotus to showcase its active ride technology, four-wheel steering and multiplex wiring. The styling lived again on a second concept, the Isuzu 4200R, designed by Lotus, but also never to make production.

Nearly three years after the Indy debuted, Jaguar revealed the XJ220, its shape and detailing also inspired by endurance racing – and a new design theme had emerged. The look was taken to its ultimate development by the 1992 McLaren F1 by Peter Stevens, also designer of the Jaguar XJR-15. Nevertheless, General Moors did finally take advantage of its breakthrough design when, in 1992, the swooping nose treatment of the Indy was reborn on the 1992 Pontiac Firebird.

> AT A TIME WHEN PRODUCTION VEHICLES — BOTH SUPERCARS AND BREAD-AND-BUTTER SEDANS — WERE CHARACTERISED BY ANGULAR EDGES, THE INDY WAS A REVELATION.

THE DODGE VIPER SENT WAVES THROUGH THE AUTO INDUSTRY AND STOKED THE FIRES OF CREATIVITY IN CHRYSLER'S DESIGN DEPARTMENT, WHICH LED IN TURN TO A STREAM OF DESIGN CONCEPTS THAT SET DESIGN TRENDS THAT INFLUENCED CAR COMPANIES ALL OVER THE GLOBE

## CHRYSLER VIPER, 1989

'TELEVISION COVERAGE WAS INCESSANT, AND IT ENDED UP BEING ON THE COVER OF EVERY AUTOMOTIVE PUBLICATION IN THE COUNTRY, IF NOT THE WORLD.'

The influence of Chrysler's 1989 Detroit Auto Show Dodge Viper concept goes much further than its dramatic look and headline-grabbing 400bhp power output.

At the time the Chrysler corporation was facing its second financial crisis in a decade and looking for an image car to boost the company's standing – both internally and externally. And in successfully doing so, it set a trend that sent creative waves around the car industry in the 1990s.

In concept, the Viper was the brainchild of Chrysler boss Bob Lutz, an enthusiastic owner of a Ford Shelby Cobra replica. Lutz came up with the idea of reinventing the iconic Ford musclecar with a Chrysler badge. His 'back-of-cigarette-packet' design, created with Chrysler design chief Tom Gale and engineering boss Francois Castaing, was a straightforward remake of the Cobra.

But Gale's team, including the car's eventual exterior designer, Robert Hubbach, came up with a modern interpretation of the musclecar, extending the proportions with a very wide stance and an enormous hood. The bright red concept car was a sensation at the 1989 Detroit Auto Show: 'It blew the roof off,' said Lutz in his account. 'Television coverage was incessant, and it ended up being on the cover of every automotive publication in the country, if not the world.'

The design clearly hit the spot and, despite carrying a hefty price tag of $50,000, far in excess of any other volume-produced US model, a waiting list rapidly built up for the car. In doing so, it injected confidence back into Chrysler and, more importantly, it re-energised a US car industry.

Chrysler then set about unleashing the series of innovative and exciting concepts that continues today.

The dramatic concepts, all beautifully executed with expensive hand-beaten metal bodies by Californian coachbuilder Metalcrafters, created an image of Chrysler as an exciting design-led company. As a result, ambitious designers at rival firms all over the world took jobs at Chrysler, further boosting the company's creative edge.

# LAGONDA VIGNALE, 1993

One of the defining trends in the automobile industry of the new millennium is super-luxury cars. Whether as remakes of established brand names, like Rolls-Royce, Bentley and Cadillac, or new entrants like Maybach and Bugatti, luxury has returned.

Back in 1993 when Ford's Turin-based design house Ghia revealed the Lagonda Vignale, luxury was nowhere near as fashionable. Rolls-Royce and Bentley were stuffy brands held back by a lack of investment, while they faced competition from solid and unflashy Mercedes-Benz.

The Lagonda showed that a middle-ground existed in which traditional design themes like imposing dimensions, an understated exterior and a luxury interior could be matched to a fresh frontal identity. So instead of a baroque grille of grandiose dimensions, the Vignale's face was distinctive, but subtle.

Designed by Moray Callum (now boss of Mazda design) and David Wilkie (now Ghia's last remaining designer), the Vignale put as much emphasis on interior detailing as the exterior.

Other luxury brands may have claimed that to be the case, but the Vignale's art deco detailing, beautifully executed in hand-stitched leather and individually crafted in metal showed standards could be taken to another level. The interior also incorporated a lofty driving position and wide-opening rear doors to ease access in and out for the rear passengers.

Bugatti toyed with similar themes in a series of show cars by Italdesign, but its then-owner was short of funding and the designs never made production. It was the mid-size Rover 75, launched in 1998, that first put ideas from the Vignale into production, its subtle body styling, chrome handles and body highlights and slightly drooping rear deckline owing something to the Lagonda. A year later Mercedes-Benz revealed its challenger in the super-luxury class, with the Maybach concept of 1999. It also employed a drooping boot.

Super-luxury is here to stay and history will record that the Geneva motor show of 1993, where the Lagonda Vignale was revealed, was the starting point for this particular renaissance.

1993 LAGONDA VIGNALE
WAS INFLUENTIAL IN PUTTING
SUPER-LUXURY MOTORING BACK
ONTO THE MAP. DESIGN CUES
SUCH AS THE DROOPING REAR
DECKLINE AND CHROME
DETAILING WERE LATER TAKEN
UP BY THE ROVER 75

# GM AUTONOMY, 2001

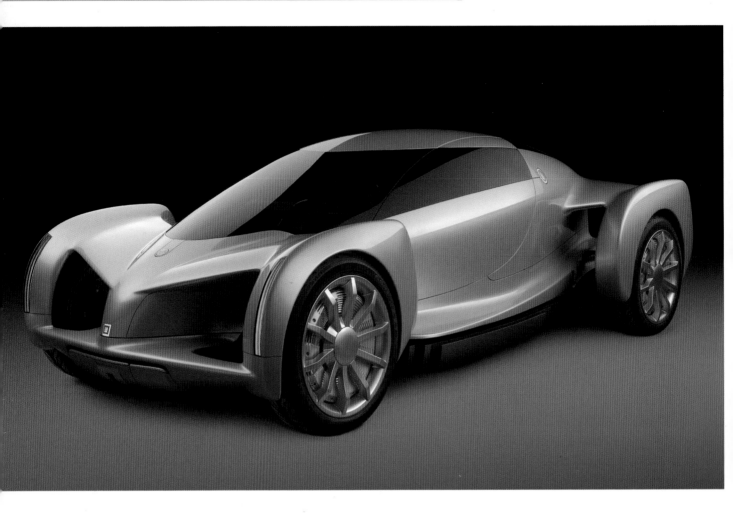

THE SKATEBOARD-LIKE CHASSIS OF FUEL-CELL POWERED GM AUTONOMY CONCEPT OF 2001 DRAMATICALLY DEMONSTRATES THE PACKAGING FLEXIBILITY MADE POSSIBLE BY THE NOVEL PROPULSION SYSTEM. ITS INFLUENCE ON FUTURE MODEL GENERATIONS MAY BE IMMENSE

Every designer in the 110-year history of the automobile has faced the same professional challenge. No matter what the concept of vehicle and its configuration, the fundamental shape of a car has had to take into account the box-like shape of an internal combustion engine, its gearbox and the mechanical controls to move the steering. The interaction of these technical parts has had an immutable influence over any designer's creativity and the final shape of any car.

Over the next 50 years of the automobile industry, the GM Autonomy concept may come to be seen as providing a glimpse of the future for car design – and in that regard it can be considered one of the most influential designs in the history of concepts.

The reason is simple: GM's Autonomy is the first study to rip up the rulebook of car design as it is powered by a fuel cell, whose size and shape has the potential to be much more flexible than the fixed silhouette a conventional engine.

Using this new freedom of expression, GM's design team, under boss Wayne Cherry, has concentrated the running gear of the Autonomy into a 'flat-pack' chassis onto which a body of almost limitless variation can be attached.

A designer's dream, the fuel cell may turn out to be the automotive equivalent of an artist's blank canvas. All the controls of a fuel cell vehicle are electric, even the steering and brakes, so there's no need to compromise the styling to accommodate pipes and steel controls inside the bodywork. There's just a series of electrical pick-ups on the 'flat-pack' chassis that the designer can connect up to. Even the suspension is enclosed in pods that form part of the front and rear of the 'flat-pack'.

Such dream-like flexibility is exploited on the Autonomy with a suitably sci-fi body. Removed from the need to heed practical considerations, the

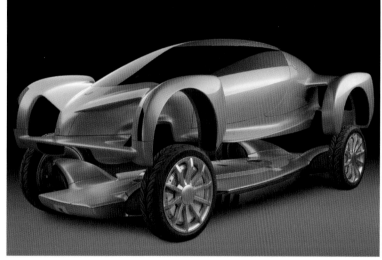

wheels and tyres are housed in racecar-style wheelarches. With no need to flow air into the internal combustion engine's radiator, there's no need for a front grille, and with modern lighting technology a narrow strip headlamp can be fitted onto the cycle-guard-style front wing.

Similar 'blue-sky' design thinking has gone into the Autonomy's body shape and tail treatment. A sharply tapering rear body section ought to be very low drag, an energy-saving feature helped by the smooth underside of the 'flat-pack' chassis.

The Autonomy's shape may be a designer's flight of fancy, but it shows how concepts can be used to explore radical new design themes. The 2050 edition of this book may well vote the GM Autonomy as the most influential design concept ever. Don't bet against it.

## LANCIA MEGAGAMMA, 1978

THE APPARENT FAMILIARITY OF
GIUGIARO'S LANCIA MEGAGAMMA OF
1978 SHOWS HOW UNIVERSALLY ITS
THEN-REVOLUTIONARY TWO-BOX
PROPORTIONS, HIGH ROOF AND UPRIGHT
SEATING HAVE NOW BEEN ADOPTED.
ALMOST EVERY PEOPLE CARRIER AND
SPACE-EFFICIENT SMALL CAR CAN TRACE
ITS ANCESTRY BACK TO THIS DRAMATIC
STEP FORWARD IN VEHICLE PACKAGING

Recreational vehicles, people carriers, MPVs – whatever you call them, high-roofed five- or seven-seat vehicles with roomy, flexible cabins are big-sellers in today's market.

Just about every carmaker has some kind of multi-purpose vehicle in its line-up – and they can all trace their ancestry back to Italdesign's seminal Lancia Megagamma design from the Turin show of 1978. At 4.3m long and with a 2.67m long wheelbase, the Megagamma was shown five years ahead of the production launch of Chrysler's Voyager minivan and six years ahead of the Renault Espace. Based on a Lancia Gamma platform, the Megagamma featured a high roofline (1.61m) to create a big interior cabin space by sitting its occupants more upright than was usual at the time. Italdesign was a pioneer of this upright seating position and a few years later introduced it in the Uno supermini.

In aesthetic terms, the exterior styling was unremarkable, simply shaped near-flat panels defining the two-box shape. But the Megagamma was all about functional design, creating the car from the inside out.

But despite being such a breakthrough design, the Megagamma was rejected as too much of a commercial risk by management at Fiat, owners of Lancia.

Italy's loss, however, was America's and France's gain. The 1983 Voyager/Caravan family was such a huge success that it saved the Chrysler Corporation from bankruptcy. It particularly worked for blue-collar families who could afford only one vehicle and needed practical, roomy transport for their families. In that sense the Megagamma can also be credited with hastening the demise of the station wagon, the vehicle that previously served this role. In contrast the Renault Espace created an upmarket niche for the people carrier.

Significantly, Renault seized the concept in more than just the top-end sector of the Espace. The Twingo and Scénic are both innovative cars that manage to provide a roomy interior package despite external dimensions that place them in two smaller market segments in Europe – city cars and small hatchbacks. Both models have spawned imitators and the two segments have grown to become huge commercial successes.

# MERCEDES VISION A, 1993

The early 1990s were a period of unprecedented expansion for Mercedes-Benz. The stolid brand, revered for its quality and exclusivity, had to respond to increasing competition and the growing realisation that small production levels might mean beautiful quality, but they didn't necessarily mean long-term survival.

A small car with high production numbers had to feature in its model line-up to suck in a new breed of young buyers who could progress through the model range, growing into the bigger luxury cars the brand had always been renowned for.

But very few car industry insiders were prepared for the shock of the revolutionary Vision A concept that stole the 1993 Frankfurt show. Designed from the inside out by Harald Leschke and Franz Lecher, the Vision A was remarkably short – close to the 3.1m of an original Mini — yet had cabin space similar to the mid-size Mercedes E-Class.

This was accomplished by a revolutionary construction method that concentrated the car's crash structure into a flat floor, allowing people and luggage to occupy as much of the concept's minimal footprint as possible. What's more, the ability to remove entirely the rear seats and front passenger seat was then unique in a small car.

The concept's styling tried to hide the Vision A's high-roof stance with a series of diagonal swage lines along the bottom of the glasshouse and on top of the wheel arches. It looked futuristic, but wasn't considered likely to deliver commercial success and was changed for production into a smoother, more curvaceous 'one-box' look.

The significance of the Vision A was to create a new approach to packaging — the art of using internal space – in a small car. And a vital secondary role was to prove at the same time that even a brand with the high-end image of Mercedes could make a small car.

Such was the threat posed by the A-Class that it soon spawned a number of rivals. BMW created the entry-level Compact and Audi the A3, although both took a much more conventional architectural approach. It was only later, with the A2, that Audi adopted a similarly radical tack.

More than a decade after the Vision A, volume carmakers are only just responding with purpose-built models with similar functions – like flexible seating arrangements – to the A-Class. Examples are the Opel Meriva and Fiat Idea, although both are longer than the A-Class. Mercedes' baby remains a radical innovation that may not ever be bettered.

THE 1993 MERCEDES VISION A WAS TASKED WITH SOFTENING UP PUBLIC OPINION FOR THE FORTHCOMING A-CLASS SMALL CAR, PREVIEWING THE SENSATIONAL PACKAGING WHICH MOUNTED THE ENGINE UNDER THE FLOOR TO PROVIDE EXECUTIVE CAR SPACE WITHIN MINI-CAR EXTERNAL DIMENSIONS

# BMW X COUPÉ 2001

If the intention of Chris Bangle's two dramatic BMW concepts in 1999 and 2001 was to shock, he could hardly have expected to score such a bulls-eye. Starting with the Z9 Coupé at Frankfurt in 1999 and culminating with the X Coupé at Detroit two years later, Bangle's concepts created the biggest talking point in car design for a decade.

Disbelief greeted the radical designs as commentators and rival designers tried to make sense of the concepts in the context of one of the world's most commercially successful carmakers whose conservative designs were matched to peerless engineering and a luxury brand equal in desirability to Mercedes-Benz. Yet Bangle's concepts reflected a fundamental review of BMW's future product direction that involved engineering, finance and marketing functions as much as design.

The Z9 and X Coupé each had a specific role and stemmed from a long-term product-planning review, called Deep Blue, convened in 1996 in California to establish a framework for new BMW products all the way to 2010. The company split its product range into what Bangle calls the 'formal' – saloons and estates – and the 'informal' – roadsters, 4x4s and coupés. The Z9 suggested a new direction for the 'formal' and the X Coupé for the 'informal'.

Both designs centred around dramatic surface treatment and radical detailing. The traditional design rulebook of delicate proportion and surface treatment was ripped up in favour of a new computer-inspired design language dubbed 'flame surfacing'. In practice this boiled down to a series of abruptly interlocking panel surfaces demarcated by unpredictable panel openings. The X Coupé had the more dramatic interpretation. The concepts' headlights had seemingly been turned upside down, while grilles hovered out

THE DESIGN OF THE BMW X COUPÉ WAS GREETED WITH DISBELIEF WHEN IT WAS UNVEILED AT THE DETROIT MOTOR SHOW IN 2001. TODAY IT IS STILL JUST AS CONTROVERSIAL

of alignment and bonnet bulges became dominant styling features.

In his defence Bangle went on the attack, saying in spring 2001: 'The fact that the new direction shocks and amazes is more of a reflection of how fixed ideas have become on what a car can be or should be. The X Coupé is an awakening, and I'm convinced it will be seen as a turning point. It's not for nothing that it is controversial.'

Commercially, the proof will come in sales. BMW has effectively bet its future on the new design direction. But by 2003 only two production vehicles featured 'flame surfacing' – the 7-Series and the Z4 roadster.

There are already signs that the production cars have a less-violent version of the new direction and that other carmakers are following in Bangle's wake. An interpretation of the controversial 7-Series trunk, for example, is rumoured to feature on the next-generation Mercedes S-Class. And Subaru has showed the B11S concept with similar design language.

Perhaps Bangle's greatest achievement is in moving the thinking of other luxury carmakers, for whom risk-adverse product development is normal. Jaguar and Audi, for example, are preparing to move their styling radically, while remaining conservative compared to BMW. Then the Z9 and X Coupé really will have fulfilled Bangle's prediction of his design vision becoming a turning point.

# FORD PROBE III, 1981

As an exercise in bold product design, the Ford Probe III concept has few equals. The star of the 1981 Frankfurt motor show, it prepared the public for the aerodynamic Sierra launched the following year.

Driven by rising fuel prices, carmakers were exploring low-drag bodyshells as a cheaper and quicker method to fuel-saving than expensive and lengthy investment in new and more efficient powertrains. As a result the Probe III concept featured a smooth and curvaceous body, faired-in rear wheels, flush windows, spoilers and a flat undertray to bring its drag coefficient down to a then-revolutionary 0.22. By way of comparison, the angular Ford Cortina, the model to be replaced by the Sierra, rated 0.44.

Ford knew the radical Sierra – created by a team under Uwe Bahnsen – would be a shock to customers used to the conservative Cortina. And in his book Guts, Ford Europe boss Bob Lutz, tells the story of how he worked Ford chief Don Petersen round to giving the design the OK. 'I gave him a small sketch to put in his pocket on his return to the US and inscribed on it the words "view daily until familiarity is achieved". It worked,' wrote Lutz.

**'AS AN EXERCISE IN BOLD PRODUCT DESIGN, THE FORD PROBE III CONCEPT HAS FEW EQUALS.'**

But cost engineering and management caution toned the production Sierra down in key areas and many of the extreme aerodynamic features were dropped. Although still radical, the production car lost the magic of the concept. The public still didn't react well and sales bombed. Design chief Uwe Bahnsen became a scapegoat for the troubles and Ford had to fend off rumours of an emergency re-skin when the press dubbed the Sierra the 'jelly-mould'.

THE FORD PROBE III CONCEPT OF 1981 SIGNALLED THE START OF THE AERODYNAMIC ERA. WITHIN FORD, ITS ROLE WAS TO PREPARE BUYERS FOR THE RADICAL, ROUNDED SIERRA DUE FOR LAUNCH IN 1982

But like all trend-setting designs, the Sierra opened the way for other car-makers to introduce the aerodynamic look. And the marketing battleground of the 1980s was dominated by advertising boasting of low Cd figures. But many rivals did not launch similiarly swooping styling until ten years later. In that period, though, there was time to perfect the look and for production techniques to catch up. By the early 1990s the aerodynamic look had been re-named 'organic' and featured in just about every carmaker's range. Even Ford North America returned to the theme with its curvaceously Sierra-like, mid-1990s Taurus replacement. Proof at last that the Probe III and its Sierra sibling were ten years ahead of their time.

## RENAULT INITIALE, 1995

Any discussion of concept cars could not ignore the efforts made by Renault in the 1990s. Under the guidance of design chief Patrick Le Quément (a member of the Ford team that created the Probe III/Sierra), the French carmaker has invested hugely in design as part of its commercial renaissance over the past ten years. Any of Renault's most important ten concepts between 1990 and 2000 could be singled out for their significance. They included the 1991 Scénic that explored the mini-MPV concept and later became a huge commercial success, and the 1994 Argos, whose exterior pre-dated the theme of the Audi TT.

But perhaps the most ambitious was the Initiale, a luxury four-door sedan that signified a French willingness to experiment in the battle for luxury car sales in the face of increasing German dominance of that market. Designed by Florian Thiercelin and exhibited at the Paris Salon in 1995, the Initiale also evolved into the striking replacement for the Laguna, a car that simultaneously established a new design language for Renault, culminating in the new Mégane at Paris in 2002. Now this new design theme is influencing cars being developed in the world's engineering centres and due for launch in the coming years.

The Initiale juggled a clever balancing act of simple body surfaces, crisp body sections and subtle detailing, adding up to a modern interpretation of luxury and quality that boasted strong ambition for a nameplate that otherwise stood for volume-produced family cars.

Its rear-end styling experimented with an extreme and angular form of the 'bustle-back' theme that is the most distinctive and original element of the new Renault design language – and the feature most likely to influence other designers. The same goes for the arching roofline and rear pillar that have been developed on the Mégane into a key part of the car's distinctive side profile.

The interior was assembled with aesthetic sensitivity, fine leather and perfectly finished metal, lending the cabin the appropriate level of luxury. Designers working in the luxury field admit that the Initiale's interior was a big influence at a time when many carmakers were exploring new design themes.

# CONCEPT CARS: THE TEN BEST FORGOTTEN

THE RESULTS ARE NOT ALWAYS PREDICTABLE WHEN AMBITIOUS AND IMPETUOUS DESIGNERS ARE LET OFF THE LEASH TO PRODUCE INNOVATIVE CONCEPT CARS. HERE WE PRESENT TEN OF THE WORST EXAMPLES OF DESIGN GONE MAD – IRRELEVANT, MISGUIDED, PRETENTIOUS OR JUST PLAIN OVER-THE-TOP CONCEPT CARS WHICH, MERCIFULLY FAILED TO CHANGE THE COURSE OF AUTOMOTIVE HISTORY.

## CITROEN 2CV METRO, 1975

THE 1948 CITROEN 2CV WAS AN ESSENTIALLY SIMPLE CAR, NOT SO MUCH STYLED AS 'PLANNED' FOR USE ON UNMADE RURAL TRACKS AT ROCK BOTTOM OPERATING COST. THE FRENCH TOOK IT TO THEIR HEARTS WHILE OFTEN DESPISING ITS LOWLY STATUS WHICH WAS WHY, 27 YEARS AFTER ITS LAUNCH, CITROEN PRESENTED AN ELABORATE RETHINK. THERE WAS AN UPGRADE FROM TWO TO FOUR CYLINDERS, BUT THE COMPANY'S STYLING DEPARTMENT CREATED A TACKILY GENTRIFIED LOOK, WITH CHINTZY FAKE HOOD IRONS, CHROME GRILLE AND FANCY WHEELS. WITH THE RENAULT 5 AND VW GOLF SETTING THE DESIGN PACE, THE 2CV METRO THANKFULLY REMAINED A ONE-OFF BUT THE 2CV STAGGERED ON ANOTHER 13 YEARS IN ITS ORIGINAL, UNADULTERATED, CLASSIC FORM.

## DAIHATSU TREK, 1985

THE TOKYO MOTOR SHOW USUALLY THROWS UP MORE WACKY
IDEAS AND QUIRKY DESIGNS THAN YOU'D FIND AT A DOZEN
EUROPEAN EVENTS. DAIHATSU, AMONG JAPAN'S SMALLER
MAKERS, BEGETS MORE THAN ITS FAIR SHARE OF CONCEPT
CARS. IN 1985, IT PRESENTED AN AMAZING 32 CONCEPTS IN
TOKYO UNDER A 'SMALL VEHICLES WITH A BIG DREAM' BANNER.
AMONG THEM, THE TREK. WITH ITS SINGLE SEAT, RUGGED
STANCE AND HIGH GROUND CLEARANCE, IT WAS APPARENTLY
INTENDED AS A PSEUDO QUAD-BIKE, BUT THE SEAT AND
STEERING COLUMN DROPPED AWAY TO TURN THE TREK INTO A
COMFY SINGLE BED, WITH A POP-UP TENT TO KEEP MOSQUITOES
AT BAY.

## DAIMLER SILVER FLASH, 1953

BRITAIN'S DAIMLER, IN THE 1950S, WAS A DINOSAUR OF THE
CAR-MAKING AGE, TURNING OUT HEAVY, OLD-FASHIONED CARS
FOR A DWINDLING MARKET OF BRITISH ARISTOCRATS.
HOWEVER, ITS CHIEF, SIR BERNARD DOCKER, TRIED TO PROJECT
AN INNOVATIVE IMAGE WITH A SERIES OF SHOW CARS FROM
1950 TO 1955 – CARS THAT BECAME KNOWN AS THE 'DOCKER
DAIMLERS'. THE FIRST, AN ENORMOUS BLACK LIMO, CAUSED A
TABLOID SENSATION WITH ITS LAVISH GOLD-PLATED TRIM, BUT
THE SILVER FLASH, UNVEILED IN 1953, WAS MORE MODEST.
BASED ON THE DAIMLER REGENCY MODEL, IT SPORTED SLIGHTLY
MORE RESTRAINED SOLID SILVER HAIRBRUSHES AND
PROPELLING PENCILS BUILT INTO THE INTERIOR, PLUS FITTED
RED CROCODILE SKIN LUGGAGE. THERE WAS A STAB AT
MODERNITY, WITH AN ALUMINIUM BODY.

## ELLIPSIS, 1992

AGED 75, PHILIPPE CHARBONNEAUX – DESIGNER OF THE
GROUNDBREAKING RENAULT 16 ALMOST THREE DECADES
EARLIER - WAS STILL HARD AT WORK, ALTHOUGH HIS ELLIPSIS
WAS, SADLY, THE LAUGHING STOCK OF THE PARIS MOTOR SHOW
IN 1992. THE RATIONALE BEHIND HIS DIAMOND WHEEL-PATTERN
RUNABOUT, WITH BOTH FRONT AND REAR STEERED WHEELS,
WAS THAT IT COULD PERFORM A U-TURN IN A SPACE BARELY
TWICE ITS LENGTH, AND ITS TWO STEERED WHEELS MEANT IT
COULD WIGGLE INTO TIGHT PARISIAN PARKING SPACES. A
SOFTLY ROUNDED 'POINT' AT EITHER END MEANT, CLAIMED
CHARBONNEAUX, THE CAR WAS MUCH SAFER IN ACCIDENTS,
DEFLECTING PEDESTRIANS RATHER THAN PLOUGHING INTO
THEM, AND 'SLIDING' AWAY FROM MOST IMPACTS.
UNFORTUNATELY, NONE OF THIS WAS EVER PROVEN.

## FORD COMUTA, 1967

FORD BUILT SIX COMUTA PROTOTYPES AT ITS UK RESEARCH &
ENGINEERING CENTRE IN DUNTON, ESSEX, IN 1967. THEY
LOOKED LIKE PHOTO-ME BOOTHS ON PEDAL CAR WHEELS, AND
TWO COMUTAS MEASURED THE SAME LENGTH AS ONE CORTINA.
IT HAD TO BE THIS COMPACT TO AVOID ANY SUPERFLUOUS
WEIGHT, BECAUSE ITS HEFTY CLUSTER OF LEAD-ACID BATTERIES
MEANT THE CAR WEIGHED MORE THAN A MINI. QUITE APART
FROM ITS AWFUL LOOKS, A POWER-SAPPING 40MPH WITH A
MERE 40-MILE RANGE CONVINCED FORD IT WAS POINTLESS
PROCEEDING WITH THE COMUTA – UNTIL 34 YEARS LATER, WHEN
THE COMPANY'S REMARKABLY SIMILAR ELECTRIC TH!NK MADE A
BRIEF AND ILL-STARRED ASSAULT ON CONVENTIONAL, PETROL-
POWERED MINI CARS.

## GENERAL MOTORS FIREBIRD XP-21, 1954

THIS WAS AMERICA'S FIRST GAS TURBINE-POWERED CAR AND,
WHILE ITS ULTIMATE TOP SPEED WAS NEVER RECORDED, IT
COULD DEVELOP 370BHP FROM COMPRESSED GAS DELIVERED
TO ITS REAR WHEELS. ITS GASIFIER SPUN AT A DAZED
26,000RPM WHILE ITS POWER UNIT GAVE 13,000RPM. THE
STYLING, HOWEVER, WAS ITS TRUE PULL – FANTASTICALLY
DRAMATIC, FANTASTICALLY IMPRACTICAL. THE WORK OF GM
DESIGN LEGEND HARLEY EARL, IT WAS FASHIONED AFTER THE
DOUGLAS SKYRAY SUPERSONIC JET PLANE AND MADE OF
GLASSFIBRE. THE FIREBIRD XP-21 TOURED AMERICA AS PART OF
GENERAL MOTORS' 'MOTORAMA' ROADSHOW, AN ANNUAL
TRAVELLING CIRCUS OF DREAM CARS. STILL, THE ONLY PART OF
THE XP-21 THAT MADE IT TO MARKET WAS THE NAME, LATER
APPLIED TO A MUCH MORE SUCCESSFUL PONTIAC.

## MINISSIMA, 1973

BMW'S ALL-NEW MINI, WHILE NOWHERE NEAR AS
REVOLUTIONARY AS THE 1959 ORIGINAL, WAS SO ENDEARING IT
GOT ORDINARY PEOPLE EXCITED BY SMALL CARS ONCE AGAIN.
YET DESIGNERS' THOUGHTS HAD TURNED TO A 'NEW MINI' LONG
BEFORE, AND THE MINISSIMA WAS A FAUX-FUTURIST
INTERPRETATION IN 1973. THE SEVERE-LINED 'ONE-BOX' CAR
PACKED THE MINI'S A-SERIES ENGINE, AUTOMATIC GEARBOX AND
FRONT-WHEEL DRIVE INTO A TINY WHEELBASE. IT WAS AS LONG
AS MOST CARS WERE WIDE – SO SHORT, IT COULD BE PARKED
END-ON TO THE KERB. YOU COULD SAFELY DISEMBARK STRAIGHT
ON TO THE PAVEMENT THROUGH THE CAR'S ONLY DOOR, SITED
CENTRALLY AT THE BACK. THE WORK OF THE LATE DESIGNER
WILLIAM TOWNS, IT REMAINS A VIEW OF THE FUTURE THAT
NEVER ARRIVED.

## VAUXHALL EQUUS, 1978

THE EQUUS, LATIN FOR HORSE, IS UNLIKE ANY VAUXHALL YOU'LL EVER SEE ON THE ROAD. FOR ANYONE WHO THINKS THE TRIUMPH TR7 WAS WEDGE-SHAPEDLY UGLY, THEN THE EQUUS TAKES THE FORM TO ANOTHER LEVEL, WITH ITS ANGULAR LINES AND KNIFE-BLADE PROFILE. IN ITS DAY THE EQUUS CLAIMED TO REPRESENT THE CUTTING EDGE IN SPORTS CAR DESIGN AND WAS WIDELY TIPPED AS A BRITISH SUCCESSOR TO THE MGB. PLANS TO MAKE IT WERE DRAWN UP BY PANTHER, ON WHOSE LIMA SPORTS CAR CHASSIS THE EQUUS WAS BASED. BUT THE DESIGN DEPARTMENT OF GM-CONTROLLED VAUXHALL CLOSED IN 1980 – AT AROUND THE TIME THE AXE FELL ON THE SLOW-SELLING TR7. STILL, IT'S HARD TO BELIEVE THIS CAR IS A QUARTER OF A CENTURY OLD.

## ZAGATO Z-ECO, 1992

THE DEBUT OF THE NEW FIAT CINQUECENTO IN 1992 WAS ACCOMPANIED BY A FLOTILLA OF SPECIALLY COMMISSIONED CONCEPT CARS BASED ON ITS MECHANICAL PARTS AND DIMENSIONS. VENERABLE ITALIAN COACHBUILDER ZAGATO REASONED THE ZAGATO Z-ECO WOULD BE THE IDEAL CAR FOR COMMUTING TO WORK. ITS TWO PASSENGERS WOULD SIT IN TANDEM UNDER A CANOPY ON ONE SIDE OF THE CAR, AS ON A MOTORBIKE, WHILE AN ADULT-SIZE BICYCLE STOOD FIXED UPRIGHT ON THE OTHER. WHEN THE TRAFFIC GROUND TO A HALT, THE Z-ECO WOULD BE PARKED IN THE NEAREST SUBURBAN AVENUE AND ONE OF ITS OCCUPANTS WOULD GRAB THE BIKE AND CARRY ON TO THE OFFICE. THE BIKE INCORPORATED AN ELECTRIC MOTOR, RECHARGED WHILE ON BOARD THE CAR AND PLUGGED IN, AND SO READY WHEN NEEDED.

## BERTONE SUZUKI GO, 1972

FINISHED IN CRISP GREEN WITH HIGHLY POLISHED WHEEL TRIMS, THIS LOW-LEVEL FUN CAR WAS SUPPOSED TO TAKE YOUR SKIS, BOOTS, MOUNTAIN BIKES AND EVEN A SNOWMOBILE TO THE EDGE OF THE ACTION, AND THEN BACK TO THE CHALET FOR A MUCH-NEEDED GLUWEIN AS THE SUN WENT DOWN. OVER THE DRIVER'S SHOULDER WAS A THREE-CYLINDER SUZUKI 750 MOTORBIKE ENGINE WITH BERTONE'S OWN CHAIN-DRIVEN GEARBOX BOASTING FIVE FORWARD AND FIVE REVERSE RATIOS; OVER THE PASSENGER'S SHOULDER, THE RADIATOR AND A LUGGAGE BOX. THERE WERE NO DOORS OR WINDSCREEN, BUT YOU COULD LOWER A RAMP AT THE BACK TO UNLOAD YOUR SNOWMOBILE, USING PULLEYS DRIVEN BY THE STEERING WHEEL. PREFER THE WATER? NO PROBLEM: JUST ATTACH AN OUTBOARD TO THE BACK TO TURN THE GO INTO A BOAT.

# 50 LANDMARK DESIGNS

WHICH ARE THE MOST SIGNIFICANT DESIGNS IN THE AUTOMOBILE'S 110-YEAR HISTORY? WHILE MOST EXPERTS MIGHT AGREE ON A SHORTLIST OF 200, NARROWING IT DOWN TO JUST 50 IS AN ALTOGETHER MORE CHALLENGING EXERCISE. SALES SUCCESS IS NOT NECESSARILY A GUARANTEE OF INCLUSION, NOR IS ENGINEERING MERIT: WE INCLUDE NEITHER THE FORD MODEL T NOR THE MCLAREN F1. INSTEAD, WE FOCUS ON THOSE DESIGNS WHICH LAUNCHED NEW SHAPES ONTO OUR ROADS; THOSE DESIGNS WHICH HAVE CHANGED THE WAY WE USE OUR CARS OR THINK ABOUT THEM, AND THOSE FRESH DESIGN IDEAS SO POWERFUL THAT THEY CHANGED THE WAY THE WHOLE AUTO INDUSTRY THOUGHT.

INEVITABLY, THERE ARE CARS WHICH NARROWLY MISSED OUT, SUCH AS THE AUDI 100, PIONEER OF THE AERODYNAMIC AGE, OR THE ROVER 2000, THE FIRST EXECUTIVE SEDAN. EVEN THE FIAT UNO, AS THE FIRST HIGH-BUILD SMALL CAR, MAKES A STRONG CASE FOR INCLUSION. BUT WHAT OUR CHOSEN 50 HAVE IN COMMON IS THAT THEY STAND STILL FURTHER OUT FROM THE CROWD AS THE TRUE LANDMARKS THROUGH WHICH THE EVOLUTION OF THE AUTOMOBILE CAN BE TRACED.

## CHRYSLER AIRFLOW, 1934

CHRYSLER BRAVELY DECIDED TO SET THE CAR WORLD ALIGHT WITH ITS STREAMLINED SEDAN AND, TO OUR EYES TODAY, THE AIRFLOW APPEARS TO BE A SEMINAL EXAMPLE OF ART DECO. SADLY, ALTHOUGH THE AMERICAN PUBLIC WAS INTRIGUED BY THE FUTURISTICALLY CURVACEOUS LINES AND WATERFALL-STYLE GRILLE, FROM THE PENCIL OF CHRYSLER'S RESEARCH HEAD CARL BREER, THIS DIDN'T TRANSLATE INTO SALES. SOME SAID IT WAS BUG-EYED, OTHERS THAT IT RESEMBLED A RHINO. THE AIRFLOW WAS A COMMERCIAL DISASTER AND ABANDONED AFTER JUST THREE YEARS, BUT WAS NONETHELESS EXTREMELY INFLUENTIAL IN MAKING AMERICAN CARS LESS LIKE BOXES ON WHEELS.

# CITROEN 2CV, 1938

BAUHAUS ARCHITECTURAL LANGUAGE TRANSFERRED TO CARS IN THE DEUX
CHEVAUX. IT WAS PLANNED AROUND THE MOST BASIC OF PRINCIPLES: TO BE ABLE
TO CARRY TWO PEASANTS AND 50KG OF PRODUCE ACROSS A PLOUGHED FIELD AT
50KMH WHILE KEEPING BOTH PEOPLE AND CARGO INTACT. WITH MICHELIN BACKING,
ENGINEER-DESIGNER PIERRE BOULANGER CAME UP WITH THE MINIMAL GOODS, AND
THE LITTLE CAR, LOOKING FOR ALL THE WORLD LIKE A METAL SNAIL ON WHEELS,
PROVIDED MOTORING FOR ECHELONS OF FRENCH SOCIETY WHO HAD NEVER KNOWN
IT BEFORE WHEN IT WAS, FINALLY, PUT ON SALE IN 1948. IT WENT ON TO STAY IN
THE CITROEN CATALOGUE FOR AN INCREDIBLE 40 YEARS.

# VOLKSWAGEN BEETLE, 1938

OF COURSE, IT WAS NEVER MEANT TO BE CALLED BEETLE: THIS WAS ADOLF HITLER'S
PERSONAL VISION FOR A 'PEOPLE'S CAR' TO PUT GERMANY ON WHEELS – ONE OF HIS
BETTER IDEAS, INDEED. IT WAS ORIGINALLY THE 'KRAFT DURCH FREUDE', THE
'STRENGTH THROUGH JOY' CAR, AND THE BASIC SHAPE FOR A REAR-ENGINED FOUR-
SEATER FAMILY CAR WAS ARRIVED AT BY DESIGNER FERDINAND PORSCHE IN 1938
AFTER MANY PROTOTYPES. THE ALLIED FORCES THOUGHT IT WAS DAFT, BUT THEY
WERE WRONG. ON FEBRUARY 17, 1972, THE 15,007,034TH EXAMPLE WAS BUILT,
MAKING IT THE WORLD'S BIGGEST-SELLING DESIGN – AND IT CONTINUES IN
MANUFACTURE (IN MEXICO) TO THIS DAY.

## 04

# JEEP, 1940

TRULY DESIGNED BY SOLDIERS, THE JEEP BECAME A SYMBOL OF THE USA. MORE
THAN 600,000 EXAMPLES WERE MADE DURING THE SECOND WORLD WAR AND
GENERAL GEORGE MARSHALL ONCE CALLED THE JEEP 'AMERICA'S GREATEST
CONTRIBUTION TO MODERN WARFARE'. IN 1938, THE US ARMY PUT OUT A TENDER
FOR A LIGHT MILITARY ALL-PURPOSE VEHICLE, AND WILLYS-OVERLAND'S CONCEPT
WAS SELECTED. IT BOASTED SELECTABLE TWO- OR FOUR-WHEEL DRIVE, AN 80IN
WHEELBASE AND A 660LB PAYLOAD. JEEP SOON BECAME A HOUSEHOLD WORD, A
SLURRING OF THE ACRONYM GP, FOR GENERAL PURPOSE. AFTER THE WAR, WILLYS
REGISTERED THE DISTINGUISHED JEEP NAME AS A TRADEMARK.

## 05

# KAISER FRAZER SEDAN, 1946

NEW ERA, NEW COMPANY, NEW CAR – WHEN THE SECOND WORLD WAR WAS
FINISHED, KAISER TURNED FROM MAKING WARSHIPS TO MOTOR CARS, AND
EMPLOYED FREELANCE INDUSTRIAL DESIGNER HOWARD DARRIN TO STYLE THEM. HIS
1946 FRONT-WHEEL DRIVE, FOUR-DOOR SEDAN, UNDOUBTEDLY SLAB-SIDED, SET THE
SCENE FOR A NEW GENERATION. ANY SUGGESTION OF 'MUDGUARDS', SEPARATE
WINGS, FREE-STANDING BONNET OR OTHER CARRIAGE THROWBACKS WAS
COMPLETELY BANISHED. THIS WAS FULL-WIDTH, 'PONTOON' STYLING AT ITS MOST
BRUTAL AND WAS MUCH COPIED IN EUROPE, MOST OPENLY BY FIAT AND SINGER.

## FERRARI 166 BARCHETTA, 1947

YOU CAN PROBABLY IMAGINE THE IMPACT THIS LITHE, PURPOSEFUL TWO-SEATER MADE IN AN AGE WHEN AMERICAN SPORTS CAR LOVERS WERE SNAPPING UP THE ANTEDILUVIAN MG TD AS THE LATEST THING FROM EUROPE. IT WAS ALMOST CERTAINLY THE PERSONAL WORK OF CARLO ANDERLONI, WORKING WITH ITALIAN COACHBUILDER TOURING, BUT NEVER PERSONALLY CREDITED WITH DESIGN OF THE BARCHETTA. AT THE TIME, THE TINY TERROR'S SCULPTED CONTOURS AND CLEVER SWAGE LINE (TO BREAK UP THE 'LITTLE BOAT' SIDE PROFILE) WERE THE LAST WORD IN SIMPLE BEAUTY. AC'S ACE AND COBRA OWE THEIR INSPIRATION TO ANDERLONI'S CLEAR THINKING BUT ARE ALTOGETHER CLUMSIER.

## CISITALIA 202, 1947

THE WORK OF PININFARINA'S GIOVANNI SOVUNUZZI, THIS IS THE FIRST GT OF ALL, AND QUITE STUNNINGLY BEAUTIFUL. IT WAS ONE OF THE EXHIBITS CHOSEN FOR A 1950 EXHIBITION AT NEW YORK'S MUSEUM OF MODERN ART ENTITLED 'EIGHT AUTOMOBILES'. THE CURATOR, ARTHUR DREXLER, CALLED THE CISITALIA 'ROLLING SCULPTURE'... AND IT WAS THE ONLY ONE OF THE CARS TO REMAIN IN MOMA'S PERMANENT COLLECTION – A UNIQUE ACCOLADE. SOVUNUZZI WAS AT FIAT WHEN HE DREW THE FIRST IDEAS, FINALLY SEEING THEM COME TO FRUITION WHEN HE MOVED TO PININFARINA. DETAILS OF THE 202 WERE TAKEN UP IN CARS AS FAR REMOVED AS THE BENTLEY CONTINENTAL AND THE PORSCHE 356..

## LANCIA AURELIA B20, 1953

LANCIA HAS A LONG HISTORY OF DISTINGUISHED DESIGN, BUT THIS EXAMPLE BY PININFARINA IS THE MOST HANDSOME OF THEM ALL: IT REPRESENTS THE ORIGINS OF THE SPORTING FASTBACK. WITH A POWERFUL V6 ENGINE AND A GEARBOX IN THE BACK AXLE, THE CAR HAD PERFECT WEIGHT DISTRIBUTION, MAKING IT A FAVOURITE FOR RALLYING IN THE HANDS OF WEALTHY SPORTSMEN, BUT THE SLEEK, ELEGANT AND SOPHISTICATED SHAPE WAS WHAT ENDEARED IT TO ONLOOKERS. ALMOST 4,000 WERE BUILT, AND TODAY THEY'RE HIGHLY PRIZED. THE LATER SPIDER VERSION, ALSO DESIGNED AT PININFARINA, WAS, IF ANYTHING, EVEN MORE GLAMOROUS, YET IN A MUCH FLASHIER WAY.

## ALFA ROMEO GIULIETTA SPRINT, 1954

THIS WAS THE CAR THAT BROUGHT THE SHOW CAR GLAMOUR AND STYLING DRAMA OF BERTONE'S BAT SHOW CARS TO THE PUBLIC AT AN AFFORDABLE PRICE... AND SAVED THE OLD-ESTABLISHED TURIN COACHBUILDER FROM FINANCIAL DOOM. THOUSANDS WERE MADE AND SOLD THROUGH ALFA ROMEO'S DEALERS UNTIL 1962. STYLIST FRANCO SCAGLIONE'S FINEST HOUR WAS SPENT IN SUCCESSFULLY UNITING A 'STRAIGHT-THROUGH' WINGLINE WITH A TEARDROP SHAPE, YET STILL ALLOWING THE CAR TO BE A PRACTICAL AND AFFORDABLE GT. THE GIULIA SS COUPÉ HE CREATED IN 1955 FOR BERTONE AND ALFA ROMEO WAS MORE EXTREME BUT TOUCHED FAR FEWER LIVES THAN THE SPRINT.

## CHEVROLET CORVETTE, 1953

WHEN 'MOTORAMA', A DAZZLING ROADSHOW FOR GENERAL MOTORS' LATEST MODELS, OPENED AT THE WALDORF HOTEL IN NEW YORK IN JANUARY 1953, NO-ONE EXPECTED A NEW SPORTS CAR TO TAKE CENTRE STAGE. BUT FOR THE FIRST TIME CHIEF STYLIST HARLEY EARL HAD CREATED A 'DREAM' CAR THAT LOOKED PRODUCTION-READY, AND THE PUBLIC REACTION TO THIS BOLD GLASS FIBRE ROADSTER WAS SO ENTHUSIASTIC THAT GM GAVE IT THE IMMEDIATE GREEN LIGHT. AMAZINGLY, THE CORVETTE WENT FROM CLAY MODEL TO SHOWROOM IN JUST 15 MONTHS, BUT SUCH EXPEDIENCY MEANT AN ANCIENT SIX-CYLINDER ENGINE WAS USED. A LATER V8 CONVERSION TURNED THE CAR'S PATCHY SALES FORTUNES AROUND.

## MERCEDES-BENZ 300SL, 1954

MUCH MORE THAN JUST A RACING CAR DRESSED UP FOR THE ROAD, THE 300SL WAS AN AWESOME MACHINE BOTH TO LOOK AT AND TO DRIVE, A HIGH-TECH, 150MPH SPORTS CAR BUILT EXPRESSLY FOR CROSSING CONTINENTS. WITH ITS GULLWING DOORS, BLISTERED WHEELARCHES AND SMOOTHLY CURVED TAIL, THE 300SL WAS ONE OF THE MOST INSTANTLY RECOGNISABLE SHAPES ON THE ROAD, AND ALSO ONE OF THE FASTEST: ONLY A HANDFUL OF HANDBUILT FERRARIS AND MASERATIS COULD CATCH IT. 'SL' STOOD FOR SUPER LIGHT BECAUSE THE BODY – BUILT IN STEEL WITH ALUMINIUM PANELS – WAS SUPPORTED BY A COMPLEX SPACEFRAME OF LIGHTWEIGHT TUBES.

## CITROEN DS19, 1955

TODAY, IT'S ALMOST IMPOSSIBLE TO IMAGINE THE IMPACT THE DS MADE AT ITS LAUNCH; EVERY OTHER CAR, WHETHER EUROPEAN OR AMERICAN, WAS RENDERED OLD-FASHIONED OVERNIGHT BY ITS SPACE-AGE LINES. IT WAS PACKED WITH NEW TECHNOLOGY, INCLUDING HYDRO-PNEUMATIC SUSPENSION, POWERED GEARSHIFT AND INDICATOR LAMPS MOUNTED IN THE PLASTIC ROOF PANEL, BUT THE PUBLIC AT THE 1955 PARIS SHOW CRANED THEIR NECKS TO SEE ITS SHAPE. IT WAS CREATED NOT BY A CAR STYLIST BUT A SCULPTOR CALLED FLAMINIO BERTONI. IT'S SAID TO HAVE INSPIRED FRENCH CULTURAL CRITIC ROLAND BARTHES TO SAY 'CARS ARE OUR CATHEDRALS'.

## CHRYSLER 300, 1955

AS WELL AS BEING A CLOSET SUPERCAR IN ITS PERFORMANCE CAPABILITY, CHRYSLER DESIGN CHIEF VIRGIL EXNER'S CLEAN, LEAN BUT BARREL-SIDED TWO-DOOR SPORTS SALOON – CHRYSLER'S TOP-OF-THE-RANGE MODEL AT THE TIME – BOASTED AN EXCEPTIONALLY STYLISH SHAPE, ESPECIALLY WHEN COMPARED TO THE CHROME-STREWN EXCESSES OF CONTEMPORARY CADILLAC AND LINCOLN RIVALS. AS THE YEARS ROLLED BY, THOUGH, THE VARIOUS SERIES OF THE 300 PUT ON WEIGHT AND DECORATIVE FLAB, AND THE ORIGINAL 300, THE INSPIRATION FOR SUCH ELEGANT CARS AS THE VOLVO AMAZON, ROVER 3-LITRE AND PEUGEOT 403, BECAME A FORGOTTEN INNOVATOR.

## BMW 507, 1955

THE PATRICIAN GERMAN ARISTOCRAT COUNT ALBRECHT GOERTZ, STILL VERY MUCH ALIVE, HAS DESIGNED A MERE HANDFUL OF CARS INCLUDING THE DATSUN 240Z, BUT HIS FIRST, THIS TWO-SEATER BMW, IS PERHAPS HIS FINEST. THAT THE CAR WAS A BIT OF A HOLLYWOOD SPECIAL DISGUISED THE FACT ITS PROPORTIONS WERE BEAUTIFULLY BALANCED – THE NOSE TREATMENT WAS STILL BEING COPIED A DECADE LATER FOR CARS LIKE THE ISO GRIFO, AND THE ENTIRE CAR HAS BEEN RECREATED, IN PASTICHE, AS THE BMW Z8. COUNT GOERTZ WAS ALSO RESPONSIBLE FOR THE BMW 503, THE GERMAN COMPANY'S FIRST LARGE COUPÉ AND THE SPIRITUAL FORERUNNER OF THE RECENT 8 SERIES.

## FIAT NUOVA 500, 1957

FIAT'S CHIEF ENGINEER DANTE GIACOSA, WHO HELD THE POSITION FOR AN ASTONISHING 40 YEARS, SAT AT THE HEAD OF THE TEAM, OF WHICH MOST OTHER MEMBERS ARE UNCREDITED, THAT CREATED THE NUOVA 500 IN 1957. IT WAS SIMILAR IN SIZE TO THE ORIGINAL 1936 TOPOLINO (ITALIAN FOR LITTLE MOUSE), BUT THE ENGINE WAS AT THE BACK, AND THE EGG-LIKE SHAPE WAS GLORIOUSLY CRAFTED AND MODERN. ONE STYLE ICON, THE VESPA SCOOTER, HAD ALREADY PUT ITALY ON TWO WHEELS; NOW THE LITTLE CINQUECENTO GAVE MANY ITALIANS THEIR FIRST TASTE OF FOUR. IT WAS MADE UNTIL 1975 BUT HAS NEVER BEEN ADEQUATELY REPLACED IN THE HEARTS OF FIAT CUSTOMERS.

## LOTUS ELITE, 1957

A TECHNICAL MASTERPIECE BY COLIN CHAPMAN, THE ENGINEER-ENTREPRENEUR, AND PETER KIRWAN-TAYLOR, A TALENTED AMATEUR STYLIST WHO WAS, BY DAY, AN ACCOUNTANT. THE ELITE WAS THE FIRST PROPER LOTUS ROAD CAR, A SOPHISTICATED LITTLE GT BLESSED WITH SUPERB HANDLING AND MEMORABLE LOOKS. IT WAS THE FIRST CAR TO HAVE A GLASSFIBRE MONOCOQUE BODY STRUCTURE. POWER CAME FROM AN OVERHEAD-CAMSHAFT 1216CC COVENTRY CLIMAX ENGINE, ORIGINALLY DESIGNED AS A FIRE-FIGHTING WATER PUMP, GIVING 118MPH IN LATER VERSIONS. THE HIGH TOP SPEED WAS ATTRIBUTABLE TO THE LOW-DRAG SHAPE: ITS AMAZING 0.29 DRAG CO-EFFICIENT IS LARGELY UNMATCHED TODAY.

## LOTUS 7, 1957

LOTUS WENT BACK IN TIME FOR THE 7, TO THE DAYS WHEN A ROAD CAR'S BODYWORK WAS ONLY THERE FOR THE MOST PRACTICAL OF REASONS – TO CLAD THE GUTS OF THE BEAST AND ITS DRIVER JUST LIGHTLY ENOUGH FOR THE PURPOSE. THE FACT COLIN CHAPMAN'S BUDGET SPORTS RACER'S HANDLING WAS FROM A DIFFERENT LIGHTNING-QUICK PLANET TO PRE-WAR SPORTS CARS MADE ITS BASIC LOOKS (WITH PROMINENT HEADLAMPS AND CYCLE-TYPE WINGS) ALL THE MORE ACCEPTABLE TO SPORTS CAR LOVERS. AND, OF COURSE, IT'S STILL VERY MUCH WITH US AS THE CATERHAM SEVEN... AND A FLOCK OF IMITATORS.

## AUSTIN-HEALEY 3000, 1959

THE HEALEY 100 PROTOTYPE WAS THE STAR OF THE 1952 LONDON MOTOR SHOW –
THE WORLD'S CHEAPEST 100MPH SPORTS CAR AND CERTAINLY AMONG THE MOST
BEAUTIFUL. OVER DINNER ON THE EVE OF THE SHOW'S OPENING, AUSTIN'S LEONARD
LORD AND RACING DRIVER DONALD HEALEY WERE DEEP IN CONVERSATION. BY THE
TIME THE SHOW CLOSED, THE CAR WAS RECHRISTENED AUSTIN-HEALEY 100: A NEW
NAME HAD BEEN ADDED TO BRITAIN'S ROLL-CALL OF SPORTING MARQUES. BY 1959,
WITH A LARGER ENGINE, A RESTYLED NOSE AND THE ADOPTION OF DISTINCTIVE TWO-
TONE PAINT, THE A-H 3000 BECAME THE ULTIMATE STYLE INCARNATION OF THE
BREED.

## CADILLAC ELDORADO, 1959

THIS WAS HARLEY EARL'S LAST CAR, AND THE ULTIMATE IN AUTOMOTIVE BAROQUE:
20FT LONG, MASSIVE TAILFINS SOARING UP AN UNPRECEDENTED 42IN, AND JET-AGE
IMAGERY ACCENTUATED BY A PAIR OF BULLET-SHAPED TURN AND STOP LIGHTS
MOUNTED IN THOSE FINS. EARL SAID ABOUT IT: 'WE HAVEN'T DEPRECIATED THESE
CARS, WE'VE APPRECIATED YOUR MIND'. FRONT-END STYLING WAS EQUALLY
DISTINCTIVE, WITH TWIN HEADLIGHTS AND A DOUBLE-DECKER GRILLE. THE 1959
CARS CAME AS TWO-DOOR COUPÉ DE VILLES, PILLARLESS FOUR-DOOR HARDTOPS OR
AS AN EVEN BIGGER FLEETWOOD 75 FORMAL LIMOUSINE. BEST REMEMBERED,
THOUGH, IS THE ELDORADO BIARRITZ CONVERTIBLE. AND BEST REMEMBERED OF
THAT IS ANY EXAMPLE PAINTED PINK.

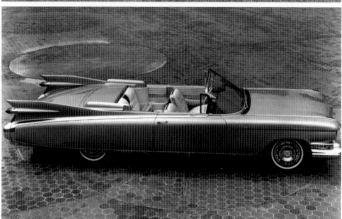

## JAGUAR MKII, 1959

IT WAS THE CUSTOM FOR JAGUAR'S FOUNDER AND INDUSTRY DYNAMO WILLIAM
LYONS TO TAKE THE CREDIT FOR HIS CARS' LOOKS. AND WHILE HE PROBABLY DIDN'T
HAVE THE TIME TO DO ALL THE PEN-WORK, HIS UNERRING EYE FOR GREAT LINES WAS
WHAT MADE JAGUARS LOOK SO GOOD. FOR THE MKII, HE WAS UPDATING AN OLDER
CAR, THE RETROSPECTIVELY NAMED MKI, BUT HIS REVISIONS TO THE CABIN, WING
LINE, FRONT AND REAR, MADE THE PREDECESSOR LOOK LIKE A SLUG IN
COMPARISON. SOME 33 YEARS ON IN THE MID-1990S, CHRYSLER APED THE
ROUNDED CURVE OF THE CABIN WINDOWS FOR ITS NEW LH SEDAN.

## AUSTIN MINI, 1959

ALEC ISSIGONIS ALWAYS RAILED AGAINST THE IDEA THAT HE EVER JUST 'STYLED'
ANYTHING, OF COURSE. YET ISSIGONIS' MINI SHAPE, ONLY THERE FOR ITS PURPOSE
OF CLOTHING WHAT WAS THEN THE MOST INNOVATIVE, BEST HANDLING AND
ROOMIEST SMALL CAR IN THE WORLD, IS NONETHELESS UNDOUBTEDLY A DESIGN
CLASSIC IN ITS PROFILE ALONE. SURPRISINGLY, CLOSE IMITATORS WERE FEW, HONDA
GETTING PERHAPS NEAREST WITH ITS N360 AND N600; BUT THEY WERE AWKWARD
AND CRAMPED, WHICH MUST HAVE MADE ISSIGONIS SMILE WRYLY THROUGH HIS
CUSTOMARY HAZE OF CIGARETTE SMOKE. HIS FORM-FOLLOWING-FUNCTION
PERSISTED IN THE BMC 1100 AND 1800 CARS, ALTHOUGH PININFARINA DID ITS BEST
TO CIVILISE HIS DESIGN BRUTALISM.

## 22

## CHEVROLET CORVAIR, 1960

COMPARED TO THE CADILLACS OF THE YEAR BEFORE, THE CORVAIR WAS ALMOST STARK IN ITS DESIGN. THE INSPIRATION OF GENERAL MOTORS DESIGNER NED NICKLES, WORKING FOR BILL MITCHELL, ITS CLEAN AND SIMPLE LINES, WITH A PROMINENT STYLING 'WAIST' RUNNING ALL ROUND THE BODY AND A DEEPLY WRAPPED-AROUND REAR WINDOW, INSPIRED A GENERATION OF CAR STYLISTS IN 1960S EUROPE: JUST LOOK AT THE NSU PRINZ, HILLMAN IMP, FIAT 1500 AND SIMCA 1000. IT WAS TECHNICALLY FASCINATING TOO, WITH AN AIR-COOLED SIX-CYLINDER ENGINE IN THE BACK, BUT TRICKY HANDLING MADE THE CORVAIR A CAUSE CELEBRE FOR AMERICAN SAFETY CAMPAIGNER RALPH NADER, AND IT'S FOREVER TARNISHED AS A RESULT.

## 23

## ASTON MARTIN DB4, 1961

A PERFECT COCKTAIL OF ANGLO-SAXON MANNERS AND ITALIAN STYLE, THIS ESSENTIALLY ENGLISH CAR HAD A BODY DESIGNED BY TOURING OF MILAN, ONE OF THE TRADITIONAL OLD *CARROZZERIE*. IT WAS THE ULTIMATE BRITISH TOURER AND THE FIRST ENTIRELY NEW ASTON MARTIN ROAD CAR UNDER THE DAVID BROWN REGIME. THE DB4 HAD A BRAND NEW CHASSIS AND DOUBLE-OVERHEAD-CAMSHAFT ENGINE DELIVERING 240BHP. TOURING PROVIDED THE SVELTE BODY STYLE AND ITS SUPERLEGGERA CONSTRUCTION SYSTEM – ALUMINIUM PANELS ON A THIN TUBULAR FRAMEWORK. IT RETAINED THE BULLDOG AURA OF THE DB2, BUT BOASTED A 140MPH TOP SPEED. THE LATER DB4 GT ZAGATO WAS JUST AS STRIKING IN A VERY DIFFERENT WAY, AND EVEN FASTER.

## 24

## JAGUAR E-TYPE, 1961

ONLY THE SECOND CAR TO BE INCLUDED IN THE PERMANENT COLLECTION OF NEW YORK'S MUSEUM OF MODERN ART, TO MANY PEOPLE THE E-TYPE IS THE MOST BEAUTIFUL CAR EVER. THERE'S SOMETHING PHALLIC ABOUT IT, CERTAINLY, BUT IT WAS THE COOL AERODYNAMIC THEORY OF A STREAMLINING EXPERT MALCOLM SAYER, TOGETHER WITH THE SHOWMANSHIP OF HIS EMPLOYER WILLIAM LYONS, THAT CREATED THE WINNING FORMULA. THAT SLEEK PROFILE WAS INSPIRED BY THE LE MANS-WINNING JAGUAR D-TYPE BUT THE FINAL SERIES III CAR OF 1971, WHICH PIONEERED JAGUAR'S AWESOME V12 ENGINE, HAD A SOFTER, FATTER BODY SHAPE TOTALLY LACKING THE ORIGINAL E'S FIERCE BEAUTY.

## 25

## LINCOLN CONTINENTAL, 1961

THE 'CLAP-DOOR' CONTINENTAL IS ONE OF AMERICA'S MOST INFLUENTIAL CARS. ESCHEWING THE FINS AND CHROME THEN STILL POPULAR ON MOST 'DOMESTIC' CARS LINCOLN LAUNCHED A CAR WITH CLEAN, UNADORNED LINES, AMERICAN IN SCALE BUT ALMOST EUROPEAN IN FEEL; SLAB-SIDED, MAGNIFICENT AND UNFORGETTABLE. MEMBERS OF THE DESIGN TEAM INCLUDED EUGENE BORDINAT, DON DE LA ROSSA AND ELWOOD ENGLE. THE REAR-HINGED REAR DOOR GAVE IT THE CLAP-DOOR NICKNAME AND IT BECAME THE 'IN' CAR WITH THE RICH AND FAMOUS. ENDORSEMENT BY THE WHITE HOUSE WAS GREAT TOO, ALBEIT WITH THE UNFORTUNATE CONSEQUENCE THAT IT WAS IN A STRETCHED CLAP-DOOR CONTINENTAL THAT PRESIDENT KENNEDY WAS ASSASINATED IN DALLAS IN 1963.

## FERRARI 250GTO, 1962

ONE OF THE GREATEST SPORTS RACING CARS OF ALL TIME, THE V12 GTO SCORED A 1,2,3 IN ITS CLASS AT LE MANS IN 1962 AND 1963, AND TOOK THE INTERNATIONAL GT RACING CHAMPIONSHIP THE FOLLOWING YEAR. TO APPRECIATE THE FRONT-ENGINED, V12 GTO IS TO DRIVE IT, SAY CONNOISSEURS, AND IT WAS SUPPOSEDLY CAPABLE OF 180MPH. YET ITS SWOOPING AND PURPOSEFUL TWO-SEATER COUPÉ BODYWORK BY GIOTTO BIZZARRINI (MAKING IT ONE OF THE FEW FERRARIS NOT DESIGNED BY PININFARINA), IS JUST AS NOTEWORTHY. IT'S PLEASINGLY UNADORNED, APART FROM SEVERAL VERY NECESSARY AIR INTAKES, AND IS AMONG THE MOST EVOCATIVE OF SPORTS CAR PROFILES FROM WHAT'S NOW SEEN AS A GOLDEN AGE OF MOTOR SPORT.

## JEEP WAGONEER, 1963

OKAY, OKAY, YOU'D NEVER CALL IT BEAUTIFUL, BUT THE CHUNKY WAGONEER REALLY DID DEFINE THE BOXY, MACHO SHAPE THAT TODAY WE TAKE FOR GRANTED (OR SNEER AT) IN THE RANGE ROVER, MITSUBISHI SHOGUN, ISUZU TROOPER AND A WHOLE RAFT OF AMERICAN TERRAIN-BUSTERS FROM THE FORD BRONCO TO THE CHEVY BLAZER. AT THE TIME, BROOKS STEVENS' MASSIVE ESTATE CAR DESIGN WAS THE MOST CAR-LIKE 4X4 YOU COULD GET, AND IT HAS HELPED CREATE A WHOLE NEW CATEGORY OF SO-CALLED SPORTS- UTILITY VEHICLES WHICH, TOGETHER WITH PICK-UPS, NOW EASILY OUT-SELL 'ORDINARY' CARS IN THE US EACH YEAR.

## PORSCHE 911, 1963

THE GREATEST-EVER SPORTS CAR, MANY THINK, WAS DRAWN BY FERDINAND ALEXANDER 'BUTZI' PORSCHE, THE ELDEST SON OF THE COMPANY FOUNDER. BUT IT CAN TRACE ITS ORIGINS DIRECTLY BACK TO HITLER'S VOLKSWAGEN, WITH WHICH THE ORIGINAL PORSCHE 356 SHARED ITS UNDERPINNINGS. AFTER 40 YEARS, TODAY'S 911 IS STILL UNMISTAKABLY RECOGNISABLE AS A DIRECT DESCENDENT OF BUTZI PORSCHE'S 1963 SLOPE-BACKED ORIGINAL. THE IMAGE HAS FLUCTUATED OVER THE YEARS, THOUGH: FOR THE 1960S AND '70S BUYER, THE 911 WAS THE CHOICE OF THE SEASONED AFICIONADO. BY THE MID-'80S, IT BECAME A YUPPIE ICON. FOR SOME, INCLUDING PORSCHE, THAT IMAGE HAS LINGERED A LITTLE TOO LONG.

## FORD MUSTANG, 1964

THE MUSTANG WAS A SPORTY COMPACT CAR WITH YOUTHFUL APPEAL THAT CAPTURED THE SPIRIT OF THE TIMES PERFECTLY. IT WAS ALSO ONE OF THE FASTEST SELLING CARS OF ALL TIME – 418,000 IN 1964 ALONE. BRAINCHILD OF HIGH-FLYING FORD EXECUTIVE LEE IACOCCA, THE MUSTANG WAS BASED ON THE FLOORPAN OF THE BUDGET FALCON RANGE, AND ITS CRISP, PSEUDO-EUROPEAN STYLING CAME IN NOTCHBACK, FASTBACK AND CONVERTIBLE FORM AND COULD BE ORDERED WITH A VAST RANGE OF TRIM AND POWER OPTIONS. THE BASIC, PRETTY SHAPE CONTINUED FAIRLY UNADULTERATED UNTIL 1968, WHEN RIVALS FINALLY CAUGHT UP WITH THEIR OWN 'PONY' CARS.

## 30

## ROLLS-ROYCE SILVER SHADOW, 1965

IT WAS A SHOCK FOR ROLLS-ROYCE TRADITIONALISTS, THE SILVER SHADOW. IN ONE BOLD MOVE, THE GENTLY FLOWING LINES OF THE OLD SILVER CLOUD WERE SWEPT AWAY. HERE WAS A BOXY, MODERN ROLLS WITH FEATURES LIKE SELF-LEVELLING SUSPENSION AND ALL-ROUND DISC BRAKES AND, THE BIGGEST SEA-CHANGE OF ALL, NO SEPARATE CHASSIS. IT WAS NOT ONLY EVEN QUIETER AND MORE SERENE TO BE IN THAN ITS ILLUSTRIOUS PREDECESSOR, BUT WAS ALSO FASTER, MORE ECONOMICAL AND MUCH LESS OF A 'CHAUFFEUR'S CAR'. LIKE THE CLOUD BEFORE IT, THE SHADOW WAS THE WORK OF JOHN BLATCHLEY, AND THERE WAS, AS USUAL, A BENTLEY VERSION, CALLED THE T-SERIES.

## 31

## RENAULT 16, 1965

FRENCH 'TWO-BOX' CARS (ONE 'BOX' FOR THE ENGINE AND ANOTHER FOR THE PASSENGERS AND THEIR STUFF) HAD BEEN AROUND FOR AGES. THINK OF THE CITROEN 2CV, RENAULT 4CV AND PEUGEOT 203. BUT THE 16 NOT ONLY MADE A VIRTUE OF ITS SHAPE WITH A PROPER HATCHBACK AND FOLDING REAR SEATS, BUT GAVE FRENCH OWNERS A LITTLE GLAMOUR WITH ITS RAZOR-EDGED LINES AND THRUST-FORWARD STANCE. IT WAS A SYMBOL: A PRACTICAL CAR FOR THE BOURGEOISIE. AND ITS DESIGNER PHILIPPE CHARBONNEAUX, IN THOSE DAYS A CONSULTANT, HAD BEEN RESPONSIBLE FOR SOME OF THE MOST GLORIOUS POST-WAR COACHBUILT FRENCH PRESTIGE CARS.

## 32

## LAMBORGHINI MIURA, 1966

FERRUCCIO LAMBORGHINI WAS A TRACTOR-MAKER DETERMINED TO RIVAL FERRARI IN THE 1960S. ALTHOUGH HE WOULDN'T LET HIS YOUNG ENGINEERS BUILD A RACER, HE WAS HAPPY TO GIVE THE GO-AHEAD FOR THIS SHOW-STOPPING TWO-SEATER, BORROWING MID-ENGINED PRINCIPLES FROM THE LATEST F1 MACHINE. THE UNITARY CHASSIS WITH V12 ENGINE SITED TRANSVERSELY BEHIND THE COCKPIT WAS CLOTHED BY BERTONE, AND NUCCIO BERTONE PUT HIS BEST MAN ON THE JOB – 25-YEAR-OLD MARCELLO GANDINI. A BOLD, SENSUAL CAR THAT HAS LOST NONE OF ITS HEAD-TURNING APPEAL, THE 'EYELASHES' AROUND THE FLIP-UP LIGHTS WERE A MEMORABLE STYLING SIGNATURE. IT'S WIDELY ACKNOWLEDGED NOW AS THE FIRST SUPERCAR.

## OLDSMOBILE TORONADO, 1966

THE OLDSMOBILE TORONADO LOOKED LIKE NO AMERICAN CAR THAT WENT BEFORE IT
- THERE WERE NO FINS AND CHROME – AND YET TOO FEW 1970S STATESIDE
DESIGNS MADE USE OF ITS SQUEAKY CLEAN NOSE, FLIP-UP HEADLIGHTS, FLARED
WHEELARCHES AND NEAT, SIMPLE FLANKS. UNDERNEATH ITS BILL MITCHELL-DRAWN
CLOTHES, HOWEVER, WAS THE MOST UNUSUAL FEATURE: FRONT-WHEEL DRIVE,
RARE EVEN TODAY ON A V8-ENGINED LUXURY COUPÉ. TODAY'S BIG COUPÉS, THE
MERCEDES-BENZ CLS AND LEXUS SCS, DERIVE MORE FROM IT THAN THEIR
IMMEDIATE PREDECESSORS – BUT THAT'S 36 YEARS ON.

## BMW 1602, 1966

CAR DESIGN IS AN INTERNATIONAL LANGUAGE AND THINGS AREN'T ALWAYS AS THEY
SEEM. THE REMARKABLE SMALL BMW SALOON DEFINED AN APPARENTLY GERMAN
STYLE BUT, IN FACT, WAS LARGELY INSPIRED BY THE WORK OF GIOVANNI
MICHELOTTI, A LEADING ITALIAN CONSULTANT DESIGNER. HE ESTABLISHED THE
MODERN BMW LOOK WITH THE 1500 OF 1961, AN ALTOGETHER BIGGER CAR, BUT
THIS ATTRACTIVE SMALL SPORTS SALOON BROUGHT ITS TECHNICAL AND AESTHETIC
QUALITIES TO A WIDER AUDIENCE. DESPITE FINE HANDLING, AND BEAUTIFUL BUILD
QUALITY, CUSTOMERS STILL CLAMOURED FOR MORE POWER, AND BMW OBLIGED BY
FITTING A 2-LITRE VERSION OF THE SAME TWIN-CAMSHAFT ENGINE, CREATING THE
CLASSIC 2002.

## NSU RO80, 1967

IN THESE DAYS OF CONSTANTLY GOOD, MODERN SALOON CAR DESIGNS, IT WOULD
BE DIFFICULT TO REPEAT THE IMPACT CAUSED BY THE RO80. NEVER MIND ITS
FASCINATING ROTARY WANKEL ENGINEERING, THE LOOKS, CREATED BY THE GERMAN
COMPANY'S OWN KLAUS LUTHE, WERE FUTURISTIC BUT NEVER UNREALISTIC. LIGHT,
FLUID AND AIRY, HIS MASTERFUL STYLING MADE THE RO80 A TRUE LANDMARK.
WHEN THE 'AERODYNAMIC' AUDI 100 APPEARED IN 1982, IT DIDN'T APPEAR TO HAVE
PROGRESSED AT ALL – THE RO80 WAS THAT GOOD. AND, REMEMBER, FOR FOUR
YEARS IT WAS IN PRODUCTION AT THE SAME TIME AS THE DESPARATELY DATED
AUSTIN A60 CAMBRIDGE.

## RELIANT SCIMITAR GTE, 1968

A BRITISH INNOVATION THAT SPRANG FROM A GROUP OF INDEPENDENT ENGINEERS
AND INDUSTRIALISTS CALLED OGLE, PLUS DESIGNER TOM KAREN'S STYLING VISION.
THIS WAS THE FIRST FOUR-SEATER 'SPORTS ESTATE', MEANING YOU COULD CARRY
YOUR SACKS WITH A BIT OF SEX. FROM A COMPANY THAT DEALT WITH DESIGNING
RADIOS AND TRUCK CABS, THE DETAIL STYLING WAS QUITE SOMETHING, BUT THE
CONCEPT – WIDELY APED BY VOLVO, LANCIA, BMW, TOYOTA, HONDA, EVEN GILBERN
– WAS WHAT MADE A SOMETIMES IMPERFECT CAR A GREAT ONE. THE WINDOW LINE,
IN PARTICULAR, INFLUENCED MANY 1970S CARS, PARTICULARLY IN THE USA AND
JAPAN.

## DATSUN 240Z, 1969

JAPAN'S FIRST SUCCESSFUL SPORTS CAR, THE RAZOR-EDGED 240Z, DESIGNED BY COUNT ALBRECHT GOERTZ (HE OF BMW 507 FAME), WAS DESTINED TO BECOME THE BEST-SELLING SPORTS CAR OF THE 1970S. WHAT THE BADGE LACKED IN ROMANCE AND CACHET, THE 240Z MORE THAN MADE UP FOR WITH ITS WELL-BALANCED AND MUSCULAR LINES. WITH ITS LONG BONNET, RECESSED HEADLIGHTS AND THOSE TENSIONED REAR HAUNCHES, THE Z CLEARLY TOOK ITS STYLING CUES FROM THE JAGUAR E-TYPE FIXED-HEAD, YET IT WAS PURE AND ELEGANT ENOUGH – ASIDE FROM ITS GRUESOME WHEELTRIMS, A TYPICAL JAPANESE WEAKNESS – TO HAVE AN APPEAL ALL ITS OWN.

## RANGE ROVER, 1970

IN THE RANGE ROVER, DESIGNER DAVID BACHE CREATED A PERFECTLY PROPORTIONED STEREOTYPE THAT HAS ONLY BEEN IMITATED, NOT BETTERED. WHEN REVEALED IN JUNE 1970, THERE WAS NOTHING ELSE LIKE IT – NOTHING COMBINING SUCH TREMENDOUS GO-ANYWHERE ABILITY WITH GREAT RIDE QUALITY, SALOON CAR COMFORT AND A LEVEL OF STYLE WORLDS AWAY FROM LAND ROVER'S CRUDE SOLIDITY. ITS BODY HAD A NEWLY-PRESSED-SUIT CRISPNESS THAT, WHILE SUPREMELY FUNCTIONAL, ALSO MANAGED TO EXUDE UPPER-CLASS STYLE. WITHIN A YEAR THE WAITING LIST STRETCHED INTO INFINITY. IT'S STILL THE ONLY VEHICLE EVER EXHIBITED AT THE LOUVRE AS A MODERN SCULPTURE, AND BECAME AS POTENT A SYMBOL OF BRITAIN AS THE CLASSIC RED TELEPHONE BOX.

## FIAT 130 COUPÉ, 1971

UNTIL PAOLO MARTIN WENT FREELANCE AS AN INDEPENDENT INDUSTRIAL DESIGNER, HIS WAS THE UNSEEN HAND BEHIND PININFARINA'S 1970S GENERATION OF 'CHUNKY' DESIGNS – THE ROLLS-ROYCE CAMARGUE, THE PEUGEOT 604 AND THIS, HIS FINEST, THE COUPÉ VERSION OF THE LARGEST POST-WAR FIAT MODEL, THE 130. THE BALANCE OF THE GLASSHOUSE, THE PASSENGER SECTION STICKING ABOVE THE REST OF THE CAR, COMPENSATES FOR THE ABRUPTLY CHOPPED FRONT AND REAR ENDS – IN FACT, EVERY VIEW OF THE CAR HAS LASER-STRAIGHT LINES UNITED BY SUBTLE CURVES. IT REMAINS A MASTERPIECE, ALBEIT OF A STYLE THAT'S NOT BEEN SO FAR REVIVED.

## LAMBORGHINI COUNTACH, 1971

IN ITS LATER YEARS THE LAMBORGHINI COUNTACH BECAME A KIND OF PARODY OF ITSELF, A TACKY, BE-SPOILERED POSEMOBILE FOR ANYBODY WITH TOO MUCH MONEY AND NOT ENOUGH VULGARITY. BUT IT WASN'T ALWAYS A BYWORD FOR POPULIST TACK. THE ORIGINAL, BRIGHT YELLOW BERTONE-STYLED PROTOTYPE OF 1971, DESTINED TO SUPPLANT THE MIURA AS FERRUCCIO LAMBORGHINI'S FLAGSHIP ULTRACAR, WAS CERTAINLY DRAMATIC YET REMARKABLY PURE AND UNADORNED. BOTH CARS WERE THE WORK OF MARCELLO GANDINI BUT, WHERE THE MIURA WAS SENSUAL AND MUSCULAR THE COUNTACH WAS A FUTURISTIC, KNIFE-EDGED WEDGE. AT 186MPH, IT WAS EVEN FASTER THAN THE MIURA, AND 'COUNTACH' WAS A PIEDMONTESE EXPLETIVE MEANING 'WOW' – OR STRONGER.

## RENAULT 5, 1972

RENAULT'S RECORD OF INNOVATION WAS SUMMARISED BY THIS, THE DEFINITIVE
THREE-DOOR SUPERMINI HATCHBACK, DESIGNED BY MICHEL BOUÉ WHO,
TRAGICALLY, DIED AGED 35 EVEN BEFORE THE CAR WENT INTO PRODUCTION.
ALMOST ONE IN THREE NEW CARS SOLD IN EUROPE TODAY IS A SUPERMINI, AND THE
ULTRA-PRACTICAL AND EASY-TO-DRIVE FRONT-WHEEL-DRIVE SMALL HATCHBACK – THE
5 IS REMARKABLY SIMILAR TO MODERN INCARNATIONS – DEFINED THE MARKET
SECTOR IN ONE DEFT MOVE. ITS CLEAN-CUT TWO-BOX PROFILE, HATCHBACK OPENING
DOWN TO BUMPER LEVEL, AND PLASTIC-MOULDED BUMPERS AND DASHBOARD
MEANT THE 5 SET THE STANDARD ALL OTHERS FOLLOWED.

## VW GOLF, 1974

THE QUINTESSENTIAL HATCHBACK AND A LANDMARK DESIGN FOR GIORGETTO
GIUGIARO, THE GOLF WAS AS PURE IN ITS DESIGN PHILOSOPHY AS THE BEETLE THAT
HAD FEATHERED THE NEST FOR IT: A SIMPLE, RELIABLE, TRULY MODERN AND HIGH-
QUALITY MACHINE FOR THE PEOPLE. JUST LIKE THE BEETLE. AND, JUST LIKE THE
BEETLE, DETROIT SCORNED. (GM'S BILL MITCHELL CALLED IT A 'BULLFROG THAT
SWALLOWED A BOX'). LIKE THE BEETLE, VW HAD THE LAST LAUGH. OLD GOLFS DON'T
DIE EASILY, SO IT WILL BE YEARS BEFORE ITS IMPORTANCE, DUE TO ITS RARITY, IS
RECOGNISED PROPERLY. IT ESTABLISHED A STANDARD OF AESTHETIC CLARITY IN ITS
SECTOR.

## RENAULT ESPACE, 1984

THE ESPACE, ACKNOWLEDGED AS THE PIONEER AND STYLE-SETTER OF EUROPEAN MULTI-PURPOSE VEHICLES, HAS A TWISTED GENESIS. IT ORIGINATED IN THE BRITISH DESIGN STUDIOS OF CHRYSLER EUROPE, AND WAS SET TO BE BUILT BY THE COMPANY'S PARTNER MATRA. THEN CHRYSLER EUROPE WAS SOLD TO PEUGEOT, AND THE DESIGN, ORIGINALLY BY FERGUS POLLOCK, WAS REFINED BY MATRA'S ANTOINE VOLANIS, THE STYLIST WHO DESIGNED EVERY MATRA MODEL FROM THE DJET TO THE RANCHO. THE ESPACE WAS AMONG THE FIRST 'PEOPLE CARRIERS'; IRONICALLY, CHRYSLER IN THE US PIONEERED THE SECTOR WITH ITS VOYAGER A YEAR EARLIER, BUT VOLANIS' ELEGANT 'ONE-BOX' DESIGN FOR SEVEN OCCUPANTS WAS STREETS AHEAD IN THE STYLE STAKES.

## 44

## FERRARI TESTAROSSA, 1984

FERRARI WAS THERE AT THE RIGHT TIME WITH THE RIGHT CAR IN THE MID-1980S. THE DRAMATIC V12 TESTAROSSA SUPERCAR, WITH ITS PININFARINA-DESIGNED AND BUILT TWO-SEATER BODYWORK AND MID-MOUNTED V12 ENGINE, WAS THE DARLING OF THE THRUSTING 1980S ENTREPRENEUR. AS A CONSEQUENCE, BETWEEN 1984 AND 1992, THE 7,177 SOLD MADE IT THE MOST POPULAR SINGLE FERRARI MODEL OF ALL TIME. WIDE, LOW AND SPORTING DISTINCTIVE HEAVILY SLATTED SIDE PANELS, PININFARINA APPLIED AS MUCH SCIENCE AS SHOWMANSHIP TO ITS DESIGN, THOROUGHLY WIND TUNNEL-TESTING THE TESTAROSSA BEFORE IT WENT ON SALE.

## 45

## TVR GRIFFITH 1990

SPORTS CARMAKER TVR COULD BEST HAVE BEEN DESCRIBED AS THE PROVIDER OF CARS FOR DEDICATED ENTHUSIASTS WHEN, IN 1990, IT UNVEILED THE PROTOTYPE FOR A SPORTS CAR SO BEAUTIFUL THAT IT ACHIEVED INSTANT CLASSIC STATUS. TWO YEARS LATER AND THE CAR, THE GRIFFITH, WAS ON SALE: MORE THAN A DECADE ON, IT HAS HARDLY DATED. TVR'S MODUS OPERANDI IS LEGENDARILY LEFT-FIELD COMPARED TO ACCEPTED MOTOR INDUSTRY PRACTICE, AND THE FACT SUCH A SIMPLE, WELL-PROPORTIONED AND THOROUGHLY EMOTIONAL DESIGN SHOULD EMERGE FROM A VIRTUAL COTTAGE INDUSTRY IS TESTIMONY TO ITS SMALL-TIME STRATEGY WORKING.

## 46

## RENAULT MÉGANE SCÉNIC, 1995

PATRICK LE QUÉMENT, DESIGN HEAD OF RENAULT, HAS BUILT UP AN ENVIABLE REPUTATION AS A CAR DESIGN MAVERICK AND, INDEED, THE RENAULT SCÉNIC BROKE NEW GROUND IN 1995 AS EUROPE'S FIRST MINI-MPV (THE FIRST OF ALL HAD BEEN THE 1991 MITSUBISHI SPACE RUNNER). APART FROM ITS ATTRACTIVE, ROUNDED EXTERIOR, THE CAR'S CLEVER INTERIOR, THE WORK OF ANTHONY GRADE, STRUCK A CHORD WITH CONSUMERS, WHO LIKED ITS VERSATILE SEATING, MULTIPLE STORAGE AREAS, AND TOUGH REAR PARCEL SHELF. THE CAR BECAME AN INSTANT BEST-SELLER ACROSS EUROPE, LEAVING RIVALS SCRABBLING TO CATCH UP.

## FORD KA, 1996

FORD'S CURVY LITTLE HATCHBACK WAS PREVIEWED IN 1994 WITH A CHERRY RED DOPPELGANGER BEARING THE SAME NAME. INDEED, 'KA' SEEMED A TYPICALLY SILLY CONCEPT CAR NAME, A TONGUE-IN-CHEEK TAKE ON 'CAR' GUARANTEED TO MAKE YOU SMIRK. IT WAS THE WORK OF CHRIS SVENSSON, WHO SHOWED OFF HIS IDEAS FOR HOW A SHARP-LOOKING, FUTURISTIC SMALL CAR MIGHT LOOK AT THE 1992 ROYAL COLLEGE OF ART GRADUATION SHOW. THE KA WENT ON SALE FOUR YEARS LATER, ITS CUDDLY CURVES SHARPENED UP INTO 'NEW EDGE' ELLIPSES AND ITS HUGE PLASTIC BUMPERS ALSO FORMING THE LOWER WINGS TO CREATE AN EFFECT, IF ANYTHING, MORE DISTINCTIVE THAN THE CONCEPT.

## TOYOTA RAV4, 1997

THE RAV4 REPRESENTED A WATERSHED IN THE MARCH OF FOUR-WHEEL DRIVE INTO THE EVERYDAY LIVES OF ORDINARY MOTORISTS. IT WAS NOT THE FIRST SMALL SPORTS UTILITY VEHICLE: THAT WAS THE 1986 JEEP WRANGLER. BUT IT WAS EASILY THE MOST SUCCESSFUL COMBINATION OF ROAD CAR DYNAMICS, OFF-ROAD ABILITY AND HIGH-RIDING DRIVING POSITION. A CURIOUS STYLISTIC COMBINATION OF HATCHBACK, SPORTS CAR AND 4X4, BUYERS LOVED BOTH ITS LOOKS AND ITS ROAD BEHAVIOUR (AND ALMOST ALL WERE USED ON THE ROAD). A MKII VERSION HAS, TO SOME DEGREE, LOST THE RAV4'S INITIAL IMPACT.

## AUDI TT, 1999

ANOTHER CAR THAT BEGAN LIFE AS A WELL-CRAFTED CONCEPT CAR, THE TT, CONCEIVED BY FREEMAN THOMAS AND PETER SCHREYER, JUMPS THE SPECIES BARRIER BETWEEN AUTOMOBILE AND PRODUCT DESIGN. ITS SMOOTH, CLEAN LINES AND DEFINED CURVES ARE INSPIRED BY THE 1930S BAUHAUS DESIGN MOVEMENT IN GERMANY. IT WAS A MASTERFULLY SELF-CONSCIOUS EXERCISE IN CONSUMER PSYCHOLOGY THAT PROVED A HIT WITH BUYERS. YET THE CAR WAS ONLY MADE A PRODUCTION FEASIBILITY BY TECHNOLOGY ADVANCES IN PLATFORM-SHARING – ESSENTIALLY, AND UNDER THAT CHARACTERFUL SHAPE, THE TT IS THE SAME CAR AS THE VW GOLF AND SKODA OCTAVIA.

## MCC SMART, 2000

THE MICRO COMPACT CAR ORGANISATION WAS ORIGINALLY CONCEIVED BY SWISS WATCH TYCOON NICOLAS HAYEK TO REJUVENATE AN INTEREST IN MICROCARS THAT HAD BEEN ABSENT IN EUROPE SINCE THE AUSTERITY DAYS OF THE 1950S BUBBLE CAR. HE INTENDED TO DO THAT WITH DESIGN, SCHEMING THE PROTOTYPE FOR AN ULTRA-SHORT URBAN TWO-SEATER WHICH WOULD BE CHEAP AND FUN TO OWN. THE FINAL CAR, THE SMART, HAD INPUT FROM HIS FIRST PARTNER VOLKSWAGEN, AND THEN FROM MERCEDES-BENZ, WHICH BROUGHT THE CAR TO THE MARKET. PUNDITS DOUBTED WHETHER THE INNOVATIVE, COLOURFUL AND UPRIGHT CITY CAR WOULD WORK. BUYERS IN EVERY TRAFFIC-CHOKED EUROPEAN CITY HAVE PROVEN THEM WRONG.

04 | **REFERENCE**

## CONTENTS

## 04.01 | HOW DO I BECOME A CAR DESIGNER?

So you want to design cars like the professionals do – but where is it best to start? What are the crucial first steps that will set you on the correct – and hopefully successful – course?

These days almost all car designers have completed a course in vehicle or transportation design. However, an increasing number of the younger designers are beginning to come from industrial or product design backgrounds – particularly those working on automotive interior design. Some of these even go on to design vehicle exteriors.

Nevertheless, it's fair to say that the majority of young car designers are recruited from transportation design courses — meaning that if you are intent on designing cars for your living, this type of course will give you the best chance of achieving your ambition.

While some car companies do welcome the fresh, out-of-the-box input that graduates in disciplines such as textiles, furniture, product or even building design can often provide, most invariably rely on transport specialists for the bulk of their intake. So, given that enrolling on a transportation or industrial design course is likely to be the mainstream option, we have concentrated our listings on colleges that provide this type of course. Needless to say, many hundreds of establishments worldwide run design courses less closely focused on automotive but which could eventually lead to a job with a car company; to find these, an online search is probably the best first step.

## STUDYING CAR DESIGN

Despite the variety of programmes on offer, selecting the right course may not be as easy as it seems. There are many factors to consider. Some are obvious – such as the school's location and tuition fees – others are less so, such as the teaching faculty and the design school's philosophy and reputation.

It is also a good idea to find out whether the course offers work experience placements outside the course and within the car industry itself, in real working design studios. Many graduates return to their placement companies for full-time employment once they have graduated.

Different courses emphasise different aspects of transportation design. Some focus more on drawing than model-making, others have a stronger engineering bias. Some focus on other areas of transportation design while others only concentrate on car design.

There is no right or wrong course necessarily: all have their own advantages and limitations. Just be sure to choose a course that reflects what you want and ultimately what you want to do.

Remember, selecting the right course may be crucial to your success.

The good news is that most transportation design schools are now online and much of this information can be gathered from their websites.

## TRANSPORT DESIGN

### EUROPE

#### FRANCE
Creapole
128 Rue de Rivoli
75001 Paris
France
Tel: +33 1 44 88 20 20
Fax: +33 1 44 88 20 22
Website: www.creapole.fr

Strate College Designers
175/205, rue Jean-Jacques
Rousseau
92130 Issy les Moulineux
France
Tel: +33 1 46 42 88 77
Fax: +33 1 46 42 88 87
Website: www.stratecollege.fr

#### GERMANY
Hochschule Pforzheim
Tiefenbronner Str 65
75175 Pforzheim
Germany
Tel: + 49 7231 28 68 91
Email: mtd@fh-pforzheim.de
Website: www.fh-pforzheim.de

#### ITALY
Istituto d'Arte Applicata e
Design – Torino
Via Lagrange 7
10123 Turin
Italy
Tel: +39 011 584 868
Fax: +39 011 584 868
Website: www.iaad.it

Istituto Europeo di Design (IED)
International Office
Via Sciesa, 14
20135 Milano
Italy
Tel: +39-0257 96951
Fax: +39-0254 68517
Website: www.ied.it

#### SPAIN
Elisava Escola de Disseny
Superior
Plaza de la Merce
C/Ample 11-13
08002 Barcelona
Spain
Tel: +34 933 174715
Fax: +34 933 178353
Website: www.iccic.edu

**SWEDEN**

Institute of Design
Umea University
SE-90197 Umea
Sweden
Tel: +46 90 786 69 90
Fax: +46 90 786 6697
Website: www.dh.umu.se

**UNITED KINGDOM**

School of Art & Design
Coventry University
Priory Street
Coventry
Warwickshire CV1 5FB
UK
Tel: +44 1203 631313
Fax: +44 1203 838 793
Website:
www.coventry.ac.uk/csad/

University of Huddersfield
School of Design & Technology
Queensgate
Huddersfield
West Yorkshire HD1 3DH
UK
Tel: +44 1484 473813
Email:
info@huddersfield3d.co.uk
Website:
www.huddersfield3d.co.uk

University of Northumbria at
Newcastle
The Centre for Industrial Design
Squires Building
Sandyford Road
Newcastle upon Tyne NE1 8ST
UK
Tel: +44 (0)191 227 4913
Fax: +44 (0)191 227 4655
Website:
www.northumbria.ac.uk

Royal College of Art
Kensington Gore
London SW7 2EU
UK
Tel: +44 171 590 4444
Fax: +44 171 590 4500
Website: www.rca.ac.uk

**NORTH AMERICA**

Academy of Art
79 New Montgomery Street
San Francisco
CA 94105
USA
Tel: +1 415 274 2200
Email: info@academyart.edu
Website: www.academyart.edu

Art Center College of Design
1700 Lida Street
Pasadena
CA 91103-1999
USA
Tel: +1 626 396 2344
Website: www.artcenter.edu

University of Cincinnati
Transportation Design
School of Design
2624 Clifton Avenue
Cincinnati
Ohio 45221
USA
Tel: +1 5135566000
Website: www.design.uc.edu/
transportation

The Cleveland Institute of Art
University Circle
11141 East Boulevard
Cleveland
Ohio 44106-1710
USA
Tel: +1 216 421 7000
Fax: +1 216 421 7438
Website: www.cia.edu

College for Creative Studies
201 E Kirby
Detroit 48202-4034
USA
Tel: +1 313 664 7400
Fax:+1 313 664 7620
Website: www.ccscad.edu

**ASIA**
**CHINA**

Tsinghua University
Beijing 100084
China
Tel: +861062782015
Fax: +861062770349
Website:
www.tsinghua.edu.cn/eng/

**INDIA**

Bhopal Institute of
Transportation Styling
Sanasar Chandra Road
India
Tel: +91 11 456892
Fax: +91 11 625432
Website: n/a

**KOREA**

Hong Ik University
Sangsudong 72
1 Mapogu
Seoul
Korea
Tel: +82 02 320 1114
Fax: +82 02 320 1122
Website: www.hongik.ac.kr

**AUSTRALIA**

Faculty of Art & Design
Monash University
900 Dandenong Road
Caulfield
East Victoria 3145
Australia
Tel: +61 3 9903 2707
Fax: +61 3 9903 2845
Website:
www.artdes.monash.edu.au

## EUROPE

### SPAIN

Escuela Universitaria de
Ingeniería Tecnica Industrial
(EUITI)
Universidad Politecnica
Camino de Vera, s/n
Valencia 46071
Spain
Tel: +34 96 387 74 64
Fax: +34 96 387 74 64
Website: ttt.upv.es/relint/

## NORTH AMERICA

### CANADA

Carleton University
School of Industrial Design
3470 MacKenize Building
1125 Colonel by Drive
Ottawa
Ontario K1S-5B6
Canada
Tel: +1 613 520 5672
Fax: +1 613 520 4465
Website: www.id.carleton.ca

Humber College
205 Humber College Boulevard
Toronto
Ontario M9W 5L7
Canada
Tel: +1 416 675 3111
Website:
appliedtechnology.humberc.on.ca

### USA

Cranbrook Academy of Art
39221 Woodward Ave
Box 801
Bloomfield Hills
MI 48303-0801
USA
Tel: +1 248 645 3300
Fax: +1 248 646 0046
Website: www.cranbrookart.edu

The Pratt Institute
New York
200 Willoughby Ave
Brooklyn
New York 11205
USA
Tel: +1 718 636 3600
Fax:  +1 718 636 3613
Website: www.pratt.edu

Savannah College of Art and
Design
PO Box 2072
Savannah
Georgia 31402-3146
USA
Tel: +1 912 525 5100
Email: info@scad.edu
Website: www.scad.edu

## ASIA
### INDIA

National Institute of Design
Paldi
Ahmedabad 380007
India
Tel: +91 79 6639692
E-mail: info@nid.edu
Website: www.nid.edu

### KOREA

Industrial Design Department
Seoul National University of
Technology
172, Gongung2-dong
NoWon-gu
Seoul
Korea
Tel: +82 02 970 6678
Fax: +82 02 970 6667
Website: www.snut.ac.kr/eng/

### JAPAN

Industrial Design Dept
Musashino Art University
1-736 Ogawa-Cho
Kodaira – ShiTokyo
187-8505
Japan
Tel: +81 42 342 5011
Fax: +81 42 342 6452
Website:
http://musabi.ac.jp/e-
home/home.html

Industrial Design Dept
Tokyo University of Art and
Design,
University of Tokyo
7-3-1 Hongo
Bunkyo-ku
Tokyo
113-8654
Japan
Tel: +81338122111
Website: www.u-tokyo.ac.jp

## DESIGN DIRECTORY

Here we list the design departments of most of the major carmakers, along with their directors where possible. The list is as up-to-date as possible, but please bear in mind that in the fast-moving world of design, personnel changes can be frequent.

**ASTON MARTIN**
*Luxury sports cars*
Ingeni building
17 Broadwick St London
W1F DDJ UK
*Design Director:* Henrik Fisker

**AUDI**
*Premium cars*
Audi Design Ingolstadt 85045
Germany
*Design Director:* Gerhard Pfeffer

**Audi Design Centre Europe**
*Premium cars*
Avda Navarra s/n Sitges
Barcelona 08770 Spain

**Audi Design Canter, California**
*Premium cars*
82 W Cochran St Simi Valley
California 93065 USA

**BENTLEY MOTORS LTD**
*Luxury cars*
Pyms Lane Crewe  CW1 3PL
Cheshire UK
*Design Director:*
Dirk van Braeckel

**BERTONE**
*Design consultants;*
*manufacturing*
Stile Bertone SpA Via Roma 1
Caprie 10040 Italy
*Design Director:* Roberto Piatti

**BMW**
*Premium cars*
Forschungs und
Innovationszentrum
Knorrstrasse 147
Munchen 80788 Germany
*Design Director:* Chris Bangle

**BMW Motorcycles**
*Premium motorcycles*
Forschungs und
Innovationszentrum
Knorrstrasse 147
Munchen 80788 Germany
*Design Director:* David Robb

**BMW Designworks**
*Vehicle and product design*
2201 Corporate Center Drive
Newbury Park, California
91320-1421 USA
*President:* Adrian van Hooydonk

**CHRYSLER**
*Volume cars*
Daimler Chrysler Technology
Center
1000 Chrysler Drive
Auburn Hills
Michigan MI48326-2756 USA
*Design Director:* Trevor Creed

**CITROEN**
*Volume cars*
Centre de Création Citroën
Centre Technique de Vélizy
Route de Gizy Velizy-Villacoublay
Cedex 78973  France
*Design Director:* Jean-Pierre
Ploué

**DAEWOO**
*Volume cars*
Design Forum 80 Dangsan-4GA
Youngdeungpa-Gu Seoul
150-044 Korea
*Design Director:* HR Kim

**DAIMLERCHRYSLER**
*Premium cars*
Mercedes-Benz Design
Department design &
Predevelopment HPC X800
Sindelfingen 711075 Germany
*Design Director:* Peter Pfeiffer

**DAIMLERCHRYSLER**
*Commercial vehicles*
Mercedes-Benz Design
Department design &
Predevelopment HPC X800
Sindelfingen 711075 Germany
*Design Director:* Gerhard Honer

**DaimlerChrysler USA**
*Advanced design*
17742 Cowan St
Irvine
California 92614
USA
*Design Director:* Karlheinz Bauer

**DaimlerChrysler Japan**
*Advanced design*
Mercedes-Benz Advanced
Design Center of Japan
1-17 Chigasaki-minami
2-Chome Tsuzuki-ku Yokohama
224-0037 Japan
*Design Director:* Jens Manske

**FERRARI AND MASERATI**
*Luxury sports cars*
Via Abetone Inferiore 4
Maranello 41093
Italy
*Design Director:* Frank
Stephenson

**FIAT**
*Volume cars*
Centro Stile Fiat
Via La Manta 22 Torino
Italy
*Design Director:*
Michael Robinson

**ALFA ROMEO**
*Premium cars*
Centro Stile Alfa Romeo
Viale Luraghi
Arese
Milano 20020
Italy
*Design Director:*
Wolfgang Egger

**LANCIA**
*Premium cars*
Centro Stile Lancia
Viale Coppi 2
Orbassano
Torino
Italy
*Design Director:* Flavio Manzone

**FIORAVANTI**
*Design consultancy*
Fioravanti Styling
Studio Emanuel 4
Moncalieri
Italy
*Design Director:* P Vittorio

**FORD OF EUROPE**
*Volume cars*
Merkenich Design Centre
Spressart Strasse
Merkenich 50725
Cologne
Germany
*Design Director:* Chris Bird

**FUORE DESIGN INTL**
*Design Studio*
c/Teodor Roviralta 31
Barcelona 08022
Spain
*Design Director:* Leo Erwin

**HEULIEZ**
*Design & Manufacturing*
Le Pin
Cerizay 79140
France
*Design Director:* M Bertet

**HONDA**
*Volume Cars*
Wako R & D 1-4-1
Chuo Wako-shi
Saitama
351-0193
Japan

**Honda**
*Volume Cars*
1900 Harpers Way
Torrence
California 90501
USA

**Honda**
*Volume Cars*
Carl-Legien Strasse
Offenbach Main 63073
Germany

**HYUNDAI**
*Volume Cars*
Europe Design Centre
Haupstrasse
185
Eschborn 65760
Germany
*Design Director:*
Seung-Dae Baek

**I.D.E.A. INSTITUTE**
*Design Studio*
Via Ferroro di Cambiano 22
Moncalieri (Torino)
Italy
*Design Director:* Justyn Norek

**ITAL DESIGN**
*Design Studio*
Via Achille Grandi 25
10024 Moncalieri (Torino) Italy
*Design Director:*
Fabrizio Giugiaro

**JAGUAR**
*Premium Cars*
Engineering Centre Design
Studio (W/3/026)
Abbey Road
Whitley
Coventry CV3 4LE
UK
*Design Director:* Ian Callum

**JOHNSON CONTROLS**
*Vehicle systems design and
manufacture*
Automotive Systems Group
Industriestrasse 20-30
Burscheid 51399
Germany
*Design Director:* Hans Hendriks

**KARMANN**
*Vehicle design and manufacture*
Wilhelm Karmann GmbH
Gesmolder Strasse 33
Osnabruck 49084
Germany
*Design Director:*
Jorg Steuernagel

**LAND ROVER**
*Premium SUVs*
G-DEC
Land Rover
Banbury Road
Lighthorne
Warwick CV35 ORG
UK
*Design Director:* Geoff Upex

**LOTUS**
*Sports cars and engineering
consultancy*
Potash Lane
Hethel
Norfolk NR14 8EZ
UK
*Design Director:* Russell Carr

**MAGNA STEYR
FAHRZEUGTECHNIK A**
*Vehicle and systems design,
manufacture*
Liebenauer Hauptstrasse 317
A-8041 Graz
Austria
*Design Director:*
Andreas Wolfsgruber

**MAZDA EUROPE**
*Volume cars*
Hiroshimastrasse 1
Oberursel 61440
Germany
*Design Director:*
Peter Birtwhistle

**MAZDA USA**
1422 Reynolds Avenue
Irvine
California 92614
USA
*Design Director:* Truman Pollard

**MG ROVER**
*Volume cars and sports cars*
P O Box 41
Lickey Road
Longbridge
Birmingham B31 2BT
UK
*Design Director:* Peter Stevens

**MITSUBISHI EUROPE**
*Volume cars and SUVs*
Europe GmbH Head Office
& Design Studio
Diamant Strasse 1
Trebur 65468
Germany
*Design Director:*
Masafumi Kunimitsu

**OPEL**
*Volume cars*
International Technical Dev
Centre (ITDC) Design
IPC 86-01
Russelheim 65423
Germany
*Design Director:* Martin Smith

**PEUGEOT**
*Volume cars*
18 Rue des Fauvells
La Garenne 92256
Colombes
France
*Design Director:* Gerard Welter

**PININFARINA**
*Design consultancy and
manufacturing*
Strade Nazionale 30
Cambiano
Turin
Italy
*Design Director:*
Lorenzo Ramaciotti

**PORSCHE**
*Premium sports cars and SUVs;
design consultancy*
Forschungs und
Entwicklungszentrum
Porschestrasse
Weissach 71287
Germany
*Design Director:* Harm Lagaay

**RENAULT**
*Volume cars*
Direction du Design Industriel 1
Avenue du Golf
Guyancourt 78288
France
*Design Director:*
Patrick le Quément

**SAAB**
*Premium cars*
S-46180
Trollhattan
Sweden
*Design Director:*
Michael Maurer

**SEAT**
*Volume cars*
Centro de Diseno
Centro Tecnico
Carretera n-2, km 585
Martorell 08760
Spain
*Design Director:* Walter De'Silva

**Skoda**
*Volume cars*
Vaclava Klementa 869
293 60 Mlada Boleslav
Czech Republic
*Design Director:*
Thomas Ingenlath

**SMART**
*Volume city cars*
Micro Compact Car
Smart GmbH
Industriestrasse 8 D
Renningen 71272
Germany
*Design Director:*
Hartmut Sinkwitz

**TOYOTA**
*Volume cars*
2650 Route des Colles
BP253 06905
Sophia-Antipolis Cedex
France
*Design Director:* Wahei Hirai

**VALMET AUTOMOTIVE**
*Specialist manufacturing;*
*design*
PO Box 4
FIN23501
Autotehtaankatu 14 23500
Uusikaupunki
Finland
*Design Director:* Aimo Ahiman

**VOLKSWAGEN**
*Volume cars*
Volkswagen AG Design –
IPC 86-01
Brieffach 1701
Wolfsburg 38436
Germany
*Design Director:*
Hartmut Warkuss

**VOLVO**
*Premium cars*
Volvo Car Corporation
Department 51000
Torslanda
Gothenburg SE-40531
Sweden
*Design Director:*
Henrik Otto

**VOLVO**
*Premium cars*
700 VLA Alondra Drive
Camarillo
California 93012
USA
*Design Director:*
Geza Loczi

**VOLVO**
*Premium cars*
Volvo Car Corporation
Calle Diputacio 246
Barcelona 08007
*Chief Designer:*
David Ancona

# INDEX